Kitchen
Witchery

Kitchen Witchery

A Compendium of Oils, Unguents, Incense, Tinctures, and Comestibles

Marilyn F. Daniel
High Priestess of Isis

WEISERBOOKS
San Francisco, CA / Newburyport, MA

First published in 2002 by
Red Wheel/Weiser, LLC
With offices at:
500 Third Street, Suite 230
San Francisco, CA 94107
www.redwheelweiser.com

Library of Congress Cataloging-in-Publication Data
Daniel, Marilyn F.
  Kitchen witchery: a compendium of oils, unguents, incense, tinctures, and comestibles/Marilyn F. Daniel.
     p. cm.
  Includes bibliographical references.
  ISBN 1-57863-189-0 (pbk.: alk. paper)
     1. Witchcraft. 2. Recipes. I. Title.
BF1572.R4 D36 2001
133.4'3—dc21

                                                      2001046719

ISBN-10: 1-57863-189-0
ISBN-13: 1-978-57863-189-6

Cover and book design by Kathleen Wilson Fivel
Typeset in ITC Garamond
Printed in the United States of America
DR
10 9 8 7 6 5 4

Blessed be those witches who have
the foresight and courage to carry on our craft
in these difficult times.

I dedicate this book to the goddesses and gods,
known and unknown, within and
extending beyond infinity.

My human counterparts to whom I dedicate this book
are all the witches worldwide—past, present, and future—
who will enhance our teachings of love and light, peace,
tranquillity and harmony among all peoples
of this galaxy and beyond.

Blessed be.

So mote it be.

Table of Contents

Note to the reader: This book is intended as an informational guide. The remedies, approaches, and techniques described herein are meant to supplement, and not to be a substitute for, professional medical care or treatment. They should not be used to treat a serious ailment without prior consultation with a qualified healthcare professional. Neither the publisher nor the author can accept responsibility for your health or how you choose to handle and use the herbs described in this book.

CHAPTER ONE

Preparing for Ritual

In the overall scheme of the powers of the cosmos, both glimpsed and unknown, certain things are everlasting, immortal, and infinite. Magic is one of the ultimate cosmic powers, the union of mind, spirit, and physical being with the infinite cosmos. Magic is one with everything past, present, and future. It belongs to no particular culture, ethnic group, or tribe.

Magic, a simple word exuding the most ancient of emotions and thoughts, returns us to our ancient ancestors who lived and worshipped the natural cycles, powers, and energies that we share with the cosmos in the turning of the Wheel of the Year. The word *witch*, even today, has the ability to stir the most ancient of memories in the most skeptical of minds, and today it is the witch who celebrates the virtues of magic.

This book is a reference book for all practitioners. Intermediate to advanced practitioners can move on to the next chapter while beginners need to study this section very carefully.

Circle Casting

The casting of the circle is the most basic ritual to perform in preparing to do magic. These simple steps will lead you through the process.

1. *Purification Bath*: This is a simple task, and yet so very important for cleansing your body, spirit, mind, and psychic areas. Start by cleaning the tub with baking soda or a commercial cleanser. Next, run hot water into the tub and place ¼ cup of sea salt or circle bath (see page 95) into the tub and stir until the salt is dissolved.

   In the tub, actually and physically force the negative energies out of your body and into the water through your hands to completely and totally destroy them. Now, visualize a blue-white light penetrating your body, spirit, mind, and psychic areas, bringing protection, purification, and an abundance of energy. Actually feel this energy entering through your crown-chakra point and engulfing you. This energy sustains and energizes you. You feel as if there is nothing you cannot accomplish! Submerge your entire body in the water and let it do its job of purification and protection, increasing your ability to cast perfect circles and spells, attuning you with deity and power. After this visualization is completed, get out of the tub, dry yourself, and enter into the sacred space of the altar room and the magic of the ancients!

2. *Purifying Sacred Space*: Walk around the areas that will become the magic circle carrying a bowl of sea salt and water (salt for the earth element, water for the water element) and an incense burner (for the fire and air elements). As you walk the path of the circle clockwise, say:

> *By water and earth, by fire and air, by spirit, be this circle*
> *bound and purified as we desire.*
> *So mote it be.*
> *Blessed be.*

3. Next, the high priest or priestess, carrying a wand, sword, or athame, walks clockwise around the circle three times, visualizing the tip of the wand, or athame, or sword creating a circle of light and energy, projecting blue-white light from the tip to create the circle of energy. In your mind's eye, see the circle as geometrically perfect and say to yourself that it is so. Say:

> *I cast this circle to protect me/us from all negative and*
> *positive energies and forces on any level that may come to*
> *do me/us harm. I bear into this circle only the energies and*
> *forces that are correct and right for me/us and most correct*
> *for my/our work.*

Walk the circle for the third time and say:

> *I create sacred space.*
> *So mote it be!*

Repeat this as you walk around the circle.

4. Invoke and invite the energies of the elements, angels, spirits, dragons, gods, and animal powers to join you in your circle from the North and ask them to add their energies to your circle.

5. Invoke and invite the energies of the elements, angels, spirits, dragons, gods, and animal powers to join you in your circle from the East and ask them to add their energies to your circle.

6. Invoke and invite the energies of the elements, angels, spirits, dragons, gods, and animal powers to join you in your circle from the South and ask them to add their energies to your circle.

7. Invoke and invite the energies of the elements, angels, spirits, dragons, gods, and animal powers to join you in your circle from the West and ask them to add their energies to your circle.

8. Give the standard goddess invocation:

> *I invoke and call upon Thee O Mother Goddess, Creator of*
> *Life and Soul of the Infinite Universe.*
> *By candle flame and incense smoke do I invoke Thee to*
> *bless this rite and grant this spell. O Goddess, Queen of All*
> *Witches, I do open my heart and soul unto Thee.*
> *Blessed be.*
> *So mote it be.*

9. Give the standard Horned God invocation:

> *I invoke and call upon Thee, O Great Horned God of*
> *Pagans, Lord of the Green Woodlands and Father of All*
> *Things Wild and Free. By candle flame and incense smoke I*
> *do invoke Thee to bless this rite and grant this spell.*
>
> *O Great Horned God of Peace and Love, I do open my heart*
> *and soul unto Thee.*
> *Blessed be.*
> *So mote it be.*

10. Close with this invocation:

> *Goddess and God, give us the wisdom and understanding*
> *of our magical workings so that they will be for our good*
> *and for the good of many!*
> *Blessed be.*
> *So mote it be.*

11. Now is the time for all magical spells and workings for the occasion. This is also the time when the drawing down of the Sun and the Moon takes place on special occasions, such as at the Full Moon or in a Full Moon rite. Earth the power by scattering salt around the circle and say:

> *This power is earthed.*
> *Blessed be.*
> *So mote it be.*

12. Thank the goddesses and gods for their attention and ask them to come again at the appointed time.

13. Close the circle by holding the wand, athame, or sword out over the circumference of the circle. Beginning at magnetic North, walk once around the circle counterclockwise as you say:

> *I send this circle into the cosmos to do my/our bidding. The*
> *circle is undone but not broken.*
> *Blessed be.*
> *So mote it be.*

Charging or Enchanting Components or Tools

Charging or enchanting components or tools programs each item with its specific duties and its vibrational level. This increases the power and effectiveness of each spell or ritual.

1. Light a candle or candles whose color is appropriate for the mixture or object you are charging (oils, tools, herbs, brews, tinctures, salves, ointments, foods, etc.). Refer to the list of colors and their representations in chapter 14, page 240, to determine the appropriate color.

2. Hold the container for the mixture or the object in your hands. Sense the nonaligned (nonspecific) energies it contains. Visualize the magical goal within yourself (power, love, energy, exorcism, protection, spirituality, etc.). Force this power and energy out of your body through your hands and into the object you want to charge. Build up your power, emotions, and intent regarding the mixture or object and say aloud the intention with which you want to charge it.

3. With this energy tingling in your hands, visualize the energy streaming into the mixture or object, perhaps as shimmering strands of blue-white or purplish-white light that pour from your palms and enter the oils, herbs, or tools. You should visualize this energy in accordance with the candles and their colors. Always go with your instincts; never go against them.

4. When you feel drained of energy, when you know that all the energy has left your body and entered the mixture or object, set it down and shake your hands vigorously for a few moments. This cuts off the flow of energy so you will not be completely drained.

   Relax your body. Pinch out the candle flame or flames (or snuff them out) and save them for use in another empowering ritual of the same type. The empowerment or charging is completed.

All tools and components must be charged before any magical workings can be performed. The vibration levels in each item must be programmed to do their specific duties. Charging or enchanting all tools and components greatly improves the possibilities of your success in any ritual or magical workings you wish to accomplish.

CHAPTER TWO

Magical Oils

In modern times, it has become quite popular to use true essential oils within the Craft for the magical working of spells, charms, amulets, and talismans. However, there are some industrious individuals who would rather make their own oils than buy them from a reputable source. For those individuals, a kind word of caution and warning. It is exceptionally difficult to ensure the quality of the oil you are extracting, because the method of extraction must be so precise that any deviation from it will cause the oil to be inferior in quality. Here are a few reasons.

It requires an enormous amount of fresh plant material to extract enough oil to fill even a dram bottle—in fact, hundreds of pounds of plant material. Also, the petals, leaves, or roots must be of the appropriate species. For example, the best rose oils are created from the "old world" varieties, which are rarely available in large quantities.

Often, the results of producing your own oils aren't worth the investment of time and money required. Most homemade oils certainly do not smell like the flowers or plants from which they were extracted. In fact, there are very few plant oils that can be extracted at home without serious problems. I recommend simply buying and blending high-quality oils for ritual use.

Buying Oils

There are many companies that claim to sell essential oils. Be wary, however, of any oil that does not actually say "True Essential Oil" on the label. The only true essential oils are those that are extracted from plants of that particular genus and species, and not from some chemical formula. Many companies sell blended oils, compounds, or bouquets that reproduce a specific scent by mixing and blending various true essential oils. Never take it for granted that an oil is either true or essential. Always check it out.

It is always best to use only authentic oils in your magic. These contain the sum of all the plant's knowledge—past, present, and future—and all of its collective magical energies. These genuine oils are the most effective for your Craftwork.

The synthetic oils that I have worked with are effective but, compared to true essential oils, they are extremely weak. While it is true that synthetic oils are much cheaper, you use them up twice as fast as true essential oils. In fact, it often takes many drops of a synthetic oil to do the work of just one drop of a true essential oil. Although it is expensive to build up a good stock of genuine essential oils, this is necessary to create quality magical oils for your work in the Craft of the Old and Wise. I recommend you buy your essential oils from a reliable source, such as a local health food store that handles the real thing.

I know that some will continue to utilize synthetic oils, but, over the years, I have found that the results are, at best, less than desirable. Although it is my recommendation that you not use synthetics at all, it is up to each individual and the quality they want to achieve in their Craft. For those essences not available in essential oil form, bouquets can be used (see "Bouquets" on page 9).

Blending Oils

There is no specific method for blending oils. Just remember when mixing the oils with a base to rotate the mixture in a clockwise direction, as when casting a circle.

1. Assemble the true essential oils (and/or bouquets) called for in the recipe.

2. In a clean, sterilized glass container, add ⅟₁₆ to ⅛ cup of any of the base oils in the following list. (I prefer the jojoba oil, simply because it is a liquid wax and will not go bad or turn rancid. Any of the other oils can go stale.) Alternatively, you can use any vegetable oil that has very little scent to it.

Safflower	*Jojoba*
Sunflower	*Almond*
Coconut	*Hazelnut*
Apricot Kernel	*Grapeseed*

3. Use any standard dropper that will dispense one drop at a time. These are usually included with each bottle of true essential oils. Add the oils one at a time, starting with a base oil, then progressing to the next oil called for in the recipe. And remember: no recipe is set in stone. Experiment, and enjoy. This is part of your learning experience. Use the recipes in this book

as guidelines, but never let your creativity be hampered by any restricting guidelines. You should, however, always err on the side of caution.

4. Always swirl the oils in a clockwise rotation within their container. Never stir. (This is true in the Northern Hemisphere. If you are in the Southern Hemisphere, swirl the contents counterclockwise. Always swirl with the gravitational pull of the planet when charging or mixing.

5. All true essential oils should be stored away from heat in a completely dark place. This helps to preserve their vibrational level. Label the oil and keep it for use in later recipes. Always remember to label your oils when you make them. I promise you that your memory will eventually fail you. Also, you need to be able to duplicate your formulas exactly, so be sure to document everything you do.

6. All oils should be stored away from heat, light, and moisture (not in the bathroom) in airtight containers. Opaque or dark-colored glass bottles work well. Always charge each oil for a specific magical goal or intention.

Charging or Enchanting Oils

Charging or enchanting an oil is done to program it with the specific duty or duties of its vibrational level in order to increase its power and effectiveness. When charging, always ask the goddess, god, elementals, dragons and angels, if you work with them, to lend their energies to the oil and further enhance its power.

1. Light a candle or candles of a color appropriate to the mixture: oils, herbs, tinctures, salves, ointments, foods, etc. (see chapter 14, page 240 for a list of color correspondences.)

2. Hold the vessel containing the mixture in your hands. Sense the non-aligned (nonspecific) energies it contains. Visualize the magical goal (power, love, energy, exorcism, protection, spirituality, etc.) within yourself and force this power and energy out of your body through your hands and into the oil. Build up your power, emotions, and intent regarding the mixture and say your intention aloud.

3. With this energy tingling in your hands, visualize it streaming into the mixture, perhaps as shimmering strands of purplish-white light that pour from your palms and enter the oils or herbs. You may wish to visualize this energy in accordance with the candles and their colors. State your magical intention in a firm voice and say:

> *I charge you_____(oil or herb) by the moon and sun*
> *to_____.*
> *Blessed be.*
> *So mote it be.*

4. When you feel drained of energy, when you know that the energy has left your body and entered the mixture, set the vessel down and shake your hands vigorously for a few moments. This cuts off the flow of energy so you will not be drained completely.

5. Relax your body. Pinch out the candle flame, or snuff it out, and save the candle for use in another empowering ritual of the same type. The empowerment or charging is completed.

Using Magical Oils

True essential oils are used in a variety of ways, from anointing candles, to anointing the human body for protection, to performing exorcisms. In fact, they can be used for all of the magical goals that are included in this book and for any you could ever possibly think of. The only restrictions are in the mind of the individual. Don't let your mind hold you back or restrict your magic. Use the full power of the ingenuity the Goddess has given you. Have fun with the Craft of the Old and the Wise.

A humble bath can be turned into a ritual simply by adding several drops of true essential oil or oils to the bath water, slipping into the tub with intention and visualization in your mind, and inhaling the fragrances of your magical goal and intention from the hot steam and aromas arising from your ritual bath. Remember always to visualize a specific magical goal while performing a ritual bath.

Quartz crystals and other stones can also be anointed with magical oils to boost and increase their energy and power during spells and rituals. These stones can then be placed in bags made of leather, velvet, or some natural fabric and carried, worn, or placed in mystic patterns to bring about specific magical goals. There are many other uses for oils that you will discover later in this chapter.

Oil Blessing

All oils to be used in ritual should be blessed by both Goddess and God. This empowers the oil with divine energy which in turn enhances and blesses you and your workings within the Craft of the Old and Wise.

Dip the blade of your athame into the oil, then raise it to the sky and say:

> *In the name of the moon,*
> *of the stars, and of the sun,*
> *I bless this oil.*

This blessing may be used with any oil or any component you might be using.

Anointing Points of the Body

This anointing must be done skyclad (in the nude) after your ritual purification bath. Place a bit of the oil on the soles of your feet, in the bend of your knees, on your genitals, at the base of your spine, on your wrists, over your heart, on your breasts, under your chin, and on your forehead.

This extensive anointing procedure should be undertaken only when you are performing a full-fledged magical ritual, and, even then, it is not completely necessary. Another method is just to dab a little on your wrists, forehead, genitals, and the soles of your feet.

Bouquets

Because some true essential oils are virtually impossible to attain due to the rarity of the live plants, it is often necessary to create a bouquet—several oils blended together—to replicate the original plant scent. Here are some examples of these oils and their bouquet recipes.

Ambergris Bouquet

6 drops Cypress oil
3 drops Patchouli oil
1 oz. or less of Base oil

This scent, a product of sperm whales, was originally found washed up on beaches. In days past, the whales were destroyed to collect this precious material. Ambergris has long been used in aphrodisiac oils and perfumes. Its odor is usually described as musty, musky, and earthy. True ambergris is to be avoided, in conjunction with the Wiccan creed: Do no harm. Artificial ambergris or ambergris compounds are widely available, and are usually sold simply as ambergris.

Bergamot Mint Bouquet

Use one part (6 drops) for each oil
Lemon oil
Lemongrass oil
Peppermint oil
1 oz. or less of Base oil

Bergamot is a small plant with a minty-lemony scent. It is commonly used in wealth and prosperity oils. Synthetic versions abound, but should not be used. Instead, make up the bouquet as suggested here.

Lotus Bouquet

Use one part (6 drops) for each oil

Rose oil

Jasmine oil

White (or light) synthetic Musk oil (Harm none!)

Ylang-Ylang oil

1 oz. or less of Base oil

Mix until the scent is heavy, floral, and "warm." All lotus oils are blends of natural essential oils or synthetics that try to duplicate the delicious aroma of the lotus. Lotus oil is used in spirituality, healing, and meditation formulas.

Magnolia Bouquet

Use one part (6 drops) for each oil

Variation One

Neroli oil

Jasmine oil

Rose oil

Sandalwood oil

1 oz. or less of Base oil

Variation Two

Orange oil

Cinnamon oil

Neroli oil

Sandalwood oil

1 oz. or less of Base oil

Variation Three

Rose Geranium oil

Ylang-Ylang oil

Jasmine oil

Sandalwood oil

1 oz. or less of Base oil

As with lotus, no genuine magnolia oil exists. Use a compound magnolia or compose your own. If possible, have a fresh magnolia flower at hand while mixing the bouquet.

This helps you duplicate the aroma. Magnolia oil is often used in recipes designed to promote harmony, psychic awareness, and peace.

New-Mown Hay Bouquet

Use one part (6 drops) for each oil
Woodruff oil or Vanilla extract
Tonka bouquet
Lavender oil or Rose oil
Bergamot bouquet
Oakmoss bouquet
1 oz. or less of Base oil

This recipe is great for simulation of the honey-fresh smell of a just-mown hay field. New-mown hay oil is used to "turn over a new leaf," to attain a fresh perspective on a difficult problem, and especially to break negative habits (such as addictions) and thought patterns.

Oakmoss Bouquet

Use one part (6 drops) for each oil
Vetivert oil or Clove oil
Cinnamon oil
1 oz. or less of Base oil

Oakmoss is any of several lichens that grow on oak and spruce trees in central and southern Europe. It has a warm, slightly spicy odor and is used in prosperity-drawing mixtures. It is most often encountered in brews in its oil form.

Sweet Pea Bouquet

Use one part (6 drops) for each oil
Neroli oil or Rose Geranium oil
Ylang-Ylang oil
Jasmine oil or Cinnamon oil
Benzoin oil
1 oz. or less of Base oil

No genuine sweet pea oil is available today. I advise creating your own using this recipe.

Tonka Bouquet

Use one part (6 drops) for each oil

Benzoin oil

Vanilla tincture (a few drops of Vanilla extract)

1 oz. or less of Base oil

Tonka beans come from eastern Ven-ezuela and Brazil. They have long been used in love, prosperity, and wealth spells, and in sachets. I advise that you try this.

Tuberose Bouquet

8 drops Ylang-Ylang oil

7 drops Rose oil

6 drops Jasmine oil or Cinnamon oil

Just a hint of Neroli oil or Rose Geranium oil

1 oz. or less of Base oil

The tuberose is a richly scented, intensely sweet white flower native to Mexico. This oil is used in love-attracting mixtures, but true tuberose essential oil is rarely available. Try this recipe to simulate it.

Oil Recipes

The proportions listed in this text are suggestions only. If you wish to deviate from them, use smaller quantities of the stronger scented oils than you do of the lighter scented oils and add the stronger oils to the mixture first. *CAUTION: All illegal or poisonous ingredients are marked with a ‡. Whether or not you use them is up to you.* Three things are important to remember when using these recipes:

1. Add these essential oils to ⅛ cup of base oil (any good vegetable oil, olive oil).

2. Visualize the goal of the oil or bouquet as you mix and smell.

3. For best results, don't use synthetic oils.

Air Oil (Elemental)

5 drops Lavender oil

3 drops Sandalwood oil

1 drop Neroli or Orange oil

Wear this to invoke the powers of air and to promote

clear thinking, for travel spells, and to overcome addiction.

Anointing Oils

Variation One

5 drops Sandalwood oil
3 drops Cedarwood oil
2 drops Lemon oil

Variation Two

5 drops Myrrh oil
2 drops Cinnamon oil

Variation Three

5 drops Orange oil
2 drops Lemon oil

Use for general ritual anointing purposes.

Candle Anointing Oil

6 drops Rose oil
6 drops Violet oil
Olive oil base
6 drops Clove oil
2 tsp. powdered Cinnamon
1 Tbsp. powdered Myrrh
1 tsp. Fennel seeds

Mix as usual, except add the dry ingredients after the oils are well blended. Place in a tightly capped bottle and store in a dark, cool place. After four weeks, strain through cheesecloth and use for candle anointing rituals.

Altar Oil

Variation One

4 drops Frankincense oil
2 drops Myrrh oil
1 drop Cedar oil

Variation Two

4 drops Frankincense oil
2 drops Camphor‡ oil
1 drop Sandalwood oil

Mix as usual in the base oil. Anoint the altar with this oil at regular intervals, calling on your chosen deity or deities to watch over you.

Aphrodite Oil

6 drops Cypress oil
2 drops Cinnamon oil
Small piece of dried Orris root
Olive oil base

Wear and use as a personal oil to increase your own powers.

Aquarius Oil

6 drops Lavender oil
2 drops Cypress oil
1 drop Patchouli oil

Wear and use as a personal oil to increase your own powers.

Aries Oil

6 drops Frankincense oil
4 drops Ginger oil
4 drops Black Pepper oil
1 drop Petitgrain oil or
4 drops Clove oil

Wear and use as a personal oil to increase your own powers.

Astral Travel Oil

6 drops Sandalwood oil
2 drops Ylang-Ylang oil
1 drop Cinnamon oil

Add to the base oil and mix as usual. Anoint stomach, wrists, back of the neck, and forehead (but remember— these essential oils are added to a base). Lie down and visualize yourself astrally projecting.

Business Success Oil

4 parts Bergamot Mint bouquet
1 part Basil oil
1 part Patchouli oil
1 pinch ground Cinnamon

Mix the oils as usual and add the pinch of cinnamon. Anoint your hands, cash register, business cards, or the front door of your place of business to increase the cash flow.

Cancer Oil (Moonchildren)

8 drops Palmarosa oil
2 drops Chamomile oil
1 drop Yarrow oil

Mix as usual with a base oil. Wear as a personal oil to increase your own powers.

Capricorn Oil

Variation One

6 drops Lemon oil
3 drops Cypress oil
1 drop Patchouli oil

Variation Two

3 drops Vetivert oil
3 drops Cypress oil
1 drop Patchouli oil

Mix as usual with a base oil. Wear as a personal oil to increase your own powers.

Citrus Purification Oil

4 drops Orange oil
2 drops Lemongrass oil
2 drops Lemon oil
2 drops Lime oil

Mix, as usual, with a base oil. Wear as a personal oil to increase your own powers.

Come and See Me Oil

5 drops Patchouli oil
2 drops Cinnamon oil
Olive oil base

Mix as usual with a base oil. Wear as a personal oil to increase your own powers.

Courage Oil

3 drops Ginger oil
3 drops Clove oil
1 drop Black Pepper oil

Mix as usual with a base oil. Prior to public speaking, wear this oil to increase your courage, especially before nerve-wracking situations.

Demeter Oil

3 drops Myrrh oil
3 drops Oakmoss bouquet
2 drops Vetivert oil

Mix as usual with a base oil. Use this oil to tune into the energies of Mother Earth. Anoint and wear to attract money, successful completion of your protections and dreams, and when planting, tending, harvesting, or working with herbs and plants to ensure a fruitful yield.

Earth Oil (Elemental)

5 drops Patchouli oil
5 drops Cypress oil

Mix as usual with a base oil. Anoint and wear to invoke the powers of Mother Earth to bring money, prosperity, abundance, stability, and foundation.

Energy Oil

6 drops Orange oil
3 drops Lime oil

1 drop Cardamom oil

Mix as usual with a base oil. Try using this oil when feeling depleted, ill, or when your own energy reserves are low. This is especially useful after heavy magical ritual to energize your body batteries.

Fast Money Oil

Variation One

7 drops Patchouli oil
6 drops Cedarwood oil
4 drops Vetivert oil

Variation Two

5 drops Basil oil
2 drops Ginger oil
3 drops Tonka bouquet

Mix as usual with a base oil. Anoint your hands, money, and or green candles to bring money. Anointing the money assures its return.

Fire Oil (Elemental)

Variation One

2 drops Rosemary oil
2 drops Cassia Bark
2 drops Clove oil

Variation Two

4 drops Ginger oil
3 drops Rosemary oil
2 drops Clove oil
1 drop Petitgrain oil

Mix in base oil. Anoint and invoke the powers of fire, such as energy, courage, strength, love, passion, etc.

Fragrance of Venus Oil

6 drops Jasmine oil
6 drops red Rose oil
1 drop Lavender (no more!)

Mix in base oil. This oil is for any woman who wishes to

be "absolutely magnetic" to men. Blend these oils together on a Friday night for maximum effect. Only women should wear this oil!

Gemini Oil

Variation One

6 drops Spearmint oil
6 drops Lavender oil
6 drops Peppermint oil

Variation Two

5 drops Lavender oil
2 drops Peppermint oil
2 drops Lemongrass oil
2 drops Sweet Pea bouquet

Mix in base oil. Anoint and wear as a personal oil to increase your own powers.

Goddess Oil

½ tsp. dried Yarrow
½ tsp. dried Basil
1 tsp. powdered Myrrh
3 drops Rose oil
3 drops Lavender oil
½ cup Olive oil base

Mix in base oil. Place all ingredients in a clear glass jar and gently swirl in a clockwise direction to slowly agitate the oils. As you do this, fill your mind with images of the Goddess and visualize her divine power as an aura of white glowing light radiating from your hands into the jar of oil, charging it with magical energy. Store in a sealed jar in a cool, dark place for at least seven days. Strain through cheesecloth and use it to anoint candles for love spells, Goddess invocations, divinations, healing rituals, and all positive (white) forms of magic.

Good Luck Oil (1)

1 Tbsp. dried Wormwood‡
1 Tbsp. ground Nutmeg

½ tsp. powdered Mandrake‡ root or Tobacco‡
13 drops Pine oil
¼ cup Olive oil base

All ingredients should be placed into a clean glass jar and gently swirled in a clockwise direction. Seal the jar tightly and allow it to sit for thirteen nights in a cool, dark place. Strain the oil through a cheesecloth and use it to anoint candles for wish-magic, jinx-breaking, and spells to attract good luck, money, and success.

Good Luck Oil (2)

Note: If you are using a homemade oil, use the full eyedropper. If you are using an essential oil, use 12 drops for each eyedropper listed.

1 eyedropper Orange oil
2 eyedroppers Rose Geranium oil
½ eyedropper Palmarosa oil
1 eyedropper Niaouli oil
12 drops Cypress oil

Mix with base oil. Anoint and wear to bring good fortune into your life. Always visualize your goal during your anointing.

Handfasting Oil

Gardenia oil (peace, harmony)
Synthetic Musk oil (passion, courage)
Jasmine oil (continuing love)
Rose Geranium oil (protection against adversity)

The handfasting ceremony is a witches' wedding ceremony. This oil can be used by any couple, regardless of their marital status. Blend the oils together using the eyedropper, a drop at a time, until the scent seems perfect. Make up 2 ounces. Then add one pinch of dried yarrow. Yarrow is used in love and marriage spells. This herb is known for keeping marriages together for seven years. (Seven is the number of Venus—the love goddess and the planet.) When you are finished mixing the oil, pour it into twin crystal jars. Give one to the bride and one to the groom. Every night, the couple should anoint one another, using their own jars. When seven nights have passed, the oils should be blended together, poured into one of the jars. The other jar should be hidden in some secret place.

Healing Oil

Variation One

4 drops Eucalyptus oil
2 drops Niaouli oil
1 drop Palmarosa oil
1 drop Spearmint oil

Variation Two

5 drops Rosemary oil
2 drops Pine oil
2 drops Juniper oil
2 drops Sandalwood oil

Variation Three

6 drops Lime oil
6 drops Lavender oil
3 drops Rosemary oil
1 drop Sandalwood oil

Mix with base oil and then add the dried mint leaf. Anoint and wear during defensive magic and rituals. This oil is also worn during the waning Moon in honor of Hecate, Goddess of the Fading Crescent.

Hoodoo Oil

¼ cup Sunflower oil
3 Tbsp. Honey
6 drops dried Pumpkin seeds
6 drops Honeysuckle‡ oil
3 drops Rose oil
3 drops Patchouli oil

Mix with base oil. On the Full Moon, crush the pumpkin seeds using a mortar and pestle, and then mix all of the ingredients together by the light of a new white candle. Use a sterilized silver pin to prick your right thumb and add 3 drops of your blood to the mixture. Spit twice into the mixture and stir thrice. Store in any airtight container until you are ready to use it. Hoodoo oil is used to anoint candles for spellcasting, divination, spirit communication, and invocation of the Voodoo Loas.

Initiation Oil

4 drops Frankincense oil
4 drops Myrrh oil
1 drop Sandalwood oil

Mix with base oil. Use this for mystic initiation ceremonies and also to increase your awareness of the spiritual realm.

Interview Oil

5 drops Ylang-Ylang oil
4 drops Lavender oil
2 drops Rose oil

Mix with base oil. Use to help make a favorable impression on a possible employer. Wear to interviews of all kinds to calm your nerves.

Jupiter Oil (Planetary)

4 drops Oakmoss bouquet
2 drops Clove oil
1 drop Tonka bouquet

Mix with base oil. Wear this oil for wealth, prosperity, help in legal matters, and all other Jupiterian influences.

Leo Oil

3 drops Petitgrain oil
2 drops Orange oil
3 drops Lime oil

Mix with base oil. Anoint and wear as a personal oil to increase your own powers.

Libra Oil

Variation One
4 drops Rose Geranium oil
2 drops Ylang-Ylang oil

1 drop Rose Absolute or Otto (Attar of Roses)
1 drop Cardamom oil
1 drop Patchouli oil

Variation Two

4 drops Rose Geranium oil
2 drops Ylang-Ylang oil
2 drops Palmarosa oil

Mix with base oil. Anoint and wear as a personal oil to increase your own powers.

Love Oil

Variation One

6 drops Lavender oil
6 drops Lotus bouquet
6 drops Sweet Pea bouquet

Variation Two

7 drops Palmarosa oil
5 drops Ylang-Ylang oil
1 drop Ginger oil
3 drops Rosemary oil
1 drop Cardamom oil

Mix with base oil. Anoint pink candles and burn while visualizing love coming into your life.

Love Potion

Use equal parts of the following oils:
Patchouli oil
Benzoin oil
Lotus bouquet
Heliotrope oil (or see substitution table in chapter 13)
Orris oil
Olive oil base

Mix with base oil. Charge the ingredients to attract love. Add a few drops to commercial perfume or cologne.

Mars Oil (Planetary)

3 drops Ginger oil
2 drops Basil oil

1 drop Black Pepper oil

Mix with base oil. Anoint and wear for physical power, magical energy, lust, and all Martian influences.

Mercury Oil (Planetary)

4 drops Lavender oil
3 drops Camphor‡ oil
2 drops Spearmint oil
4 more drops Lavender oil
3 drops Eucalyptus oil
2 drops Peppermint oil

Mix with base oil. Anoint, visualize, and wear to attract Mercurial influences such as communication, intelligence, and travel into your life.

Moon Oil

1 drop Jasmine oil
1 drop Rose oil
1 drop Sandalwood oil

Mix with base oil. Anoint and wear to induce psychic dreams, speed healing, facilitate sleep, increase fertility, and for all other lunar influences. Also wear to attune with the Full Moon's vibrations.

Pan Oil

4 drops Patchouli oil
3 drops Juniper oil
1 drop Pine oil
1 drop Oakmoss bouquet
1 drop Cedarwood oil

Mix with base oil. Anoint and wear to be infused with the spirit of Pan. Ideal for attuning with Mother Earth, magical or ritual dancing, music making, singing, etc.

Peace Oil

4 drops Ylang-Ylang oil
3 drops Lavender oil

2 drops Chamomile oil

1 drop Rose Absolute or Otto (Attar of Roses)

Mix with base oil. Anoint and wear as a personal oil to increase your own powers.

Pisces Oil

4 drops Ylang-Ylang oil

3 drops Sandalwood oil

2 drops Jasmine oil

Mix with base oil. Anoint and wear as a personal oil to increase your own powers.

Power Oil

4 drops Orange oil

1 drop Ginger oil

1 drop Pine oil

2 drops Carnation oil

Mix with base oil. Anoint to infuse yourself with additional power during potent rituals.

Protection Oil

Variation One

6 drops Bergamot Mint bouquet

3 drops Rose Geranium oil

1 drop Patchouli oil

1 drop Cypress oil

Variation Two

5 drops Basil oil

3 drops Rose Geranium oil

2 drops Pine oil

1 drop Vetivert oil

Variation Three

6 drops Petitgrain oil

6 drops Black Pepper oil

Mix with base oil. Anoint and wear for protection against all forms of attacks. It is also important to anoint windows, doors, and other parts of your home to guard against negativity.

Protection/Uncrossing Oil

3 parts Sandalwood oil
3 parts Patchouli oil
3 parts Myrrh oil
1 drop Ammonia

The mixture as a whole should equal one dram. Mix with base oil. Anoint and wear to destroy negativity within your personal sphere that is hindering the peace and harmony in your life.

Psychic Oil

5 drops Lemongrass oil
3 drops Lemon oil
1 drop Yarrow oil

Mix with base oil. Anoint and wear to increase psychic powers, especially when working with rune stones, quartz-crystal spheres, and other such tools.

Purification Oil

Variation One
6 drops Eucalyptus oil
3 drops Camphor‡ oil
2 drops Lemon oil

Variation Two
4 drops Frankincense oil
2 drops Myrrh oil
2 drops Sandalwood oil

Mix with base oil. Anoint and wear or add to the bath for destruction of negativity.

Sabbat Oil

Variation One
2 drops Pine oil
1 drop Ginger oil
1 drop Cinnamon oil
2 drops Sandalwood oil
Any base oil

Variation Two

3 drops Frankincense oil

2 drops Myrrh oil

2 drops Sandalwood oil

3 drops Orange oil

3 drops Lemon oil

Olive oil base

Mix with base oil. Anoint and wear as a personal oil to increase your own powers.

Satyr Oil

4 drops synthetic Musk oil (Harm none!)

4 drops Patchouli oil

3 drops Cinnamon oil

3 drops Carnation oil

Mix the oils with a base oil until the scent seems right to you. The above recipe is my personal favorite. Use your instincts. This should be blended on a Tuesday and should be worn only by women. Its smell will vary with the amount of each oil that is used. It works as an aphrodisiac and the results can be quite amazing!

Sexual Energy Oil

2 drops Ginger oil

2 drops Patchouli oil

1 drop Clove oil

1 drop Sandalwood oil

Mix with base oil as usual. Anoint and wear to attract sexual partners. Most important of all, please have safe sex.

Sleep Oil

Variation One

3 drops Rose oil

1 drop Mace oil

1 drop Nutmeg oil

Variation Two

3 drops Rose oil

3 drops Jasmine oil

1 drop Chamomile oil

Variation Three

2 drops Rose oil

2 drops Myrrh oil

3 drops Eucalyptus oil

Variation Four

2 drops Nutmeg oil

2 drops Camphor‡ oil

2 drops Mace oil

Mix with base oil as usual. Anoint your temples and neck, the insides of both wrists and the soles of both feet. This oil relaxes the senses and allows your body to rest.

Spirit Oil

1 Tbsp. powdered Orris or Serpentaria Root

1 Tbsp. dried Solomon's Seal

1 Tbsp. dried and crushed Rosemary

Small pinch powdered Jade or Turquoise

3 drops Sandalwood oil

3 drops Mint oil

¼ cup Safflower oil base

The gemstones can be powdered using a metal file. Mix all of the ingredients together and store in an airtight jar for at least three weeks in a cool, dark place. Strain through a cheesecloth and use to anoint candles for exorcisms, seances, counterspells, purification rituals, protection against evil influences, and spells to increase clairvoyant powers of all kinds.

Sun Oil

Variation One

1 tsp. Cinnamon, ground

1 tsp. Juniper berries, mashed

1 Bay leaf, crumpled

Scant pinch Saffron (genuine)

Variation Two

5 drops Frankincense oil

2 drops Cinnamon oil
1 drop Petitgrain oil
1 drop Rosemary oil

Gently heat the first recipe over low heat in ¼ cup base oil. Strain and anoint for all purposes relating to the Sun. Mix the second recipe with base oil as usual. Anoint for all purposes relating to the Sun.

Taurus Oil

2 drops Oakmoss bouquet
2 drops Cardamom oil
1 drop Patchouli oil

Mix as usual in base oil. Anoint and wear as a personal oil to increase your own powers.

Temple Oil

4 drops Frankincense oil
3 drops Rosemary oil
1 drop Bay oil
1 drop Sandalwood oil

Mix as usual in base oil. Anoint and wear during religious rites, such as promoting spirituality, "temple workings," etc.

Venus Oil (Planetary)

3 drops Ylang-Ylang oil
3 drops Geranium oil
1 drop Cardamom oil
1 drop Chamomile oil

Mix as usual in base oil. Anoint and wear to attract love and friendships, to promote beauty, and for other Venusian influences.

Virgo Oil

8 drops Oakmoss bouquet
2 drops Patchouli oil

1 drop Cypress oil

Mix as usual in base oil. Anoint and wear as a personal oil to increase your own powers.

Visions Oil

5 drops Lemongrass oil
3 drops Bay oil
1 drop Nutmeg oil

Mix as usual in base oil. Anoint your forehead to produce psychic awareness.

Water Oil (Elemental)

4 drops Palmarosa oil
2 drops Ylang-Ylang oil
1 drop Jasmine oil

Mix as usual in base oil. Anoint and wear to promote love, healing, psychic awareness, purification, and any water elemental rituals.

Wealth Oil

Variation One
5 drops Tonka bouquet
1 drop Vetivert oil

Variation Two
½ eyedropper Clove oil
3 eyedroppers Honeysuckle‡ oil
3 eyedroppers Tonka bouquet
1 eyedropper Cassia oil
4 drops Patchouli oil

Mix as usual in base oil. Anoint green or black candles while visualizing to bring wealth into your life. Also wear to attract wealth.

Oils of the Elemental Winds

When desiring a change in your life use the appropriate oil. These oils should also be worn during rituals to boost your magical workings.

Lavender oil: East Wind, the wind of intelligence

Musk oil: South Wind, the wind of passion and change

Rose oil: West Wind, the wind of love and the emotions

Honeysuckle‡ oil: North Wind, the wind of riches

CHAPTER THREE

Tinctures

The stimulation of ritual consciousness through the sense of smell using oils adds the energies of the oils to spells, amulets, ointments, talismans, perfumes, and our own bodies. Tinctures, which are scented liquids, are just as effective as oils for this purpose. In magical perfumery, a tincture is created by soaking dried plant materials in alcohol, thus capturing the odor. The process of tincturing is fairly fast and easy, and creates wonderful products that can be used in much the same way as oils in magic. Only ethyl alcohol—also known as ethanol, grain alcohol, and Everclear—can be used to make magical tinctures. Ethyl alcohol is a completely natural product distilled from grain, sugar, or grapes. Although some may be inclined to believe that rubbing alcohol can be substituted for the ethyl alcohol, this is not the case. Rubbing alcohol is distilled from petroleum products. Its sharp odor thus makes it completely unsuitable for tincturing.

Unfortunately, ethyl alcohol is usually very expensive and is sometimes difficult to find. While Everclear, which is 192 proof, is available in the United States, it is quite costly. (192-proof alcohol indicates that it contains 96 percent alcohol and only 4 percent carriers.) You can purchase a quart of Everclear from your local liquor store. When making the tinctures, you do not use much ethyl alcohol, so a bottle of this size should last quite a long time. I have personally found that adding a little water to the dried herbs and letting them set for a couple of hours before you add the alcohol helps to improve the power of the tincture.

For tincturing, you must have alcohol that is at least 70 percent, or 140 proof. Even Vodka is only 90 proof, or 45 percent alcohol, and is thus unsatisfactory for tincturing. As I stated previously, check with liquor stores, supermarkets, and drug stores for sources of ethyl alcohol. Once you have found a supplier for the ethyl alcohol, you are ready to begin making the tinctures.

When making tinctures, start with a good supply of dried plant materials. Do not use fresh herbs, for they will not work. The water content in the plant prevents it from working. Some plants, however, are not soluble in alcohol—in other words, the scent of the plant will not transfer to the ethyl alcohol. You will find a list of herbs that work well for tincturing on page 33, but you should feel free to experiment on your own as well. Have fun crafting and tincturing.

Processing Tinctures

The herbs used for making your tincture must be powdered to an extremely fine consistency. I've found that, in some cases, a small coffee grinder works extremely well for this purpose. Of course, you can always use the tried-and-true mortar and pestle. Whichever method you use, be sure to reduce your herbs and plants to the finest powder possible. You might even consider buying pre-powdered herbs, especially with woods such as sandalwood.

Place the herb to be used in a small sterilized bottle with a tight-fitting lid. Using a small funnel, pour just enough Everclear into the bottle to wet and cover the herb. Cap tightly. Shake the bottle vigorously. Be sure to charge the tincture for its specific purpose. For the next two weeks, shake vigorously every day. As you shake the tincture, visualize its magical goal.

Next, strain the tincture. There are several methods of doing this. You can use a coffee filter, cheesecloth, or any clean fabric that will strain out the used-up herbs. At this time, the scent may be strong enough—it usually is with gums and resins such as frankincense and myrrh. If not, add more herb to the Everclear and repeat the 2-week process again. You must do this quickly, as alcohol evaporates when exposed to air.

The alcohol should become heavily scented and colored. In fact, this may happen soon after you add the Everclear to the herbs. If it doesn't, the plant isn't readily soluble in alcohol. Add a bit of water to the alcohol and try again, or select one of the herbs mentioned on page 33.

To determine if the tincture is properly scented, apply a drop or two to your wrists. Wait until the alcohol has evaporated and smell. Many tinctures will not have a "true" scent in the bottle. After the plant's smell has completely overpowered the sickly-sweet odor of the Everclear, filter it one last time, bottle it, and add a few drops of castor oil or glycerine to stabilize the fragrance. Label the bottle and store it in a cool dark place until needed.

Using Tinctures

Virtually all tinctures can be used in any magical ritual, just as oils may be used in any magical ritual. Unless your psychic intuitions tell you otherwise, always use equal parts of herbs for tincturing. *CAUTION: Never eat or drink magical tinctures. Many of the herbs used in making them are deadly to both animals and humans and are marked with a ‡ in the lists and recipes to follow.*

Herbs Recommended for Tincturing

Try not to sniff tinctures until after the alcohol has evaporated. Once the alcohol has evaporated, the true scent of the tincture comes through.

Benzoin: Purification, prosperity, increasing business success, and sharpening mental powers. A few drops of benzoin tincture can be added to scented oils and ointments to preserve them. This has an antiseptic smell.

Camphor‡: Chastity, health, divination. Sniff to lessen sexual desires or set beside the bed for this purpose. This has a penetrating, cool odor.

Cinnamon: Spirituality, success, healing, power, psychic powers, lust, protection, and love. This tincture has a beautiful rich scent.

Clove: Protection, exorcism, love, and money. A fantastic scent.

Copal: Love and purification. This one has a lemony scent.

Frankincense: Protection, exorcism, spirituality, love and purification. Once you have smelled the full, bold scent of the real thing, you will realize that most frankincense oil is synthetic.

Galanga: Protection, lust, health, money, psychic powers, and hex-breaking. This tincture smells of ginger and camphor‡.

Lavender: Love, protection, sleep, chastity, longevity, purification, happiness, and peace. This is a very relaxing scent.

Myrrh: Protection, exorcism, healing, and spirituality. This scent recalls ancient times and is extremely evocative when mixed with frankincense. It is well suited for use with incense paper.

Nutmeg: Luck, money, health, fidelity. Try this for a spicy smell.

Patchouli: Money, fertility, lust. This is a stimulating and earthy scent.

Peppermint: Purification, sleep, love, healing, psychic powers. Though this herb takes a lot of time to cure, it is well worth the effort. Try spearmint as well.

Rosemary: Protection, love, lust, mental powers, exorcism, purification, healing sleep, youth.

Sage: Immortality, longevity, wisdom, protection, wishes. The scent is similar to camphor‡, with a strong "green note."

Sandalwood: Protection, wishes, healing, exorcism, spirituality. This tincture seems to take an enormous amount of time to cure, but when finished, it smells like sandalwood, with a slight cedary smell.

Star anise: Psychic powers and luck. This is a Sassafras-smelling tincture.

Tonka: Love, money, courage, wishes. This tincture has a vanilla scent.

Vanilla: Love, lust, mental powers. A rich, delicious-smelling tincture.

Wood aloe: This Malaysian bark smells of ginger and pepper and is highly resinous. It is perfect for anointing luck and spirituality amulets and talismans.

The herbs above are only a few of the many good for tincturing. Experiment with others and have fun with your Craft.

Tincture Recipes

Astral Projection Tincture
Benzoin
Cinnamon
Sandalwood

Anoint your chakra points and visualize your astral body separating from your physical body as you go into your altered state of consciousness. Use dried herbs only.

Courage Tincture
Frankincense
Tonka

Anoint your chakra points and visualize your own courage increasing to the point that you feel invincible. Use dried herbs only.

Deity Tincture
Frankincense
Myrrh
Benzoin

Anoint your body to attune and increase your involvement with spiritual activities, especially prior to meditation and religious rituals of all kinds. Use dried herbs only. Visualize as usual.

Divination Tincture

Camphor‡
Clove

Anoint your chakra points and visualize your ability to see into the past and future for scrying by any of the several methods: crystal spheres, rune stones, tarot cards, I-Ching sticks, etc. Use dried herbs only.

Exorcism Tincture

Myrrh
Rosemary
Sandalwood

Anoint your chakra points and visualize a heavy cleansing of your self. Visualize all negative energy being totally destroyed. Use only dried herbs.

Good Luck Tincture

Nutmeg
Star Anise
Tonka

Anoint your chakra points and visualize good fortune entering your life. Use only dried herbs.

Happiness Tincture

Lavender

Anoint your chakra points and visualize your emotions turning into a happy, easygoing mood. All negative emotions are completely destroyed. Use only dried herbs.

Healing Tincture

Rose Hips
Sage
Myrrh
Rosemary

Anoint healing amulets (sachets), your body, blue candles, etc., to speed healing and to retain good health. Use dried herbs only. Visualize as usual.

Love Tincture

Lavender
Rosemary
Patchouli

Anoint your body or love sachets to attract a love and to expand your ability to give and receive love. Visualize as usual.

Lust Tincture

Patchouli
Peppermint
Rosemary
Clove

Anoint your chakra points and sexual organs; visualize lustful desires. Use only dried herbs.

Power, Magical Tincture

Vanilla Bean

Anoint your chakra points. Visualize magical power and energy bombarding your body, spirit, soul, and psychic powers with energy. Use only dried herbs.

Protection Tincture #1

Cedar
Cinnamon
Sandalwood
Clove

Anoint objects or yourself for protection. Use dried herbs only. Visualize as usual.

Protection Tincture #2

Clove
Lavender

Peppermint
Wood Aloe

Anoint your chakra points. Visualize protective energy entering, surrounding, and engulfing your body, spirit, soul, and physical being. Use only dried herbs.

Psychic Dreams Tincture

Star Anise
Clove
Nutmeg
Deerstongue

Anoint your wrists and forehead before using your natural psychic abilities, even while dreaming. Also, anoint your pillow for psychic dreams. (Be careful; this causes stains. Use one pillowcase just for this purpose.) Use dried herbs only. Visualize as usual.

Purification Tincture

Frankincense
Myrrh
Sandalwood

Anoint your chakra points. Visualize purification energy entering your body, spirit, and soul. Use only dried herbs.

Wealth Tincture

Patchouli
Clove
Nutmeg
Cinnamon

Anoint your purse, wallet, cash register, money before spending it, or money amulets. Use dried herbs only. Visualize as usual.

These recipes are only suggestions. Use your imagination. See the substitution lists in chapter 13 for further herb tincture possibilities.

Chapter Four

Magical
Incense

Incense is used for magical purposes as well as for practical household tasks and aroma therapy. Its uses are as varied and diverse as the human mind. Never allow yourself to be limited by books when planning your magic. Always use the intuitive feelings with which the Goddess and God have endowed you when working in the Craft of the Old and Wise.

During magical rituals, incense is burned to promote ritual consciousness, the state of mind necessary to conjure and direct personal energy. This can also be achieved through the use of magical tools—by standing before an altar laden with softly glowing candles radiating slivers of light that reflect from the altar, by using altar tools and the altar mirrors, by intoning Goddess-inspired poetry or chants, and by speaking the symbolic words of an invocation to the Goddess and God.

When incense is burned prior to and during magical workings, fragrant smoke purifies the altar and the surrounding areas, cleansing them of negative, disturbing vibrations. It helps restore the appropriate mental state necessary for the successful practice of magic.

Each incense is specifically designed and crafted for a magical goal. Each component of the incense is carefully chosen for its magical goal and scent when burned. These formulas are specially prepared and burned to attract specific energies to the magician and to aid her or him in charging personal power with the ritual's magical goal, eventually creating the change necessary to bring that goal to manifestation in the physical world.

Incense possesses specific vibrations, as do all things. Magicians choose an incense for its magical purpose and use only components with these specific vibrational levels. If performing a healing ritual, they burn a mixture composed of herbs that promote healing in their vibration levels.

For over 5,000 years, incense has smoldered on magicians' altars, fulfilling different purposes. It is burned during magical ritual to promote cosmic consciousness—the state of mind necessary to rouse and direct personal energy. Priestesses, priests, and magicians choose the incense that best fits their magical goals. If performing a love ritual, they burn a mixture of herbs promoting love. Any incense burned in a ritualistic setting undergoes a transformation. No longer trapped in a physical form, the vibrations of the herbs are released into the environment to perform and manifest their magical goal or goals.

Not all of the incenses included here are strictly for ritual or magical use. Some can be burned in thanks or as an offering to a variety of aspects of deity. Just as lavender was burned as an offering to Isis over 5,000 years ago in Egypt, other blends are used to enhance Wiccan rituals.

Always remember, you needn't limit incense use to ritual or magical purposes. Do not, however, burn healing incense just because you love the smell of it or to enhance your house with a wonderful smell. Burning magically endowed and empowered incenses when they are not needed is a waste of materials and magical energy. If you wish to burn a pleasant-smelling incense, compound a household mixture for this purpose only.

Incense is made up of a variety of flowers, leaves, barks, roots, resins, woods, gums, oils, and tinctures. Semiprecious stones may also be added to incense to lend their energies to the mixture. Indeed, emeralds were once burned in fires by ancient Meso-American peoples, and the Eastern peoples dissolved pearls in wine and drank the wine as an aphrodisiac.

Incense Burners: Censer or Thurible

Whether you use raw incense, cones, sticks, blocks, or incense papers, you must have an incense burner. A censer can be anything from the type that hangs from a chain that is used in churches, to a bowl filled with sand or salt to distribute the heat so the bowl will not break. There are many occultists who have chosen to use the bowl-and-salt method for years, although they could have afforded to purchase other censers.

You can even use a mortar that has been carved from lava and stands on three legs. This can be absolutely perfect for a censer. Indeed, it is a prime example of a thurible! A thurible is also a censer, defined in the lexicon of witchcraft and Wicca as a shallow, three-legged dish used in magical workings as an incense burner.

In the Craft of the Old and Wise, your own intuitions, feelings, and emotions should always govern what you choose for your Craft tools. These feelings are the Goddess and God telling you in their own way what is right and correct for you as an individual. Always listen to your inner feeling and you will not go wrong!

The bowl-and-sea-salt (or sand) method can always be used if nothing else is available. In this case, use a bowl half-filled with sea salt, or sand or dirt, and just get on with your work! The sand, salt, or dirt protects the bowl and the surface on which it sits against heat. It also provides a wonderful place to put stick incense. In fact, you can even use a bowl specifically for stick incense if you prefer stick incense to any other type.

Two Forms of Incense

Incense in any magical practice is virtually a necessity, and there is great mystery surrounding its composition. No one seems to know who first came up with the idea or where it was first used. Fortunately, it's extremely easy to make—with practice.

There are basically only two types of incense used in our magical traditions: combustible and noncombustible. Combustible incense contains saltpeter (or potassium nitrate); noncombustible does not. Combustible incense can, therefore, be burned alone, without any other heat source. Combustible incense is available in cones, sticks, blocks, and other shapes. Noncombustible incense, on the other hand, must be sprinkled onto glowing charcoal blocks to release its fragrance and energies.

Ninety-five percent of the incense used in the magical traditions is of the noncombustible, granular, or raw type. This is, perhaps, because it's easier to make. Herbalists and herbal magicians are notoriously practical people! They would rather spend their time working in the Craft than spend it making combustible incense. I know that this is my reason for using and preferring noncombustible incense in my own personal practice.

There are also some spells and rituals that call for billowing clouds of smoke (particularly divinatory and evocational rites). This effect is impossible to achieve with cone, stick, or block incense, since they burn at a steady rate.

The advantages of combustible incense can outweigh its drawbacks, however, depending on the circumstances. If you need to do a money-drawing ritual, you could take out the censer, incense, and a charcoal block, light the charcoal, place it in the censer, and sprinkle incense onto the hot burning charcoal. But you could also just pull out a stick of money-drawing incense, light it, set it in the censer, and get on with the money-drawing ritual.

There are many different types of magicians in the world, and no two will agree on what is the best type of incense. Always use your Goddess- and God-given instincts and intuition. This is how they communicate with each and every one of us! Only those who are attuned to and with the deities can hear and react to their voices. Only those who listen will hear! The wise magician is always prepared for emergencies. I recommend that you keep both types of incense available for use. Although I personally prefer non-combustible incense, I always have some combustible incense on hand for emergencies. I have included directions and recipes for both types for just this reason.

Using Combustible Incense

Combustible incense is easy to use. Simply set it in a censer or thurible, light it, and snuff out the flame after the tip begins to glow. As the incense burns, visualize your magical goal manifesting into physical reality and into your life. You may also wish to add powdered rocks, colored candles, true essential oils, and possibly even herbs and/or oils mixed with or added to the candles for greater magical power. To powder the rocks, simply sand them with a diamond-grit fingernail file, then use the powdered rock for your magical workings.

Making Combustible Incense

Combustible incense can be made as cones, sticks, or blocks. Each type is fairly complicated to make, but many feel the results are worth the extra effort and work involved. Some of the ingredients in combustible incense are difficult to acquire, and the procedures tend to be messy and frustrating. Some people even question whether combustible incense is as effective as noncombustible. If you consider, however, that the charcoal used to burn non-combustible incense contains the same potassium nitrate found in the combustible variety, one is just as effective as the other! The only difference is that one will burn by itself and the other has to be placed on the hot charcoal. Another concern is that since potassium nitrate is related to Mars, it might add aggressive traits or energies to the incense. But again, since the use of both types of incense involves potassium nitrate, neither would be any more affected by these energies than the other. Thus, it is simply a matter of personal preference and intuition which you use.

At first, making combustible incense may seem an impossible task. But take heart, and you will be rewarded with wonderfully scented and smelling incense cones, blocks, or sticks, whichever you choose to make.

To make the base for combustible incense, you must have a bonding mucilage such as gum tragacanth. This is the best ingredient for all molded incenses. Gum tragacanth is available at some herb stores. In the past, most drugstores carried it. It is very expensive, but a little goes a long way. If you cannot find gum tragacanth, you can substitute gum arabic.

Tragacanth Glue

1 tsp. Gum Tragacanth
Approx. 8 oz. of warm water

Mix thoroughly until all particles are dissolved. You may also use a whisk or eggbeater to help dissolve the gum. The foam that rises can easily be skimmed off or allowed to subside on its own. Gum tragacanth has enormous absorption qualities; one ounce will absorb up to a gallon of water in a week. Let the tragacanth absorb the water, until it becomes a thick, foul-smelling paste. The consistency of the mixture depends on the form of incense desired.

- For sticks, the mixture should be relatively thin. This is the most difficult to make;

- For blocks and cones, the mixture should be much thicker, since you must be able to form the shapes desired.

It may take several tries to get the right consistency for each type. After you have made the tragacanth glue, cover it with a wet cloth and set it aside. It will continue to thicken as it sits. If it becomes too thick, just add a little water and stir thoroughly. Just be careful not to add too much!

Cone Incense

Next, make up the cone incense base—either #1 or #2. All herb mixtures used in combustible incense should be mixed with one or the other of these two base formulas.

Cone Incense Base #1

6 parts ground Charcoal (Do not use the self-starting
   variety.)
1 part ground Benzoin
2 parts ground Sandalwood
1 part ground Orris root (a scent stabilizer)
6 drops true essential oil (Use an oil made from one
   of the ingredients above.)
2 to 4 parts mixed and charged incenses that you
   have made yourself
Potassium nitrate

Mix the first four ingredients until well blended. Add the essential oil and mix again with your hands. The goal is to create a very fine powdered mixture. If you wish, run the mixture through your mortar and pestle, or a coffee grinder until you are satisfied with its consistency. Add 3 to 4 parts of the completed, charged, noncombustible incense (see page 46). Mix well with your hands. Then weigh the entire mixture on a small kitchen scale and add 10 percent potassium nitrate. If you have made 10 ounces of incense, add one ounce of potassium nitrate. Mix until the white powder is completely blended.

CAUTION: Under no circumstances should the Potassium nitrate (saltpeter) constitute more than 10 percent of the completed mixture. If any more is added, it will burn too fast; less and it might not burn at all.

Next, add the tragacanth or gum arabic mixture, 1 teaspoon at a time, mixing it with your hands in a large bowl until all the ingredients are well moistened and attain a pasty consistency. For cone incense, a very stiff dough-like texture is required. If it is too thick, however, it will not form properly into cones and will take forever to dry. The mixture should mold easily and hold its shape. Always use the cone shape, or the incense may not burn properly.

On a piece of waxed paper, shape the mixture into cones, similar to those you have purchased. Place the cones in a warm, dry place and leave them undisturbed for seven days.

Cone Incense Base #2

6 parts powdered Sandalwood (or Pine, Cedar, Juniper)
2 parts powdered Benzoin (or Myrrh, Frankincense, etc.)
1 part powdered Orris root
7 drops essential oil (use the oil form of one of the components)
4 to 5 parts of charged incense mixture

Gum Tragacanth
Postassium nitrate

In place of the charcoal, wood has been substituted. Use sandalwood if it's included in the incense recipe, otherwise use cedar, pine, or juniper, depending on your magical goal. Try to match the wood base of this incense to its recipe if you can't use sandalwood.

Mix the first 3 ingredients until combined. Add oils and mix thoroughly, then add 4 to 5 parts of incense. This should be a very fine powder. Weigh and add 10 percent potassium nitrate, then add the gum tragacanth. Mix well and shape as described above.

It is important to follow three simple rules when making this recipe, or your incense will not burn properly. There is much less room for error with combustible incense than there is with noncombustible incense.

1. Never use more than 10 percent potassium nitrate (saltpeter).

2. Keep all woods and resins in their proper proportions (at least twice as much powdered wood as resin).

3. Depending on the type of incense you are adding to the base, you may have to adjust some proportions. Just make sure that the powdered woods never account for more than a third of the final mixture.

Block Incense

Make a ⅛-inch-thick square of the stiff dough on waxed paper. Cut with a knife into one-inch cubes, as if you were cutting small pieces of fudge. Separate slightly and let dry.

Stick Incense

To make stick incense, simply add more tragacanth or gum arabic glue to the mixed incense and base until the mixture is wet, but still rather thick. The trick here is to determine the proper thickness of the tragacanth mixture and find appropriate materials to use. Professional incense manufacturers use thin bamboo splints, which aren't generally available. Try making them at home out of wood or bamboo splints, broom straws, very thin twigs, or the long wooden cocktail skewers available at some grocery and oriental food stores.

Dip the stick into the mixture, let it sit upright, then dip again. Several dippings are usually necessary. This is a most difficult process. When the sticks have accumulated enough of the incense on them, poke them into a slab of clay or some other substance so that they stand upright and allow them to dry for seven days.

Another variation on stick incense uses a much stiffer incense dough. Pat down the dough onto waxed paper until it is very thin. Place the stick on the dough and roll a thin coating of dough around the stick. Press or squeeze it onto the stick so that it stays put and let it dry for seven days. Stand the sticks up in clay or other suitable material for drying.

These are only a few of the many ways of making combustible incense. Have fun and be creative when practicing the Craft of the Old and Wise.

Using Noncombustible Incense

Light a self-igniting or normal charcoal block and place it in a censer or thurible. Once the block is glowing, sprinkle approximately ½ teaspoon of the incense onto the glowing coal. Use a small spoon, the blade of a knife, or anything you choose to add the incense. It will begin to smolder immediately. In so doing, it releases its energies and fragrant smoke.

Always use just a small amount of incense at first. Wait until the smoke begins to clear to add more. Do not dump on a large amount or it will probably extinguish the charcoal or cause billowing clouds of smoke that are sure to set off the smoke detectors in your home! Incenses that contain large amounts of frankincense, myrrh, and other resins burn longer than those made mainly of woods, leaves, or oils.

Never knock off the ash that forms on top of the coal unless the incense starts to smell foul. In this case, scrape off the burning incense and the ash with a spoon or knife and add a fresh amount of incense. Frankincense and myrrh both tend to smell odd after smoldering for long periods of time.

Incense burning is used for direct acts of magic, such as to clear the house of negativity. It is also burned as part of magical ritual, to honor higher forces, and to place peaceful vibrations throughout your sacred space and/or home.

Components of Noncombustible Incense

Before you start to process or make anything in the Craft, I recommend that you check your supply cabinet and make sure you have all of the components needed to complete the task at hand. It is so frustrating to get into the middle of making something and then, to your dismay, realize that you are lacking something you need. If you find that something you need is missing, choose an appropriate substitution from the lists in chapter 13.

Grind all the ingredients for your noncombustible incense to a fine powder, using either a mortar and pestle or an electric grinder (such as a coffee grinder). Most resins are not easily powdered, but I have found that a coffee grinder works wonders! If you must use a mortar and pestle, don't get frustrated if the material sticks to the sides of the implements. This can add negative energies to the incense or formula that you are working on. With practice, you will become proficient and the gum resin you are working on will come out just fine.

When all is ready, visualize the magical goal of your incense: love, health, protection, etc. In a large wooden, ceramic, or glass bowl, mix the resins and gums together with your hands or a wooden spoon. *CAUTION: Never use aluminum utensils for any magical project!* While visualizing the magical goal of your incense, start to mix the ingredients together, forcing the energy out of your body, through your hands, into the incense itself. This is the first step in charging your incense—before you ever get it to the altar for permanent charging. It is this process that makes homemade incense more effective than its commercial counterparts.

Next, add the powdered leaves, barks, flowers, and roots, always concentrating on the magical goal at hand. This is imperative. Then add any oils or liquids (honey, wine, etc.) that are included in the recipe. Only use true essential oils; a few drops are usually sufficient. If there is a sufficient amount of dry ingredients in the recipe, you can substitute oil for any herb you are missing. You can also substitute any tincture for any herb you are missing. Simply ensure that the oil is an essential oil, for synthetics smell like burning plastic when smoldering.

Mix the ingredients thoroughly, then add any powdered gemstones or other power boosters. Not many of the recipes in this text call for any powdered stone, but it can be added to each and every one of them for added power.

Powdering Semiprecious Stones or Gems

Take a small stone of the appropriate type and pound it in a metal mortar and pestle, smash it with a hammer, or take a diamond fingernail file and file away at the stone until you have a pile of powdered stone. Grind the resulting pieces into a fine powder and add no more than the scantest pinch to the incense. One general power-boosting "stone" is amber. A pinch of this fossilized resin added to any mixture will increase its effectiveness, but this can be rather expensive.

The fully compounded incense is now ready to be taken to the altar and charged. Once charged, it is ready to be used in rituals or spells. All incense should be stored in dark, tightly capped containers that are carefully labeled with the name of the incense, the date it was made, and the page number and title of the book in which you found the recipe. I don't recommend that you use magical charged incense for household purposes. If you want to do so, however, use your intuition as to where and when and which one.

The Fourteen Most Frequently Used Incense Herbs

The following herbs are the most frequently utilized within the Craft. Of course, it is always wonderful to add to your magical component supplies as the need arises.

Frankincense	*Pine needles or resin (pitch)*
Myrrh	*Juniper*
Sandalwood	*Benzoin*
Copal	*Cedar*
Rose Petals	*Thyme*
Bay	*Basil*
Cinnamon	*Rosemary*

Be aware that some plants that smell extremely sweet turn horribly sour when burned. Conversely, some plants that smell horribly sour turn sweet when burned. It's quite curious how this works. It never ceases to amaze me!

I recommend that you start a notebook of herbs, flowers, leaves, bark, roots, etc. Try burning a small amount of each one on a hot coal and record what the scent is, whether you have any psychic reaction, and whether or not you like the scent. This will help you learn about the smells each plant produces when burned and whether you want to use them or not.

You must remember that the scent itself is not a magical factor. However, scent is power. It allows you to slip into ritual consciousness, thereby allowing you to raise magical power, infuse it with programming energies, and send it forth to do your magical bidding.

In the end, it is your obligation to train your nose to accept exotic scents. The art of incense burning will then become a joy and a natural occurrence in your daily life.

You may obtain your herbs in one of two ways. You can gather them yourself or purchase them from local establishments. Personally, I do both. I love working in my gardens. If I had my way, I would grow everything, but my energy and time do not permit that. This is a personal choice. However, the herbs you grow and collect from the wild will have more power and greater magical properties than the ones you purchase.

Charcoal Blocks

These are an absolute necessity for using noncombustible incense. Simply light the coal, wait until it glows all over with a reddish-orange color, then add a small amount of your own handcrafted incense. Unfortunately, some charcoal blocks aren't fresh, have been exposed to moisture, or haven't been properly saturated with potassium nitrate. If this happens to you, simply stick the block on your kitchen stove burner until it is sufficiently ignited. This works well, I have found, even with stubborn coals.

One Herb Incenses

The following herb list could be useful when you need incense but don't have the time to prepare a special recipe. They are quite efficient and take very little time to make.

Allspice: Attracting money, good luck, and providing extra physical energy.

Arabic(gum): Purification and protection of the home.

Bay: Purification, healing, protection, and enhancing psychic powers.

Benzoin: Purification, prosperity, and increasing mental powers.

Cedar: Purification, protection, speed healing, promoting spirituality, and obtaining money.

Clove: Protection, exorcism, money, love, and purification.

Copal: Protection, cleansing, purification, spirituality, and purifying quartz crystals and other stones before use in magic ritual.

Dragon's blood: Love, protection, sexual prowess, and exorcism.

Fern: House purification, or, when burned outdoors, bringing rain.

Frankincense: Protection, spirituality, love, exorcism, and consecration.

Juniper: Exorcism, protection, healing, and love.

Myrrh: Healing, protection, peace, consecration, exorcism, and meditation.

Pine: Money, healing, exorcism, and purification.

Rosemary: Protection, purification, healing, exorcism, and to induce sleep; to restore or maintain youth, bring love, and increase mental and intellectual powers.

Sage: Spirituality and to promote healing.

Sandalwood: Spirituality, healing, protection, and exorcism.

Thyme: Purification, promoting health, and healing.

These are just a few of the herbs you can use. Any and all herbs may be used as incense, either alone or mixed with other herbs. Remember: experimentation is the name of the game! Just keep your magical goal in mind and make sure that the herbs you use coincide with that goal.

Incense Recipes

The following recipes have been collected over more than forty years of my life. All proportions are suggestions. Feel free to experiment. *CAUTION: All illegal or poisonous herbs are marked with a ‡. Whether you use them or not is up to you.*

I have often wondered where some of the incense names came from. Some are names of individuals, spirits, deities, etc. Sometimes, however, a name shows up that defies explanation. I guess this is just one of those things that will always be a mystery.

Abramelin Incense

3 parts Myrrh
1½ parts Wood Aloe
Few drops Cinnamon

This incense is used to contact spirits during ritual, or for the consecration of altars or magical tools.

Air Incense

4 parts Benzoin
2 parts Gum Mastic
3 parts Lavender
1 pinch Wormwood‡
1 pinch Mistletoe‡

This incense is used to invoke the element air and its powers. It increases intellectual powers, promotes communication and study, facilitates travel, enhances concentration, and is useful in divinatory rituals or to end addictions.

Altar Incense

4 parts Frankincense
2 parts Myrrh
2 parts Cinnamon

This incense is used for general purification, and as an altar incense.

Anti-Anxiety Incense

4 parts Frankincense
2 parts Mullein
2 parts Mums (Chrysanthemums)

This incense is to be used when you are distraught over the passing of a loved one or friend.

Anti-Incubus Incense

3 parts Sandalwood
3 parts Benzoin
3 parts Wood Aloe
3 parts Cardamom
1 part Calamus
1 part Birthwort
1 part Ginger
½ part Cinnamon
½ part Clove
½ part Carnation
½ part Nutmeg
1 part Mace
1 part Cubeb seed
Few drops Brandy

This ancient incense is burned to ward off the incubus—a demon or evil spirit in medieval folk legend that takes on the shape of a handsome man and seduces women as they sleep in order to possess their souls. The female equivalent of the incubus is the succubus.

Anti-Theft Incense

4 parts Frankincense
2 parts Juniper berries
2 parts Vetivert
½ part Cumin

Burn this incense during the day in a censer before the front door, then move it to each opening in the house (doors, windows, cellars, etc.) through which thieves might enter. Visualize its smoke forming an invisible but impregnable barrier. Move in a clockwise circle throughout your home, replenishing the incense as necessary. Repeat monthly at the time of the Full Moon, if possible, or use as needed. This incense is designed to "lock" your home against unwanted intruders—but don't forget to lock your home as well.

Aphrodite Incense

1 part Cinnamon
3 parts Cedar
Several drops Cypress oil

This incense is used to attract love. Be careful, however, for it works extremely well!

Apollo Incense

5 parts Frankincense
2 parts Myrrh
2 parts Cinnamon
2 parts Bay

This incense is used in healing rituals and for divination.

Apparition Incense

3 parts Wood Aloe
2 parts Coriander
1 part Camphor‡
1 part Mugwort
1 part Flax
1 part Anise
1 part Cardamom
1 part Chicory
3 parts Hemp‡

This incense is used to make apparitions appear.

Aries Incense

4 parts Frankincense
2 parts Juniper
6 drops Cedarwood oil

This incense is used to increase your own powers and for a personal altar or household incense.

Astral Travel Incense

Variation One

Equal parts Poplar, Cinnamon, and Sandalwood
6 drops Jasmine oil

Variation Two

Equal parts Sandalwood and Gum Arabic

1 part Mugwort

1 part Dittany of Crete

Variation Three

½ oz. Sandalwood powder

½ oz. Lavender powder

½ oz. Bayberry powder

¼ oz. Orris root powder

½ oz. Rose petal powder

1 oz. powdered Charcoal

30 drops Frankincense oil

15 drops Patchouli oil

1½ oz. tincture of Benzoin

¹⁄₁₆ oz. Potassium nitrate or Saltpeter

This incense is used to aid in projecting the astral body.

Aquarius Incense

Equal parts of Sandalwood, Cypress, and Pine resin

This incense is used as a personal altar or household incense for your own powers.

Babylonian/Sumerian Incense

3 parts Cedar

2 parts Juniper

2 parts Cypress

2 parts Tamarisk

This incense is burned during Babylonian and Sumerian magical rites, or when attuning with deities such as Inanna, Enlil, Marduk, or Tiamat.

Bast Incense

4 parts Frankincense

3 parts Acacia gum

2 parts Myrrh

1 part Catnip

1 part Cedar

1 part Cinnamon

½ part Juniper

2 drops Civet oil

Mix all herbs to a fine powder. Blend in oil. Visualize and worship the Cat Goddess, Bast.

Beltane Incense

4 parts Frankincense
3 parts Sandalwood
2 parts Woodruff
2 parts Rose petals
Few drops Neroli oil
Few drops Jasmine oil
Few drops Orange oil

This incense is used on Beltane (April 30th) or on May Day (May 1st) for fortune and favors, or to attune to the changing of the seasons. These dates are Wiccan Sabbats.

Binding Incense

Equal parts Nettle, Thistle, and Knotgrass
¼ part Nightshade‡
¼ part Aconite (Wolfsbane)‡

This incense is used during outdoor rituals to destroy baneful (harmful or negative) habits and thoughts. Use small amounts only and be sure not to inhale the fumes.

Business Incense

2 parts Benzoin
1 part Cinnamon
1 part Basil
1 part Mustard seed

This incense is used to attract customers. Place a few mustard seeds in your cash register drawer as well.

Cancer Incense (Moonchildren)

3 parts Eucalyptus
2 parts Myrrh
1 part Sandalwood
1 part Lemon peel (or a few drops Lemon oil)

This incense is used to increase your personal powers, and as an altar or household incense.

Capricorn Incense

3 parts Sandalwood
2 parts Benzoin
Few drops Patchouli oil

This incense is used to increase your personal powers, and as an altar or household incense.

Ceremonial Magical Incense

Variation One

3 parts Frankincense
2 parts Wood Aloe
Few drops synthetic Musk oil (Harm none!)
Few drops Ambergris bouquet

Variation Two

3 parts Frankincense
2 parts Gum Mastic
2 parts Mace
1 part Brandy
1 part Wood Aloe
1 part Vervain

This incense is used to raise power and for purification. This incense is an adaptation from one found in the Key of Solomon.

Circle Incense

4 parts Frankincense
2 parts Myrrh
2 parts Benzoin/Gum Arabic
1 part Sandalwood
½ part Cinnamon
1 part Rose petals
1 part Vervain
1 part Rosemary
¼ part Bay
½ cup Orange peel

This incense is used for general workings in the Circle, the ritual working space of Wiccans and magicians, and as a general ritual incense. (The Circle is created by directing personal power to form a sphere of energy surrounding the ritual area [see page 1]).

Clearing Incense

3 parts Frankincense
3 parts Copal
3 parts Myrrh
1 part Sandalwood

This incense is used to clear, exorcise, and purify your home of all negative vibrations, especially when household members are arguing or when the house seems heavy and thick with anger, jealousy, fear, negative emotions, or depression. Leave the windows open while burning this mixture so the negativity can escape and not be trapped in your home. This one really works well!

Consecration Incense

2 parts Wood Aloe
1 part Mace
1 part Nutmeg
1 part Gum Arabic
1 part Benzoin

This incense is used to purify and consecrate magical tools, jewelry, quartz crystals, and other stones. Visualize the fumes purifying the tool as you pass it through the smoke several times.

Courage Incense

2 parts Dragon's Blood
2 parts Frankincense
1 part Rose Geranium leaves or a few drops Rose Geranium oil
Few drops Tonka bouquet
Few drops synthetic Musk oil (Harm none!)

This incense is used to increase your courage when needed. If you are in a situation you cannot bear, recall its scent and be strong. If tonka bouquet is not available, use tonka or vanilla tincture (vanilla extract).

Crystal Purification Incense

2 parts Frankincense
2 parts Copal
2 parts Sandalwood
2 parts Rosemary
1 pinch finely powdered salt
1 small, purified Quartz Crystal point

Before mixing any of the above ingredients, place the small crystal point into the jar in which your incense will be mixed. Next, place all the ground herbs in the bowl and mix them together. Visualize and charge the incense as usual. Place a bit of the incense on a burning coal and pass the crystal or crystals to be purified through the smoke, visualizing the smoke destroying the impurities within the stone. This incense can be used in any purification rituals.

Curse-Breaker Incense

Variation One

3 parts Clove
3 parts Sagebrush
3 parts Cedar

Variation Two

3 parts Sandalwood
2 parts Bay
1 part Tobacco‡

Variation Three

2 parts Frankincense
2 parts Rosemary
1 part Dragon's Blood

If you feel you are cursed, you are—your psychic intuition is trying to protect you. To use this incense, burn it near an open window, visualize it banishing all negativity from you and your area. Repeat this ritual for seven nights during the waning Moon.

Divination Incense

Variation One
2 Tbsp. Orange peel
2 Tbsp. Clove
2 Tbsp. Hyssop
½ Tbsp. each Nutmeg and Cinnamon

Variation Two
2 parts Clove
1 part Chicory
1 part Anise
1 part Cinquefoil

Variation Three
2 parts Sandalwood
2 parts Orange peel
1 part Mace
1 part Nutmeg

Smolder any of these during or directly before using tarot cards, magic mirrors, quartz crystal spheres or rune stones, or any divination method or methods. The second recipe given above does not smell very good.

Dream Incense
2 parts Cedar
2 parts Rose petals
1 part Camphor‡
1 part Lavender
Few drops Tuberose bouquet
Few drops Jasmine oil

To produce psychic dreams, smolder on a hot coal in your bedroom prior to sleep. If you cannot find real camphor‡, use spirits of camphor‡, available at most drug stores. Just a few drops will do nicely.

Earth Incense (Elemental)
3 parts Pine resin/needles
2 parts Patchouli
2 parts powdered salt

Few drops Cypress oil

This incense is used for invoking the powers of the element of Mother Earth for stability, money, etc.

Earth Incense (Planetary)

2 parts Pine needles
2 parts Thyme
Few drops Patchouli oil

This incense is used for honoring the Earth, and for all Earth-revering rituals.

Egyptian Incense

4 parts Frankincense
3 parts Gum Arabic
2 parts Myrrh
2 parts Cedar
2 parts Juniper
1 part Camphor‡
1 part Cinnamon

This incense is used during Egyptian rites and to honor any ancient Egyptian deity, such as Isis, Osiris, Thoth, Anubis, Selket, or Heket.

Egyptian Thief Incense

2 parts Crocus
2 pinches Alum

In ancient Egypt, this incense was placed on a brazier and the seer stared into the coals to see the thief. Visualize as always.

Eightfold Hearth Incense

3 parts Dragon's Blood
3 parts Myrrh
2 parts Juniper
1 part Sassafras
1 part Orange flowers
1 part Rose petals

This incense is used to guard, protect, and create a safe, warm, loving home environment. This makes a wonderful gift.

Emergency Incense

(inspired by Jim Alan's song "Talkin' Wicca Blues")

3 parts Frankincense
3 parts Dragon's Blood
2 parts Myrrh
2 parts Rosemary
1 part Asafoetida‡
1 part Cayenne
1 part Grains of Paradise
1 part Rue
1 part Garlic

This incense is used to banish wrathful spirits, foul demons, drunks, tax collectors, or anything that is detrimental to one's physical, psychic, or mental safety. *CAUTION: This incense is irritating to the eyes, nose, and lungs. I recommend that you ignite it and then leave the room.*

Esbat Incense

4 parts Frankincense
3 parts Myrrh
2 parts Benzoin
2 parts Sandalwood
2 parts Gardenia petals
1 part Orris root
½ part Thyme
½ part Poppy seed
½ part Rose petals

This incense is used during rituals and spells at the thirteen monthly coven meetings held, one during each Full Moon.

Exorcism Incense

Variation One

2 parts Cumin

2 parts Mistletoe‡
2 parts Bay
1 part Avens
1 part Mugwort
1 part St. John's Wort
1 part Angelica
1 part Basil

Variation Two

3 parts Frankincense
2 parts Rosemary
1 Tbsp. Cayenne Pepper
2 parts Pine
1 part Sagebrush
1 part Thistle
3 parts Yarrow oil

Variation Three

¼ tsp. Brimstone (powdered)
1 tsp. Mistletoe‡
1 Tbsp. Orris powder
1 tsp. Jalop powder
2 Tbsp. Rosemary (powdered)
1 pinch Saltpeter
2 Tbsp. powdered Charcoal
1 Tbsp. all-purpose flour
30 drops Patchouli oil
30 drops Jasmine oil
1 oz. tincture of Benzoin

This incense is to be burned with open windows in disturbed places as a heavy purifying incense. Breathe through your mouth while smoldering this.

Fire Incense (Elemental)

3 parts Frankincense
3 parts Dragon's Blood
1 part Red Sandalwood
1 pinch Saffron
Few drops synthetic Musk oil (Harm none!)

This incense is used to summon the powers and beings of fire, and for success, strength, protection, health, and passion. If you have no real saffron, substitute orange peel.

Fire of Azrael Incense

2 parts Sandalwood

2 parts Cedar

2 parts Juniper

This incense is to be burned while scrying, or it can be thrown onto the coals of an outside fire once the flames have burned down.

Frankincense Incense

2 Tbsp. Frankincense

1 Tbsp. Orris root

1 tsp. Clove

1 Tbsp. Lemon oil

Grind the herbs with a mortar and pestle, add the oil, and mix. This incense is for general ritual and altar use. It is also excellent for worshipping any of the gods or goddesses of any pantheon. Visualize while charging.

Full Moon Incense

Variation One

2 parts Sandalwood

2 parts Frankincense

1 part Gardenia petals

½ part Rose petals

Few drops Ambergris oil

Variation Two

3 parts Frankincense

2 parts Sandalwood

Variation Three

2 parts Cedar

2 parts Copal

2 parts Lemon

12 drops Jasmine oil

Variation Four

3 parts Gardenia petals

2 parts Frankincense

1 part Rose petals
1 part Orris root
Few drops Sandalwood oil

This incense is used at the thirteen Wiccan Full Moon
Esbats, for worship and attuning with deity.

Gamblers Incense

Equal parts Gum Mastic and Frankincense

This incense is to be burned before gambling of any
kind.

Gemini Incense

2 parts Gum Mastic
2 parts Citron
½ part Mace

This incense is used as a personal altar or household
incense to increase your powers.

Goddess Incense

15 drops Cypress oil
15 drops Olive oil
½ oz. dried Rose petals
½ oz. White Willow bark
3 dried Rowan berries
1 tsp. Anise seeds

This incense is to be mixed when the Moon is new.
Visualize as usual, grind the herbs, add the oils, and mix.
Use this to worship the Triple Goddess in rituals.

Good Omen Incense

1½ oz. Myrrh
1 oz. Dragon's Blood
½ oz. Sassafras
½ oz. Orange blossoms
½ oz. Juniper
½ oz. Sage
15 drops Frankincense oil
10 Rose Petals

Grind the herbs with a mortar and pestle, mix oil in with the herbs, and visualize your needs and desires while charging. Make this incense on the night of the New Moon.

Greek God and Goddess Incense

5 parts Frankincense (sacred to Apollo)
4 parts Myrrh (Demeter)
3 parts Pine (Poseidon)
3 parts Rose petals (Aphrodite)
2 parts Sage (Zeus)
2 parts White Willow bark (Persephone)
Few drops Olive oil (Athena)
Few drops Cypress oil (Artemis/Hecate)

This incense is used to honor the Greek gods and goddesses in circle and ritual worship.

Hathor Incense

5 parts Orris root
5 parts Rose petals
3 parts Myrrh
2 parts Spikenard
2 parts Calamus
7 drops Civet oil
9 drops Henna oil (oil from Henna plant)

All herbs must be ground into a fine powder and mixed. Add the oils. Blend, visualize, and burn to worship the goddess of inspiration and strength (also known in Egypt as Het Heret or Hat Hor). These names all refer to the same goddess.

Healing Incense

Variation One
2 parts Rosemary
2 parts Juniper berries

Variation Two
2 parts Myrrh
2 parts Cinnamon
2 pinches Saffron

Variation Three

3 parts Myrrh

2 parts Nutmeg

2 parts Cedar

2 parts Clove

½ part Lemon Balm

½ part Poppy seeds

Few drops Pine oil

Few drops Almond oil

Variation Four

3 parts Myrrh

2 parts Rose petals

2 parts Eucalyptus

2 pinches Saffron

Few drops Cedarwood oil

Variation Five

4 parts Juniper berries

2 parts Rosemary

Grind all ingredients into a fine powder and mix. Charge the incense and then burn on charcoal.

Hecate Incense

Variation One

4 parts Sandalwood

3 parts Cypress

2 parts Mint

Variation Two

½ tsp. dried Bay leaves

½ tsp. dried Mint leaves

½ tsp. dried Thyme

Pinch Myrrh resin

Pinch Frankincense resin

3 drops Camphor‡ oil

13 drops Cypress oil

Variation Three

½ tsp. dried Bay leaves

½ tsp. dried Mint leaves

½ tsp. dried Thyme

Pinch Myrrh resin

Pinch Frankincense resin

13 drops Cypress oil
4 drops Camphor‡ oil

This incense is ignited to honor Hecate. It should be burned at a crossroads or during ritual at the waning of the Moon. On August 13th it should be burned to honor the Goddess, or at Full Moon rituals as a powerful visionary incense.

Honors Incense

2 parts Benzoin
2 parts Wood Aloe
½ part Pepperwort/Rue

This incense is to be burned for honors and favors. Visualize.

Horned God Incense

2 parts Benzoin
2 parts Cedar
2 parts Pine
2 parts Juniper berries
Few drops Patchouli oil

This incense is to be burned in honor of the Horned God in his many disguises, especially during Wiccan rites and rituals.

House-Purification Incense

Variation One

3 parts Frankincense
3 parts Dragon's Blood
1 part Myrrh
2 parts Sandalwood
1 part Wood Betony
½ part Dill seed
Few drops Rose Geranium oil

Variation Two

3 parts Hyssop
3 parts Chamomile
3 parts Yarrow

2 parts Lemon Verbena
1 part Dill

This incense is to be burned in your home at least once a month, and perhaps on the Full Moon. Additionally, never move into a new home without burning this mixture.

Imbolc Incense

3 parts Frankincense
3 parts Dragon's Blood
½ part Red Sandalwood
1 part Cinnamon
Few drops red wine

Add a pinch of the first flower (dried) that is available in your area at the time of Imbolc. Burn this incense to attune to the symbolic rebirth of the Sun—the fading of winter and the promise of spring to come. Also burn it for our Wiccan ritualistic ceremonies on Imbolc (February 1st).

Isis/Kyphi Incense

Variation One

3 parts Myrrh
2 parts Sandalwood
1 part Frankincense
3 parts Rose petals
2 eyedroppers Lotus bouquet

Variation Two

3 parts Lemon balm
3 parts Cedar
1 part Copal
1 part Jasmine oil

Variation Three

3 parts white Sandalwood
2 parts Myrrh
2 parts Orris root
1 part Rose petals
1 part Frankincense
5 drops Lotus bouquet (see recipe on page 10)

Variation Four

½ oz. Benzoin

½ oz. Cinnamon

½ oz. Frankincense

½ oz. Galangal

1 oz. Myrrh

4 drops Lotus bouquet

4 drops Honey

These recipes are for attuning with the Egyptian goddess, Isis.

Jupiter Incense (Planetary)

Variation One

2 parts Wood Aloe

1 part Benzoin

2 parts Gum Arabic

¼ part Ash seed

1 pinch powdered Lapis Lazuli

Few drops Olive oil

Variation Two

3 parts Frankincense

2 parts Mace

1 part Cardamom

½ part Balm of Gilead

¼ part pulverized Oak leaves

⅛ part pulverized Pomegranate rind

2 pinches Saffron

Few drops Ambergris bouquet

Variation Three

1 part Clove

1 part Nutmeg

1 part Cinnamon

1 part Lemon Balm

1 part Citron peel

Mix, visualize, and burn for spells involving expansion, law, luck, and riches. The stone Lapis Lazuli can be charged for a Jupiterian talisman.

Kyphi/Isis Incense

Variation One

4 parts Frankincense
2 parts Benzoin
2 parts Gum Mastic
2 parts Myrrh
1 part Cedar
1 part Galangal or Ginger
½ part Calamus or Vetivert
½ part Cardamom
½ part Cinnamon
½ part Cassia
½ part Juniper berries
½ part Orris root
½ part Cypress
Few drops Lotus bouquet
Few drops red wine (Malmsey)
Few drops Honey
30 Raisins

Grind and mix the dry herbs thoroughly. This must sit in an airtight container for two weeks. After the two-week period, mix the oil, wine, honey, and raisins into the dry herbs and blend with your hands. Let this sit another two weeks. Then, if desired, grind to a fine powder. Kyphi incense is used in night rituals, to invoke Egyptian goddesses and gods, and as a general magical incense.

Kyphi/Isis Incense

Variation Two

4 parts Frankincense
2 parts Benzoin
2 parts Myrrh
1 part Juniper berries
½ part Galangal
½ part Cinnamon
½ part Cedar

4 drops Lotus bouquet

2 drops red wine (Malmsey)

2 drops Honey

15 Raisins

Mix and burn as you would Kyphi incense, Variation One.

Kyphi/Isis Incense

Variation Three

½ oz. Benzoin

½ oz. Cinnamon

½ oz. Frankincense

½ oz. Galangal

1 oz. Myrrh

3 drops Lotus bouquet

3 drops Honey

Using your hands, mix together the benzoin, cinnamon, frankincense, galangal, and myrrh in a large nonmetallic bowl. Add the lotus bouquet and honey and mix thoroughly. Cover the bowl tightly with a plastic wrap and let it sit undisturbed for two weeks in a dark place. With a mortar and pestle, grind the ingredients into a fine powder and burn on a hot charcoal block as a magical incense or to invoke ancient Egyptian deities.

Kyphi/Isis Incense

Variation Four

½ pint Cyperus (a type of bulrush used as a thickener)

½ pint Juniper berries

12 lbs. of Stone Plum Raisins

5 lbs. of resin

1 lb. of Aromatic Rush

1 lb. Asphalatus (Cystisus lanigerus, Genista acantho-clada—a thickener)

1 lb. Iuncus odoratrus (Cymbopogon schoenan-nathus)

1½ oz. Myrrh

8½ pints aged red wine (Malmsey or Egyptian Wine)

2 lbs. Honey

Using a mortar and pestle, grind the stone plum raisins with the wine and myrrh. Holding back the honey, pound and sift the remaining ingredients together with the raisins. Let sit for a day. Boil the honey to thicken it. Strain and mix with the other ingredients. Store in an earthenware pot or jar. This complicated incense tends to improve with age, and is intended to be burned over charcoal. Kyphi was added to wine as a flavoring and used as a purge by Egyptian physicians. It induced trance states and promoted sleep. This incense is reported to be the recipe of Dioscorides. I personally do not know, but it is quite interesting, so I have included it here.

Leo Incense

2 parts Gum Mastic
2 parts Sandalwood
1 part Juniper berries

This incense is used as a personal altar or household incense to increase your personal powers.

Libra Incense

3 parts Sandalwood
2 parts Thyme
Few drops Rose oil

This incense is used as a personal altar or household incense to increase your personal powers.

Love Incense

Variation One

½ oz. Sweet Bugle
½ oz. Cinnamon
1 oz. Sandalwood powder
¼ oz. Anise seed
⅛ tsp. Potassium nitrate or Saltpeter
¼ oz. Frankincense
7 oz. powdered Charcoal
6 oz. tincture of Benzoin

Variation Two

3 parts Sandalwood
½ part Basil
1 part Bergamot bouquet

1 part Lavender

Few drops Rose oil

Few drops Lavender oil

Variation Three

2 parts Dragon's Blood

1 part Orris root

½ part Cinnamon

1 part Rose petals

Few drops synthetic Musk oil (Harm none!)

Few drops Patchouli oil

Variation Four

2 parts Dragon's Blood

1 part Mint

1 part Orris root

1 part Violet

Few drops Patchouli oil

2 parts Lavender

Lughnasadh Incense

Variation One

2 parts Frankincense

2 parts Daisy

2 parts Lilac

1 part Rosemary

Few drops Ambergris oil

Variation Two

2 parts Frankincense

2 parts Heather

1 part Apple blossoms

1 pinch Blackberry leaves

Few drops Ambergris oil

This incense is burned during Wiccan rites and rituals on August 1st or 2nd, and to attune to the coming harvest. Always visualize.

Mabon Incense

3 parts Frankincense

2 parts Sandalwood

2 parts Cypress oil

1 part Juniper

1 part Pine
1 part Oakmoss bouquet
1 pinch pulverized Oak leaf
1 part Sage

This incense is burned during Wiccan rites and rituals on September 21st or 22nd, Autumnal Equinox, or Circa, or at that time to attune with the change of the seasons. Always visualize.

Mars Incense (Planetary)

Variation One

3 parts Galangal
1 part Coriander
2 parts Cloves
1 part Basil
Scant pinch Black Pepper

Variation Two

4 parts Benzoin
2 parts Pine needles (resin)
Scant pinch Black Pepper

Variation Three

3 parts Dragon's Blood
1 part Cardamom
2 parts Clove
2 parts Grains of Paradise

This incense is burned to attract Martian influences, or during rituals and spells involving lust, exorcism, competitions, physical strength, or men. Always visualize.

Medicine Wheel Incense

2 parts Sage
2 parts Lavender
1 part Sweetgrass
1 part Pine resin or needles
1 part Angelica root
Scant pinch Tobacco‡

This incense is burned during rites and rituals revering the American Indian deities and spirits. It is also used to attune to Mother Earth energies. Always visualize.

Meditation Incense

1 part Gum Arabic
1 part Sandalwood
1 part Cedar

This incense is burned prior to meditation to relax the conscious mind. Always visualize.

Mercury Incense (Planetary)

Variation One

2 parts Benzoin
1 part Lavender
1 part Mace
1 part Frankincense

Variation Two

2 parts Benzoin
1 part Lavender
1 part Marjoram
Few drops Lavender oil

Variation Three

2 parts Sandalwood
1 part Gum Mastic
1 part Lavender
Few drops Lavender oil

This incense is burned to invoke the powers of Mercury, or during rites and rituals involving travel, divination, or intelligence.

Mexicali Magic Incense

2 parts Copal
2 parts Frankincense
2 parts Rosemary

This incense is burned during Mexican-American folk magic rituals and spells.

Midsummer Incense (June 21)

Variation One

2 parts Sandalwood

1 part Mugwort
2 parts Chamomile
1 part Gardenia petals
Few drops Rose oil
Few drops Lavender oil
Few drops Yarrow oil

Variation Two

3 parts Frankincense
2 parts Benzoin
2 parts Dragon's Blood
1 part Thyme
1 part Rosemary
1 pinch Vervain
Few drops red wine

This incense is burned at Wiccan rituals at the Summer Solstice or around that time to attune to the seasons and the Sun.

Moon Incense

Variation One

2 parts Frankincense
2 parts Sandalwood
Few drops Eucalyptus oil
Few drops Jasmine oil
Few drops Camphor‡ oil

Variation Two

4 parts Sandalwood
2 parts Wood Aloe
1 part Eucalyptus
1 part pulverized Cucumber seed
1 part Mugwort
1 part Ranunculus blossoms
2 parts Selenetrope
Few drops Ambergris oil

Variation Three

2 parts Juniper berries
2 parts Orris root
1 part Calamus
Few drops Spirits of Camphor‡ oil
Few drops Lotus bouquet

Variation Four

2 parts Myrrh
2 parts Gardenia petals
2 parts Rose petals
2 parts Lemon peel
½ part Camphor‡
Few drops Jasmine oil

This incense is burned to attract the Goddess's influences, and also during psychic workings, love magic, healing, and rituals involving the home and dream magic.

Moonfire Incense

3 parts Rose
2 parts Orris root
1 part Bay
1 part Juniper
3 parts Dragon's Blood
½ part Potassium nitrate or Saltpeter

This incense is burned for love and harmony, divination, or anything concerning the workings of the Moon. *CAUTION: If too much potassium nitrate is added, the mixture will explode!*

Nine Woods Incense

Use equal part of the following woods:
Rowan or Sandalwood
Apple Wood
Dogwood
Poplar Wood
Juniper Wood
Cedar Wood
Pine Wood
Holly Wood‡
Elder or Oak Wood

Grind each into sawdust, mix them together, and burn indoors on charcoal when a ritual fire is necessary or desired, but not practical. This incense smells of an open campfire.

Offertory Incense

3 parts Frankincense
2 parts Myrrh
1 part Cinnamon
1 part Rose petals
1 part Vervain

This incense is to be burned to honor the goddesses.

Ostara Incense

2 parts Frankincense
1 part Benzoin
2 parts Dragon's Blood
½ part Nutmeg
1 part Violet flowers
1 part Orange peel
2 parts Rose petals

This incense is burned from March 20th to the 24th, depending when the Spring Equinox falls, to celebrate Ostara, or to welcome the spring and to refresh your spirituality and the return of the Sun and abundance of life.

Pele Incense (Hawaiian Volcano Goddess)

3 parts Frankincense
3 parts Dragon's Blood
1 part Red Sandalwood
2 parts Orange peel
1 part Cinnamon
Few drops Clove oil

This incense is burned when you wish to be filled with additional strength, when you feel manipulated by others, or for fire spells in general.

Pisces Incense

2 parts Frankincense
2 parts Eucalyptus oil

2 parts Lemon peel
Few drops Sandalwood oil

This incense is burned to increase your own powers or as a personal altar or household incense.

Planetary Incense (General)

Use all the following ingredients in equal parts:

Myrrh
Gum Mastic
Costus
Opoponax
Frankincense
Camphor‡
Red Sandalwood
Wood Aloe
Storax
Thyme
Euphorbium‡

This incense is used for any general rituals pertaining to the workings of all the planets. Check the substitution lists in chapter 13 for any needed changes.

Prophecy Incense

Mix the following ingredients in equal parts:

Fleawort seed
Violet root
Parsley
Hempseed‡

This incense is burned for divination and psychic work.

Prophetic Dream Incense

2 parts Frankincense
1 part Buchu
1 part Rose
1 part Marigold

This incense is burned before going to bed to encourage the psychic mind to surface and produce prophetic dreams. It will also ensure that the conscious mind remembers the dreams in the morning.

Protection Incense

Variation One

2 parts Frankincense

3 parts Dragon's Blood

½ part Wood Betony

Variation Two

2 parts Frankincense

2 parts Sandalwood

½ part Rosemary

Variation Three

1 part Frankincense

2 parts Myrrh

1 part Clove

Variation Four

2 parts Frankincense

1 part Clove

1 part Rosemary

Variation Five

4 parts Hyssop

2 parts Myrrh

2 parts Juniper Berries

1 part Rosemary

½ part Avens

½ part Mugwort

½ part Yarrow

½ part St. John's Wort

½ part Angelica oil

½ part Basil

2 parts Clove oil

Variation Six

2 parts Frankincense

1 part Copal

2 parts Dragon's Blood

This incense is burned for protection, both physical and psychic. Visualize as usual.

Psychic Incense

Variation One

3 parts Frankincense

2 parts Bistort

Variation Two

2 parts Sandalwood
1 part Gum Acacia
1 part Cedar

Variation Three

2 parts Frankincense
2 parts Sandalwood
1 part Cinnamon
1 part Nutmeg

This incense is to be burned to increase and enhance your psychic abilities.

Purification Incense

Variation One

4 parts Frankincense
2 parts Bay
2 parts Camphor‡
1 pinch sea salt finely powdered
1 pinch Sulfur‡

Variation Two

3 parts Sandalwood
1 part Cinnamon
1 part Frankincense
1 part Vervain

This incense is to be burned to purify the atmosphere of a disturbed home. *CAUTION: Open the windows when working with sulfur and do not breathe the fumes!*

Rain Incense

5 parts Heather
2 parts Fern
½ part Henbane‡

This incense is burned out of doors on a deserted hilltop to attract rain. *CAUTION: Do not inhale the fumes!*

Raise Spirits Incense

Mix equal parts of the following:

Pepperwort

Red Storax

Saffron

Few drops synthetic Musk oil (Harm none!)

According to ancient texts, this incense causes spirits and ghosts to gather if burned about the tombs and graves of the dead. Visualize as always.

Riches and Favors Incense

2 parts Gum Arabic

2 parts Wood Aloe

½ part Pepperwort

1 part Clove

This incense is to be burned when you need favors and wealth. Visualize as always.

Sabbat Incense

4 parts Frankincense

2 parts Myrrh

2 parts Benzoin

½ part Bay

½ part Fennel

½ part Thyme

½ part Pennyroyal

1 part Solomon's Seal

¼ part Rue

¼ part Wormwood‡

½ part Chamomile

½ part Rose petals

1 part Snapdragons

This incense is burned during Wiccan Sabbats for purification and general magical workings.

Sagittarius Incense

2 parts Frankincense

2 parts Myrrh

2 parts Clove

This incense is burned to increase your own personal powers and as an altar incense.

Sahumerian Azteca Incense

4 parts Copal
3 parts Frankincense
2 parts Rosemary
1 part Sage
2 parts Lemongrass
2 parts Bay
1 part Marigold
1 part Yerba Santa

This incense is used for ancient Aztec rituals and all Mexican-American folk magic. It is also used as a general purification incense.

Saturn Incense (Planetary)

Variation One

3 parts Cypress
2 parts Ash leaves
1 part Alum
1 part Gum Scammony
1 part Asafoetida‡
1 part Sulfur‡
½ part Nightshade‡

Variation Two

2 parts Frankincense
2 parts Poppy seed
1 part Gum Arabic
2 parts Myrrh
¼ part Henbane‡ seed
¼ part Mandrake‡ root
Few drops Olive oil

Variation Three

2 parts Sandalwood
2 parts Myrrh
2 parts Dittany of Crete
Few drops Cypress oil
Few drops Patchouli oil

Variation Four

1 part Pepperwort
1 part Mandrake‡

1 part Myrrh
Few drops synthetic Musk oil (Harm none!)
Few drops Cypress oil

This incense is burned for Saturnian influences and for spells dealing with buildings, studying past lives, and banishing illnesses, pests, and negative habits. *CAUTION: This incense can be dangerous. Henbane‡ and mandrake‡ are baneful plants!*

Scorpio Incense

2 parts Frankincense
1 part Galangal
1 part Ginger root
1 part Pine resin

This incense is burned to increase your personal powers and as an altar incense. Visualize as always.

Scrying Incense

2 parts Mugwort
2 parts Wormwood‡

This incense is burned prior to scrying in your quartz crystal ball. It signifies flames, water, smoke, etc. *CAUTION: This is a foul-smelling incense.* Visualize as always.

Sight/Scrying Incense

2 parts Gum Mastic
2 parts Juniper
2 parts Sandalwood
2 parts Cinnamon
2 parts Calamus
Few drops Ambergris bouquet
Few drops Patchouli oil

This incense is burned to promote and increase psychic awareness. Visualize as always.

Spirit Incense
Variation One
1 part Anise

1 part Coriander

1 part Cardamom

1 part Lavender

1 part Sandalwood

1 part Willow bark

Variation Two

5 parts Coriander

1 part Smallage (Parsley)

¼ part Henbane‡

¼ part Hemlock‡

1 part Sandalwood

1 part black Poppy seed

Variation Three

2 parts Sandalwood

3 parts Wood Aloe

1 part Crocus

1 part Costus

Few drops Ambergris Bouquet

Few drops synthetic Musk oil (Harm none!)

Variation Four

3 parts Frankincense

2 parts Coriander

2 parts Fennel root

1 part Cassia

½ part Henbane‡

Few drops Ambergris bouquet

These incenses are burned to make spirits and strange shapes appear. *CAUTION: You never know exactly what you will get!*

Spirit Dismissal Incense

Variation One

2 parts Calamint

2 parts Peony

1 part Mint (Spearmint)

¼ part Castor beans‡ or Castor oil‡

Variation Two

1 part Parsley

1 part Asafoetida‡

1 part Frankincense

Variation Three

3 parts Fennel seed

3 parts Dill seed

1 part Rue

This incense is burned to banish the spirits you have called. I do not recommend calling any kind of spirits! Magic is a direction of personal power (the energy within your being), as well as of the Elementals, not summoned spirits!

Study Incense

2 parts Gum Arabic

2 parts Rosemary

This incense is burned to strengthen the conscious mind, develop concentration, improve the memory, and for study.

Success Incense

3 parts Wood Aloe

2 parts Frankincense

1 part Cedar

1 part Nutmeg

1 part Cinnamon

This incense is to be burned for success in all undertakings.

Sun Incense

Variation One

3 parts Frankincense

3 parts Sandalwood

2 parts Bay

2 pinches Saffron

Few drops Orange oil

Few drops honey

Variation Two

3 parts Frankincense

3 parts Galangal

2 parts Bay

¼ part Mistletoe‡

Few drops red wine

Few drops honey

Variation Three

3 parts Frankincense

3 parts Myrrh

1 part Wood Aloe

1 part Balm of Gilead

½ part Bay

½ part Carnation

Few drops Ambergris bouquet

Few drops synthetic Musk oil (Harm none!)

Few drops Olive oil

Variation Four

3 parts Frankincense

2 parts Clove

½ part Red Sandalwood

½ part Sandalwood

½ part Orange flowers

3 pinches Orris root

This incense is burned for spells involving promotions, friendships, energy, magical power, healing, or any magical workings pertaining to the Sun's influences.

Talisman Consecration Incense

2 parts Frankincense

2 parts Cypress

1 part Ash leaves

1 part Tobacco‡

1 pinch Valerian

1 pinch Alum

1 pinch Asafoetida‡

This incense is used to consecrate any type of talisman. *CAUTION: This incense does not smell very good. I recommend any of the other consecrating incenses listed here.*

Taurus Incense

3 parts Sandalwood

2 parts Benzoin

1 part Rose

Few drops Rose oil

This incense is used to increase your powers and as a personal altar and household incense.

Temple Incense

3 parts Frankincense
3 parts Myrrh
2 parts Lavender
Few drops Lavender oil
Few drops Sandalwood

This incense is burned in the temple or "magic room," or as a general magical incense. It also increases spirituality. Visualize as always.

True Love Incense

1 part Cinnamon
1 part Orris root
2 parts Roses
Few drops Patchouli oil

This incense is burned to bring love into your life. *CAUTION: Do not use this unless you want true love!*

Universal Incense

3 parts Frankincense
2 parts Benzoin
1 part Myrrh
1 part Sandalwood
1 part Rosemary
1 part Clove

This incense is burned for all positive magical purposes. The incense above is not to be used for any negative magical purposes. It will totally cancel out the spell or ritual.

Venus Incense (Planetary)

Variation One

2 parts Violet
2 parts Rose petals
½ part Olive leaves

1 part Orchid (optional)
Few drops Violet oil

Variation Two

3 parts Wood Aloe
2 parts red Rose petals
1 part crushed red Coral
Few drops Olive oil
Few drops synthetic Musk oil (Harm none!)
Few drops Ambergris bouquet

Variation Three

2 parts Sandalwood
2 parts Benzoin
2 parts Rosebuds
Few drops Patchouli oil
Few drops Rose oil

This incense is burned to bring love and healing, and in rituals involving women and partnerships. Use the above mixture for any Venusian influences.

Virgo Incense

2 parts Mace
2 parts Cypress
1 part Almond
Few drops Patchouli oil
2 parts Peppermint
2 parts Bergamot Mint
1 part Honeysuckle‡
Few drops Lavender oil

This incense is burned as a personal altar or household incense to increase your personal powers.

Visionary Incense

3 parts Frankincense
1 part Bay
1 part Damiana
1 part Pomegranate skin
1 part Calamus
2 parts Fennel root
1 part Red Sandalwood

1½ parts Henbane‡

This incense is burned prior to psychic workings.

Water Incense (Elemental)

Variation One

2 parts Benzoin
1 part Myrrh
1 part Sandalwood
1 part Lotus bouquet
Few drops Ambergris bouquet

Variation Two

3 parts Lemon balm
1 part Gardenia
1 part Passion Flowers
1 part Lemon
1 part Sweet Pea bouquet

This incense is burned to develop psychism, and promote love, fertility, or beauty. It is also used to attract the influences of the element water.

Wealth Incense

Variation One

1 part Pine
1 part Nutmeg
1 part Pepperwort
1 part Saffron

Variation Two

2 parts Frankincense
1 part Cinnamon
1 part Nutmeg
2 parts Lemon balm
2 parts Citron

Variation Three

4 parts Pine needles
1 part Cinnamon
1 part Galangal
Few drops Cedar oil
Few drops Patchouli oil

Variation Four

3 parts Frankincense

1 part Cinnamon

1 part Nutmeg

1 part Clove

1 part Ginger

6 parts Orange peel

2 parts Bergamot bouquet

1 part Patchouli oil

This incense is burned to attract wealth. This really works! Try it! You will like it!

Yule Incense

3 parts Frankincense

2 parts Pine needles

2 parts Cedar

2 parts Juniper berries

6 drops Pine oil

This incense is burned at Wiccan rituals on Yule, around December 21st, and during the winter months to cleanse the home and to attune to the forces of nature amid the cold days and nights.

CHAPTER FIVE

Bath Salts

Bath salts are an easily prepared alternative to herbal baths and are much preferable to the caustic chemical mixtures sold by manufacturers today, most of which can irritate your skin and aggravate your allergies. The basic ingredients of these homemade salts are all natural: Epsom salts, baking soda, borax, and sea salt.

From this base, you can make many different bath salts, in any quantity needed. If you need several different types, simply divide the base and set aside those portions to be separately scented and colored.

Color as well as scent empowers these bath salts. Use plain food coloring for this purpose, letting it fall drop by drop onto the salt base. For exotic hues (such as purple), mix the required colors in a spoon first and then add to the bath salts, adding enough food color to make the hue you desire.

Always mix bath salts with a wood spoon. Never mix essential oils in anything but glass, pyrex, pottery, enamel, or stainless steel. *CAUTION: Never use aluminum utensils when preparing or handling essential oils, as a toxic reaction can occur.*

Add your true essential oils drop by drop, one ingredient at a time. Let your Goddess- and God-given instincts tell you when the scent seems right. Mix with a wooden spoon until all the salt particles are moistened. It will take some time—perhaps thirty minutes to one hour—to get the oils mixed into the base properly. As you mix the oils into the base, visualize the oils' energies merging, mingling, and blending with each other and with the bath salts base.

Charging or Enchanting Bath Salts

This ritual can be used for any charging in the Craft.

1. Turn on the proper type of music.

2. Start the coal smoldering.

3. Cast a 9-foot circle (see Circle Casting in chapter 1).

4. Cast out all negative and harmful energies from the jar of bath salts by saying:

    In the name of the Goddess and God,
    I cast off all negative energies from these_____bath salts.

    Cast off all negative energies by moving your hands from the middle of the jar to the bottom, and then from the middle of the jar to the top, going in a complete circle around the jar in a clockwise motion.

5. Charge the bath salts by saying:

    In the name of the Goddess and God,
    I charge these_____bath salts for_____.

    Force the energy from the cosmos and your body into the jar of salts for whatever particular magical intent you are charging them. Say:

    Blessed be.
    So mote it be.

6. Ask the candles of the appropriate color to lend their energies to the charging of these_____bath salts. (The candle colors and correspondences are listed on page 240) and say:

    In the name of the Goddess and God,
    I ask these candles to lend their energies
    to these_____bath salts.

    Actually pass the jar through the flames of the candles or candle.

    Blessed be.
    So mote it be.

7. Charge the bath salts in the incense, saying:

    In the name of the Goddess and God,
    I ask this incense to lend its energies
    to these_____bath salts.

    Blessed be.
    So mote it be.

At this point, either another jar or component can be charged, starting the process all over again, or the Circle can be closed.

To use the bath salts, add from ¼ to ½ cup of salts to the water in your bath tub and stir with your hand, visualizing the energies of the salts and water, visualizing the magical intent of the ritual bath. Allow yourself to receive this energy, or to release specific negative energies from yourself into the water.

Always clean the bathtub before you get into the ritual bath. A ritual bath taken in an unclean tub will not have the desired effect. Clean the tub with either a commercial cleanser or with a damp cloth covered with baking soda.

Generally speaking, there shouldn't be more than 10 drops total of essential oil per half cup of bath salts. Use only genuine true essential oils and experiment to find what works best for you and your recipes.

Preparing the Bath Salts Base

The following bath salts recipe is easy to make. It acts as a water softener as well as performing its magical goals. Bath Salts also make wonderful gifts. Have fun and enjoy.

Bath Salts Base

3 parts Epsom salts
2 parts Baking soda
1 part Borax

OR

½ part sea salt and ½ part Borax

Mix all the above ingredients thoroughly. With this base, you can create a wide variety of bath salts. If you want to make more than one type of salt, simply divide the base and set aside the portions to be separately fragranced and colored.

To add the power of colors to your bath salts, use food coloring. Add it drop by drop into the base mixture. If an exotic color is required, mix the colors in a spoon before adding them to the base mixture. This will keep the tint even. Color recommendations for the bath salts are included with the following recipes. For those that read "Color: White," simply leave the base mixture untinted. For darker colors, just add more food coloring. Mix with a wooden spoon until evenly distributed.

Next, add the true essential oils drop by drop, one oil at time, until the scent seems right to you. Mix with a wooden spoon until all of the oils are completely blended with the base mixture. This can take up to thirty minutes, depending on the quantity of base and oils used. At all times, keep in mind the magical goal of the salts.

Your next step is to visualize the magical goal of the bath salts. Picture the goal in your mind's eye. Send energy from your inner being into the salts, through your body, out through your hands, and into the salts.

Proportions

Although each recipe below lists relative proportions, rely on your nose to determine the exact quantities used. The stronger the finished product's scent, the less you will have to use for each bath. All bath salts should be strongly scented.

To a full tub of hot bath water, add from 2 tablespoons to ¼ cup of the ritual bath salts. As you are sitting in the tub, soak up the power. Allow yourself to receive the power, or alternately, to release specific negative energies from yourself into the water.

Bath Salts Recipes

When mixing these bath salt recipes, use only true essential oils. *CAUTION: All illegal or poisonous ingredients are marked with a ‡.* Apply the following conversions:

1 part   =   6 drops
1 part bouquet   =   2 eyedroppers

Air Bath (Elemental)

4 parts Lavender oil
1 part Rosemary oil
1 part Peppermint oil
1 part Bergamot Mint bouquet
Color: Yellow

Use for divination, theorizing, aiding the memory, concentration, clear thinking, visualization, study, and anything pertaining to the Air elemental.

Celibacy Bath

5 parts Lavender oil
3 parts Camphor‡ oil
Color: White

Add to a tub of cool—not hot—water. When you wish to cool down, bathe in this blend.

Circle Bath

Variation One

4 parts Rosemary oil
3 parts Myrrh oil
2 parts Sandalwood oil
1 part Frankincense oil
Color: Purple

Variation Two

4 parts Clove oil
5 parts Lemon oil
2 parts Cedar oil
2 parts Carnation oil
Color: Purple

In preparation for any magical ritual, bathe in these salts to strengthen, purify, and prepare yourself.

Earth Bath (Elemental)

3 parts Patchouli oil
4 parts Cypress oil
1 part Vetivert oil
Color: Green

For spells involving money, foundation, stability, creativity, fertility, and ecology. Use for anything pertaining to Mother Earth.

Exorcism Bath

Variation One

3 parts Frankincense
3 parts Sandalwood oil
2 parts Rosemary oil
3 drops Clove oil
Color: White

Variation Two

4 eyedroppers Copal oil
4 eyedroppers Cedar oil
1 eyedropper Rosemary oil

3 drops Clove oil
Color: White

For a heavy psychic cleansing, bathe in these salts. Rinse off your entire body in cool, fresh water after your bath.

Fire Bath (Elemental)

3 parts Frankincense oil
2 parts Basil oil
1 part Juniper oil
1 part Orange oil
Color: Red

For rituals involving strength, courage, passion, and lust. Use for anything pertaining to the element Fire.

Energy Bath

8 parts Carnation oil
3 parts Lemon oil
1 part Cassia Bark oil
s1 part Patchouli oil
1 part Oakmoss bouquet
Color: Red

Bathe in a cool tub. Visualize your body and spirit being energized with colorful riplets of energy from the water.

Flowery Love Bath

4 parts Palmarosa oil
4 parts Lavender oil
2 parts Rose oil
1 part Jasmine oil
Color: Pink

Bathe in these salts to expand your ability to give and receive love. Visualize love coming into your life.

Healing Bath

Variation One

4 parts Niaouli oil
2 parts Eucalyptus oil

1 part Sandalwood oil
1 part Rosemary oil
Color: Dark Blue

Variation Two

3 parts Palmarosa oil
2 parts Eucalyptus oil
2 parts Honeysuckle‡ oil
1 part Orange oil
Color: Dark Blue

Use to speed healing. Visualize the release of the ailment into the water. Rinse your body with fresh water before toweling off. *CAUTION: Do not bathe if your condition does not allow it.*

High Awareness Bath

4 parts Cedarwood oil
2 parts Sandalwood oil
2 parts Frankincense oil
Color: Purple

Bathe in these salts to promote spirituality and for the destruction of Earth obsessions, such as uncontrollable spending, overeating, sluggishness, and any form of unbalanced materialism.

Love Bath

Variation One

1 eyedropper Tonka bouquet
3 parts Orange oil
3 parts Rose Geranium oil
2 parts Jasmine oil
Color: Pink

Variation Two

3 parts Rosemary oil
2 parts Lavender oil
6 drops Patchouli oil
1 part Yarrow oil
Color: Pink

Variation Three

3 parts Palmarosa oil

3 parts Lavender oil
2 parts Rose Geranium oil
1 part Orange oil
Color: Pink

Variation Four

2 eyedroppers Sweet Pea bouquet
2 eyedroppers Lotus bouquet
2 parts Lavender oil
1 eyedropper Jasmine oil
Color: Pink

Visualize the ability to promote and attract love into your life.

Lust Bath

Variation One

3 parts Sandalwood oil
1 part Patchouli oil
1 part Cardamom

Variation Two

2 parts Patchouli oil
2 eyedroppers Rosemary oil
2 eyedroppers Ambergris bouquet
Color: Red

Bathe in this salt to promote lustful desires. Visualize as usual.

Protection Bath

Variation One

3 parts Rosemary oil
2 parts Frankincense
2 parts Lavender oil
Color: White

Variation Two

4 parts Lotus bouquet
4 eyedroppers Copal oil
20 drops Lavender oil
20 drops Eucalyptus oil
Color: White

To fend off all manner of attacks—physical, mental, spiritual, psychic, and emotional—bathe with this salt. Visualize as usual.

Psychic Bath

4 parts Yarrow
2 parts Bay oil
10 drops Clove oil
20 drops Orange oil
16 drops Camphor‡ oil
7 drops Honeysuckle‡ oil
Color: Light Blue

To strengthen your psychic awareness and powers, use this salt. Visualize as usual.

Purification Bath

3 parts Rose Geranium oil
3 parts Rosemary oil
2 parts Frankincense oil
Color: White

To purify your body, spirit, and soul bathe in this salt. Visualize as usual.

Sea Witch Bath

3 parts Lotus bouquet
3 parts Lavender oil
1 part Rosemary oil
Color: Dark Blue

For a gentle purification prior to magical ritual, bathe in this salt. Add a bit of sea salt to the base mixture. Visualize as usual.

Spiritual Bath Oil

12 drops Sandalwood oil
12 drops Myrrh oil
4 eyedroppers Lotus bouquet
1 part Frankincense

1 drop Cinnamon oil

Use to increase your awareness of the divine, especially before religious rituals. Visualize as usual.

Water Bath (Elemental)

Variation One

3 parts Palmarosa oil
2 parts Sandalwood oil
1 part Myrrh oil
2 parts Geranium oil

Variation Two

3 Chamomile oil
1 part Yarrow oil
2 parts Ylang-Ylang oil
2 parts Palmarosa oil
Color: Dark Blue

Use for love, psychic awareness, friendships, healing, or anything to do with the element Water. Visualize as usual.

Zodiac Bath Salts

You can invoke the powers of the various signs of the zodiac by keeping in mind their separate traits and characteristics as you prepare your salts. Below is a list of the traits and characteristics of the signs of the zodiac as they relate to magical workings.

Aries: Energetic, impatient, lacking in foresight, short-tempered, sarcastic, witty, lucky, demanding, sharp-minded, cutting, egocentric, adventuresome, feisty.

Taurus: Patient, loyal, emotionally stable, stubborn, practical, dependable, organized, materialistic, possessive, plodding, sweet, calm, determined, security-oriented.

Gemini: Versatile, fickle, curious, high-strung, a flirt, changeable, anxious, petty, superficial, communicative.

Cancer: Caring, nurturing, moody, clinging, dependent, lazy, retentive memory, receptive, changeable, sensitive, a pack rat, emotional, overprotective, messy, money-oriented.

Leo: Positive, optimistic, warm, dogmatic, organizational, hardworking, persistent, dramatic, colorful, generous, flamboyant, arrogant, inspiring, a performer.

Virgo: Neat, fussy, conservative, efficient, studious, retiring, worrier, practical, logical.

Libra: Refined, diplomatic, vacillating, vain, social, just, artistic, gentle, tactful, gracious, peace-loving.

Scorpio: Secretive, intelligent, psychic, manipulative, passionate, stubborn, well organized, deceitful, resourceful, vindictive, tenacious, methodical.

Sagittarius: Outspoken, freedom loving, independent, warm, outgoing, spiritually oriented, athletic, opportunist, inspiring.

Capricorn: Rigid, practical, a loner, managerial, persistent, opinionated, sarcastic sense of humor, prudent, efficient, miserly, cold, pessimistic, patient, ruthless, ambitious.

Aquarius: Perceptive, temperamental, organized, erratic, cool, detached, ingenious, impersonal, goal-oriented, insightful, outgoing, self-expressive, unconventional.

Pisces: Refined, shrewd, impractical, nagging, unstable, con-artist, impressionable, compassionate, escapist or drifter, paranoid, a dreamer, intuitive.

Zodiac Recipes

The following recipes were deisgned to invoke the powers of the various signs of the Zodiac. Always keep in mind your magical goals when utilizing and preparing these bath salts.

Aries Bath Salts

1 eyedropper Frankincense oil
½ eyedropper Ginger oil
4 drops Black Pepper oil
4 drops Clove oil

Bathe with this salt to increase the powers of your own zodiac signs. Visualize as usual.

Taurus Bath Salts

8 drops Oakmoss bouquet
2 drops Patchouli oil
2 drops Ylang-Ylang oil
2 drops Cardamom oil

Bathe with this salt to increase your own zodiac powers. Visualize as usual.

Gemini Bath Salts

6 drops Lavender oil
½ eyedropper Peppermint oil
½ eyedropper Spearmint oil
1 drop Lemongrass oil
½ eyedropper Sweet Pea bouquet

Bathe with this salt to increase the power of your own zodiac signs. Visualize as usual.

Cancer Bath Salts (Moonchildren)

8 drops Palmarosa oil
4 drops Chamomile oil
2 drops Yarrow oil

Bathe with this salt to increase the power of your own zodiac signs. Visualize as usual.

Leo Bath Salts

6 drops Cinnamon oil
4 drops Orange oil
2 drops Lime oil

Bathe with this salt to increase the power of your own zodiac signs. Visualize as usual.

Virgo Bath Salts

8 drops Oakmoss bouquet
2 drops Patchouli oil
4 drops Cypress oil

Bathe with this salt to increase your own zodiac powers. Visualize as usual.

Libra Bath Salts

6 drops Rose Geranium oil
3 drops Ylang-Ylang oil
3 drops Palmarosa oil
2 drops Rose Absolute or Otto (Attar of Roses)

1 drop Patchouli oil

Bathe with this salt to increase your own zodiac powers. Visualize as usual.

Scorpio Bath Salts

6 drops Pine oil
2 drops Myrrh oil
2 drops Patchouli oil
1 drop Black Pepper oil
2 drops Cardamom oil

Bathe with this salt to increase your own zodiac powers. Visualize as usual.

Sagittarius Bath Salts

8 drops Oakmoss bouquet
4 drops Rosemary oil
1 drop Cinnamon oil

Bathe with this salt to increase your own zodiac powers. Visualize as usual.

Capricorn Bath Salts

6 drops Lemon oil
4 drops Cypress oil
1 drop Patchouli oil

Bathe with this salt to increase the power of your own zodiac signs. Visualize as usual.

Aquarius Bath Salts

8 drops Lavender oil
4 drops Cypress oil
1 drop Patchouli oil

Bathe with this salt to increase the powers of your own zodiac signs. Visualize as usual.

Pisces Bath Salts

5 drops Ylang-Ylang oil

4 drops Sandalwood oil

4 drops Jasmine oil

Bathe with this salt to increase your own zodiac powers. Visualize as usual.

CHAPTER SIX

Magical Soap

Today, most soaps are made with caustic chemicals and are artificially perfumed. Have you ever been soaking in a tub of herb-scented water, preparing for ritual, relaxing by the light of a candle's flame, the smoke of the incense drifting on the air, then you reach for the soap, only to be jerked back to reality by the obnoxious, heavy, artificial scent of your soap? I have. This is extremely disconcerting, to say the least. Although soaping isn't necessary in magical baths, a ritually correct soap can give a boost to any spell's effectiveness. Even if you don't bathe before rituals, it is wise to wash your hands. Even such a minor purification ritual can trigger a state of ritual consciousness. Spell soaps are ideal for this purpose.

The only way to obtain these soaps is to make them yourself. This can be quite tricky, but, if you follow precise measurements for both the solid and liquid ingredients, you should be successful.

It is best to start with pure, natural castile soaps. These can be purchased at most drugstores or supermarkets. Oils or herb brews are then added to the soap. The magical power is in the scent of the soap.

You should use castile soap made from coconut oil. I recommend a soap made by Kirk's, a company in the Philippines. Be aware, however, that castile soap can be very drying to your skin. To avoid this, add 1 to 2 teaspoons of apricot, almond, or coconut oil to the water prior to mixing, reducing the amount of water accordingly.

There are two types of ritual soaps: spherical and liquid. Directions for both follow.

Magical Soap Spheres

Using a very sharp, thick-bladed knife, cut a 4 oz. bar of coconut-oil castile soap into ¼" square cubes. The smaller the square, the better. Place these in a heat-proof, nonmetallic container. If you choose to add 1 to 2 teaspoons of coconut, almond, or apricot oil at this time, reduce the amount of water accordingly. I always add almond oil.

Heat slightly less than ⅓ cup water until nearly boiling. Pour the steaming hot water over the cut-up soap. Let it sit until the water has cooled sufficiently to allow you to handle it. Mix the soap and water with your hands. This will moisten the soap chips, but they shouldn't be floating on the surface of the water. If they are, add more soap. Let the soap and water sit for about nine minutes, or until mushy. If the soap cubes are still hard, set the bowl in a pan of water and reheat it gently until the soap is soft.

While the soap is melting, mix together the oils and charge them with your magical goal. Then add 20 to 50 drops of your combined or single oil to the soap and water mixture. Extremely warm water evaporates the oils, so wait until the water has cooled. Mix them thoroughly. The scent should be extremely strong. If not, add more oils.

The quality and strength of the essential oils you use determines the quantity needed to overpower the natural, antiseptic smell of the castile soap. Just add oils until you are satisfied with the scent.

Divide the soap mixture into 3 or 4 parts. Form these into spheres with your hands. Place each on a 9"-square piece of cotton cheesecloth. Pull the ends of the cloth tightly around each sphere, gather the cloth ends at the top and twist them together. The cloth should be tightly wrapped around the soap spheres. Tie the ends closed with strong twine. Repeat for each sphere.

Hang the soap spheres in a warm place for three days, or until the soap is completely hardened. When the spheres won't yield to your finger pressure, remove the cloth wraps. The soaps are ready to be used in ritual baths. Or, they can be wrapped in clean cheesecloth, labeled, and given as gifts to friends who will appreciate them.

Magical Liquid Soap

Add 5 to 6 tablespoons of mixed dried, ground, and charged herbs to your 3 cups of hot water (substitute the herbs for the oils in the following recipes or any recipes that you choose to create on your own.) Take the mixture off the heat, let it steep for ten to thirteen minutes, and strain. Add 2 teaspoons of almond, coconut, or apricot oil, then reduce the water accordingly. Gently reheat the water. Add 1 cup of coconut castile soap shavings, whisk, and allow to cool. It is ready for use. Bottle.

The scent will change drastically when you add dry herbs to the castile soap. Experiment with small quantities, until you perfect the scents you prefer. You may also add a few drops of the oil from one of the suggested herbs, if you choose.

Almost any of the oil recipes in this book can be used to make the soap. Experiment and use your instincts. Remember, however, to use only true essential oils, including rose or orange oils, and to store unused soaps with your herbs in your altar room. Use ritual magical soaps with visualization and power.

Soap Recipes

Herbal Soap

Place 2 tablespoons finely chopped lemon verbena or lavender into 2 tablespoons warmed glycerin. Place in a warm area for several days. Strain and finely grate 12 tablespoons of coconut castile soap and melt in the top of a double boiler. Remove from the heat and add the scented glycerin to the melted soap. Add 1 tablespoon of honey. Mix well. Pour into greased molds, any shape. Allow to set until the soap is cool and hardened.

You may use either the oil or herb form of the soap ingredients. However, oils are usually preferred. Remember to decrease the amount of water you use if you have added oil to any of the following recipes.

Good Fortune Soap

3 parts Vetivert
3 parts Orange
1 part Nutmeg

Use to bring positive energies into your life or to change your luck. Orange flower water may be substituted in place of plain water when making soap.

Isis Soap

2 parts Myrrh
3 parts Frankincense
3 parts Lotus bouquet

Use before any Egyptian or Isian ritual, or any ritual to develop spiritual awareness. Substitute rose water for the water in which the soap chips are melted.

Love Soap

4 parts Geranium
4 parts Palmarosa
3 parts Neroli
1 part Ginger

Use to attract love, or prior to love rituals. Again, rose water may be used in the same proportions as plain water in preparing the soap.

Money Soap

3 parts Patchouli
4 parts Peppermint
2 parts Basil
2 parts Pine
1 part Cinnamon

Use to attract money, or use prior to money-drawing rituals.

Moon Soap

3 parts Sandalwood
3 parts Camphor‡
2 parts Lemon
2 parts Eucalyptus

Use before rituals on the Full Moon to attune with her energies.

Protection Soap

4 parts Rosemary
4 parts Basil
2 parts Frankincense
1 part Bay
3 parts Mint

Use daily for protection and before rituals or casting spells.

Psychic Soap

4 parts Lemongrass
3 parts Bay
1 part Cinnamon

Use to increase your psychic abilities, especially prior to divinatory or psychic workings and rites.

Sabbat Soap

4 parts Sandalwood
4 parts Rosemary
2 parts Patchouli
1 part Cinnamon
1 part Myrrh
1 part Bay
3 parts Lemon
1 part Ginger

Use during ritual baths prior to Sabbats, or as a general magical cleanser.

Witch's Soap

4 parts Rosemary
3 parts Pine
1 part Cinnamon
4 parts Orange

Use before rituals of all kinds to increase your personal power.

These are just a few of the recipes for ritual soaps. Use your intuition and have fun with your Craft.

CHAPTER SEVEN

Ointments

In this chapter, you will learn how to prepare your own ointments. As always, cleanse and charge the ointment before use (see chapter 1 for charging rituals and Circle casting). It is a good idea to prepare ointments for future use. It saves time and, if you prepare ointments in advance, you will have them on hand for emergency use, as well as for everyday life. I personally keep a list of frequently used recipes taped inside the door of my herbal cabinet. Of course, there are always some recipes that you simply can't make up ahead of time, but their ingredients can be stored in tightly closed glass jars that are correctly labeled. Always sterilize your containers and be sure each is labeled clearly and correctly with the contents, use, and dosage.

It takes time to build up the herbs and oils you need for your remedies, but it is well worth the effort and time. If you are going to have a large supply of herbs and oils, you must first make sure you have the containers in which to store them. Dark glass bottles and jars are acknowledged as the best for storing herbs and oils. I have several bookshelves in my living room that hold bottles and jars filled with all sorts of herbs. My house may look like a witch's abode, but it is very handy to go into the living room and just grab the jar or bottle I need.

If you are going to keep your prepared ointments for any amount of time, you must add a preservative to the recipe, or the mixture will go rancid very quickly. Honey and vitamin E are both preservatives, and benzoin tinctures also work well. If honey is used in the recipe, that is usually sufficient. If you are not using honey, you can add the fluid from several vitamin E capsules instead. Gum benzoin also acts as a preservative if it is in the recipe.

Preparing Magical Ointments

Ointments consist simply of herbs or oils and a base. They are easily made. The best results are attained by using beeswax or vegetable shortening as a base. The base must be a greasy substance that melts over heat, but is solid at room temperature. Some herbalists actually use dinosaur fat (i.e., Vaseline, which is prepared from petroleum)!

There are two basic ways to create magical ointments—the shortening method and the beeswax method.

Shortening Method

Gently heat four parts shortening over low heat until liquified. Be careful that it doesn't burn. Add one part dried herbal mixture, blend with a wooden spoon until thoroughly mixed, and continue heating until the shortening has extracted the scent. You should be able to smell it in the air. Make sure to keep the heat low enough so you don't burn the shortening. You may even prefer to use a double boiler. The double boiler must be glass or enamel-coated to prevent contaminating the ointment.

Strain the mixture through cheesecloth into a heatproof container, such as a canning jar. Add ½ teaspoon tincture of benzoin (See chapter 3, or buy at a drugstore) to each pint of ointment as a natural preservative. Store in a cool, dark place, such as the refrigerator. Ointments should last for weeks or months. Discard any that turn moldy, and make up a fresh batch.

Beeswax Method

I actually prefer this way of making ointments, because it creates a more cosmetic ointment, one without a heavy, oily feeling. This is best prepared with oils rather than herbs, as it is difficult to strain.

Use unbleached beeswax. If this is not available in your area, use what you can find. Chip the beeswax with a large, sharp knife so that you can pack it into a measuring cup. Try a potato peeler. Place ¼ cup of beeswax in the top of a double boiler (a coffee can set into a larger pot of water will work, too). Add about ¼ cup olive, hazelnut, sesame, or vegetable oil. Stir with a spoon until the wax has melted into the oil.

Remove from the heat and let cool very slightly, until it has just begun to thicken. (This step is taken so that the hot wax won't evaporate the oils, so don't skip this step.) Now add the mixed oils to the wax. Stir thoroughly with a wooden spoon and put into a heatproof container. Label and store in the usual way.

Charging Ointments

Ointments are usually rubbed into the body to effect various magical changes. As with oils, this is done with visualization and with the knowledge that the ointment will do its work.

Once the ointment is made and has cooled in its jar, charge it with its particular magical intention. This vital step, remember, directs the energy within the ointment, readying it for your ritual use.

Ointment Recipes

CAUTION: Although most of the ointments included here are fairly harmless, some are poisonous and may be lethal. By including these ointments, I am in no way advocating the use of such dangerous and possibly deadly mixtures. These ointments form a part of the herbal magic lore of long-gone days, and are included solely for their historical interest. All illegal or poisonous ingredients are marked with an ‡. Please take care in how you use them.

Remember to use a mortar and pestal to crush all herbs before adding them to the mixture.

Exorcism Ointment

4 drops Frankincense
4 drops Peppermint
1 drop Clove
2 drops Ping

Add the oils to the beeswax/oil base. Anoint your body when you feel the need for a strong purification. Charge as usual.

Flying Ointment: Nontoxic #1

CAUTION: Flying ointment is intended for external use only.
2 parts Dittany of Crete
2 parts Cinquefoil
2 parts Mugwort
2 parts Parsley

Add the herbs to shortening and prepare in the usual way. Anoint your body prior to attempting astral projection. Charge as usual.

Flying Ointment: Nontoxic #2

4 drops Sandalwood oil
2 drops Jasmine oil
2 drops Benzoin oil
2 drops Mace oil

Add the oils to a beeswax/oil base. Use as the above formula. Charge as usual.

Flying Ointment: Nontoxic #3

½ tsp. Clove oil
1½ tsp. chimney soot
¼ tsp. dried Cinquefoil
¼ tsp. dried Mugwort
¼ tsp. dried Thistle
¼ tsp. dried Vervain
½ tsp. tincture of Benzoin

Add the oils to a beeswax/oil base. Use as the above formula. Charge as usual.

Ancient Witches Flying Ointment

The notorious "Witches Flying Oint-ment," a dangerous herbal concoction producing psychedelic effects, is said to have been used by witches in the Middle Ages. It consisted mainly of parsley, hemlock‡, water of aconite‡, poplar leaves, soot, bat's blood, deadly nightshade‡ (or belladonna‡), henbane‡, and hashish‡. Tradition has it that these ingredients were mixed together in a large cauldron over a fire with the melted fat of an unbaptized infant, and then rubbed on various parts of the witch's body to enable her (or him) to "fly" off to the Sabbat. (Of course, witches didn't literally fly; however, the ointment did induce incredible hallucinations, psychic visions, and astral projections.) Because these recipes are hundreds of years old, the quantities of the ingredients are no longer known.

Ancient Witches Flying Ointment: Toxic #1

CAUTION: This mixture can be deadly.

Cinquefoil
Parsley
Aconite‡
Belladonna‡
Hemlock‡
Cowbane‡

Ancient Witches Flying Ointment: Toxic #2

CAUTION: This mixture can be deadly.
Hogs lard
Hashish‡
Hemp flowers‡
Poppy flowers‡
Hellebore‡

Healing Ointment

4 drops Cedarwood
3 drops Sandalwood
2 drops Eucalyptus
1 drop Cinnamon

Add the oils to a melted beeswax/oil base, cool, and anoint your body to speed healing. *CAUTION: Do not apply to wounds, burns, or broken skin.*

Hex-Breaker Ointment

3 parts Galangal
3 drops Ginger root, dried
2 drops Vetivert
1 drop Thistle

Steep the herbs in shortening, strain, cool, and anoint your body at night. Charge as usual.

Love Ointment

4 drops Ylang-Ylang oil
6 drops Lavender oil
1 drop Cardamom oil
1 drop Vanilla extract
4 drops Rose oil

Add the oils to a beeswax/oil base. Make in the usual way and anoint your body when looking for love. Charge as usual.

Lust Ointment

1 whole Vanilla Bean
3 parts Galangal
2 parts Dill
3 parts Ginger root, dried
2 parts peppermint

Prepare with shortening in the usual way. Anoint your body (but not areas that are too tender). Charge as usual.

Moon Goddess Ointment

8 drops Sandalwood
5 drops Lemon
2 drops Rose

Prepare with beeswax/oil base. Anoint yourself to attune with the Goddess of the Moon and during our Wiccan Full Moon rituals. Charge as usual.

Protection Ointment

3 parts Mallow
3 parts Rosemary
2 parts Vervain

Make in the usual way, with shortening. Rub onto your body to drive out negative influences and to keep them far from you. Charge as usual.

Psychic Powers Ointment #1

4 parts Bay
4 parts Star Anise
3 parts Mugwort
2 parts Yerba Santa

Make in the usual way, with shortening. Anoint your temples, the middle of your forehead, and the back of your neck to improve psychic powers. Charge as usual.

Psychic Powers Ointment #2

4 drops Lemongrass
2 drops Bay
2 drops Yarrow

Mix with the beeswax/oil base and anoint as with the above formula. Charge as usual.

Riches Ointment

5 drops Patchouli oil
4 drops Oakmoss Bouquet
1 drop Clove oil
2 drops Basil oil

Mix with beeswax/oil base and anoint the body and hands daily to attract riches. Charge as usual.

Sun God Ointment

4 drops Frankincense oil
6 drops Orange oil
1 drop Cinnamon oil

Mix with a beeswax/oil base and anoint the body to attune with the Solar God, especially on Wiccan Sabbats. Charge as usual.

Visions Ointment: Toxic

Hemp‡
Angelica
Kava Kava

Mix with shortening base. Anoint to produce visions. Substitute star anise for the hemp to have legal visions. Charge as usual.

Witches' Ointment: Nontoxic #1

4 parts Vervain
4 parts Sandalwood
3 parts Cinnamon
1 part Carnation petals

Make in the usual way with shortening. Store in a container marked with a pentagram (a five-pointed star with one point facing up). Anoint the body prior to Wiccan rituals to become one with the Goddess and God and that which lies beyond them.

Witches' Ointment: Nontoxic: #2

4 drops Frankincense oil

3 drops Myrrh oil

2 drops Sandalwood oil

3 drops Orange oil

3 drops Lemon oil

Mix with the beeswax/oil base. Use as the above ointment. Charge as usual.

Witches' Ointment: Toxic

Hemlock‡

Poplar

Aconite‡

Soot

Mix with the beeswax/oil base. Use as with the above ointment. Charge as usual.

Youth Ointment

5 parts Rosemary

4 parts Rose petals

2 parts Anise

2 parts Fern

1 part Myrtle

Mix with the shortening base. For preserving or reattaining youth, stand nude before a full-length mirror at sunrise and lightly anoint your entire body, visualizing yourself as you would like to be. Charge as usual before using.

These are just a few recipes. Any of the true essential oils mentioned in this book can be converted to ointments simply by adding them to melted beeswax or solid vegetable shortening.

Calendula Ointments

These natural skin remedies are prepared from the golden flower of the calendula plant, which has been used for medicinal purposes since the six-
teenth century. To make calendula ointment, an oil-based infusion is
produced from flower petals and then mixed with a base oil. This essential
oil has wound-healing and anti-inflammatory properties. In addition, it has
carotenoids, which can help to regenerate skin cells. As a result, calendula
ointment is useful for treating skin wounds and inflammation, as well as
frostbite. *CAUTION: Calendula should never be used for burns.* To use,
simply apply a thin layer onto affected areas of the skin several times daily.

Medicinal Effects of Calendula

Calendula ointment has two principal effects on skin wounds. First, it acts as a
natural antibiotic to kill germs, thereby cleansing the wound and helping to prevent infection. Second, it promotes blood-cell growth in regenerating skin tissue,
speeding the healing process and helping to minimize the formation of scars.

Components

Calendula ointment contains volatile constituents, yellow-orange carotenoids,
and other natural pigments, flavonoids, saponins, alcohols, enzymes, and various organic acids. Depending on the manufacturer, store-bought products
may contain additional substances, which I do not recommend using.

Using Calendula Ointments

Calendula can used to alleviate a number of skin ailments.

Chapped Skin and Cold Sores: Helps moisturize and heal chapped or cracked
skin and lips. It may be a particularly effective remedy against cold sores.
These painful sores, also known as fever blisters, appear on the lips and
are caused by a type of herpes virus.

Varicose Veins: Gently apply calendula ointment to affected areas twice a day.
The ointment promotes blood circulation and helps speed healing. *CAU-
TION: Do not rub or massage the ointment into affected areas.* Instead,
gently spread a thin layer of ointment over the affected sections and let it
soak into the skin. This will avoid damaging fragile veins.

Bedsores: If you are confined to a bed for a long period of time, sores (decu-
bitus ulcers) often develop, especially on heels, elbows, collarbone, and
the tailbone area. To help them heal, gently rub calendula ointment into
the bedsores several times daily. If necessary, bandage with gauze.

Nail Infections: The ointment's anti-inflammatory and germ-killing actions are very useful for infections of the nail bed. Simply apply the ointment directly to the affected area or areas several times daily.

Wounds: Calendula can help soothe cuts or abrasions that are already scabbed over, but have a light rose-colored border, indicating possible infection.

Other uses for Calendula: Skin wounds that are superficially inflamed, wounds that are discharging pus, painful areas of the skin, lips that are dry, cracked, and highly sensitive, athlete's foot or any other skin infections.

To ensure a ready supply of fresh ointment, simply refrigerate small amounts of the olive-oil infusion—the oil in the ointment without the beeswax and cocoa butter—in covered containers. The oil will keep for more than a year.

Calendula Recipes

Calendula Ointment

½ cup dried powdered Calendula flowers
1 cup Olive oil, extra virgin

Place both ingredients into a glass bottle or jar and soak for fourteen days, then strain well and refrigerate. Be sure to purchase calendula and not the American marigold, tagetes. Charge as usual for healing and regeneration of skin cells.

Calendula Salve

1 oz. Beeswax
½ to ¾ cup Olive oil, extra virgin
½ cup Calendula flowers
Cocoa butter for base

Melt the beeswax in a double boiler and add to the oil and flower mixture. Mix until all ingredients are well combined, pour into container with a tight-fitting lid, and let cool. Charge as usual for healing and regeneration of skin cells.

CHAPTER EIGHT

Magical Potpourri

Throughout recorded history, aromatic mixtures of herbs have been created in many lands. The fragrance of simple herbs, rare spices, and exotic flowers were mixed and used for purposes both medicinal and magical.

The aromatic mixtures of ancient Egypt, Rome, and Greece are considered the forerunners of our modern-day potpourri. It wasn't until the Renaissance that the art of creating what we now know as potpourri (po-poo-ree) reached the peak of its popularity. By then, however, potpourri and other fragrant mixtures were rarely made for magical purposes, for the magic of the herbalist had been largely forgotten. Thus was lost a very valuable part of our magical history!

During these ancient and almost forgotten times, bathing was uncommon and sewers were unheard of. Air circulation was usually poor, since there were few windows in any home or building. It is not surprising, under these conditions, that people would use the delightful scents and aromas of fragrant herbs, exotic flowers, and spices to brighten everyday life.

Rich and poor alike devised many ingenious methods to use fragrant flowers, herbs, and spices to perfume themselves and their homes and businesses. Admittedly, more options were available to the upper class than to the lower class. Traders brought rare and costly spices from overseas for those with money who could afford them. It wasn't long before pomanders, tussy-mussies, sachets, and scent rings were made and carried to sweeten the air. Incenses were smoldered, sweet herbs were strewn onto rugs to release their exotic scents when walked upon, and sachets were tied onto beds, couches, chairs, tables, doors, and anywhere one could be tied.

Potpourri was also used to cleanse the air of foul smells and illness. These mixtures of either fresh or dried herbs, spices, and flowers were kept in tight-lidded jars. To release the exotic scent, the box or jar was opened, allowing the aroma to mask the baleful smells, making the home a much more pleasant place to live.

Several of these herbs were once thought to have healing powers, but the witchcraft and heresy trials encouraged the populace to forget about the magical qualities of these herbs. Thus, potpourri came to be viewed either as a pleasant smelling mixture, or as a weapon in the arsenal against disease, but not as a magical tool. Today, however, we create specific magical results with our knowledge of the subtle powers of these plants. Remember always to visualize your magical goal when using potpourri. The power of the mixture lies in its aromatic scent.

Locating the Ingredients of Potpourri

Many flowers and herbs, and some spices, can be found in local gardens or in the wild. For those not easily obtained, I recommend trying local herb shops and occult or health food stores. Many are available in supermarkets and gourmet shops. If you still can't find the ingredients you need, check with your local nursery. They may be able to recommend a place where you can find the herbs you seek. You can also substitute one herb for another, using the substitution lists in chapter 13.

Most witches like to collect and dry at least some of the components for their potpourri. They pick them in the morning, after the dew has dried from them, lay the flowers, herbs, or spices on trays, and place them out of direct sunlight, preferably in a place with good air circulation. You can also use a dehydrator if you have access to one. I personally use a dehydrator to make sure that no moisture is left in the plant material that can cause mold! This takes only hours, whereas the other method can take 10 days minimum (with good weather). Once the plant materials are dried, you are ready to begin.

Storing Your Potpourri

Potpourri should be stored in closed boxes or jars, from which the lids can be lifted to release the aromatic smell and scents. Any type of jar or box with a tight-fitting lid is suitable for this purpose. Special potpourri containers, made of ceramic with perforated holes, are available in some specialty shops. These release the mixture's aromatic smells and scents and, of course, their power continuously. Those mixtures that are used over a long period of time, such as those that attract money, protect the home, or attract love and health, should be placed in this type of container. You can also use an open jar, or even a large seashell.

Using Magical Potpourri

The power of potpourri is released through its aromatic scent. Thus, smelling potpourri is actually an act of magic, for by doing so, you move energy contained in the mixture into yourself. Release the potpourri's aromatic fragrance only when you need its energies.

Once you have opened the closed box or jar of potpourri, breathe deeply for a few moments. Next, visualize your need or magical goal. (If you've made a money potpourri, the need is obviously money.) Inhale, breathing deeply. Feel the energy flowing into your body, spirit, mind, and psyche, creating real and tangible changes. Continue to visualize and allow the potpourri to affect you. Repeat as many times a day as needed.

If the potpourri is in an open container, run your fingers through the mixture at least once a day. Bend and smell the wonderful evocative aroma several times a day. The effects of the magical potpourri will be subtle, but they will occur if you've correctly mixed and used them. Open yourself to change, and change will manifest.

Every 3 months, or sooner if the aromatic smell diminishes, your magical potpourri must be replaced. Bury the spent potpourri in the earth and create a new one, if necessary. Potpourri kept in closed containers can last indefinitely. Some potpourris are still fragrant twenty years after their preparation. You shouldn't have to replace them very often.

Mixing Potpourri

Technically, this is quite simple. Magically, it is the most important step.

1. Gather the necessary ingredients. All ingredients should be completely dried. Don't substitute an oil for an herb unless recommended.

2. Place the first ingredient into a large bowl. Touch it. Stroke it. Smell its aroma, visualize its purpose.

3. Add each ingredient separately, following the same system: touch, smell, visualize its purpose.

4. Rub the herbs together with your fingers, mingling their powers and fragrances. Deepen your visualization. Feel the power under your fingertips. Sense its reality.

5. Place the potpourri in a suitable container and use as needed.

You may use any of the many charging methods given here. Use your own personal favorite, or experiment with others.

Potpourri Recipes

The following potpourri recipes will stimulate your imagination and creativity. They smell wonderful and last for quite long time. Experiment with color, texture, scent, and oils—the only limitations are in your own mind. Have fun and enjoy!

16th-Century Potpourri Mix

1 part Peppermint leaves, cut
1 part Lavender flowers
1 Tbsp. well-crushed Caraway seeds
1 part Thyme
1 Tbsp. crushed Cloves and Coriander
1 Tbsp. crushed Gum Benzoin or Orris root

Lightly mix together all the ingredients. Put into a potpourri jar with a few dried rose and marigold petals on the top for color.

Courage Potpourri

½ cup black Pepper berries, whole
½ cup Allspice, whole
⅛ cup Thyme

Forest Potpourri

2 oz. Geranium leaves (pine-scented)
1 oz. Balsam Fir needles
4 oz. Sweet Woodruff
3 Tbsp. Cedar chips
1 Tbsp. Violets
1 tsp. Vanilla
2 oz. German Rue
2 Tbsp. Pine needles
1 oz. powdered Orris root
1 drop Bergamot Mint bouquet

German Witch's Potpourri

2 oz. Witch Hazel
1 oz. Rue

1 oz. Sweet Woodruff

¼ tsp. Ginger

2 drops Pine oil

1 oz. Rosemary

1 oz. powdered Myrrh gum

1 tsp. Lemon or Orange peel

2 tsp. Vanilla

Healing Potpourri

1 cup Rosemary, whole

¼ cup Coriander seed, whole

¼ cup Sandalwood, ground/chips

⅛ cup Sassafras, whole

2 Tbsp. Peppermint

1 pinch Poppy seed

Place in a small jar with a lid. Remove the lid when you want to perfume the room.

Lammas Ritual Potpourri

20 drops Clove bud oil

25 drops Sandalwood oil

1 cup Oakmoss

2 cups dried pink Rose buds

2 cups dried red Peony petals

1 cup dried Amaranth flowers

1 cup dried Heather flowers

½ cup dried Cornflowers

Mix the clove bud and sandalwood oils with the oakmoss and then add the remaining ingredients. Stir well and store in a tightly covered ceramic or glass jar.

Place in a cup or bowl on the altar at Lammas as a fragrant ritual potpourri, or cast it into an open fire or sprinkle it on hot charcoal blocks to burn it as a powerful ritual incense. (Lammas Potpourri may also be put into a mojo bag and carried or worn to attract a lover.)

Love Potpourri

1½ cups Rose petals or Rose buds

1 cup Lavender

¼ cup Chamomile

¼ Vanilla bean, chopped

2 Tbsp. Calamus or Benzoin, ground

2 Tbsp. Cardamom seed, ground

Medieval Lady Potpourri

1 pt. red Rose blossoms

3 Tbsp. Damiana

1 oz. powdered Orris root

½ pint white Rose petals

1 oz. dried Hawthorn berries

1 Tbsp. Lavender flowers

Money Potpourri

1 cup Oakmoss

1 cup Cedar shavings

1 cup Patchouli

¼ cup Vetivert, powdered or pulled apart

1 Tbsp. Nutmeg, ground

1 tsp. Cinnamon, ground

1 pinch Ginger, ground

Passion Potpourri

2 oz. Violet

2 oz. Orris root

1 oz. Lovage

¼ oz. Rose leaf

½ oz. Rose petals

1 oz. Rosemary

1 oz. Tonka beans

½ oz. Lemon leaf

Cut and collect the herbs on a dry morning, after the dew has dried. Tie the herbs together securely with a red string and hang them to dry in an attic or other warm, dark, airy place. Remove the string after the herbs are dry and brittle, and break them into large coarse pieces. (It is important that the herbs be completely dry, otherwise mold will develop and ruin the potpourri.) Stir the ingredients together with a large wooden spoon and place in a large glass jar, bottle, or jug. Seal with a tight-fitting lid. Keep the potpourri in a cool dark place for 3 months, removing the lid and stirring the contents with wooden spoon at least once a week.

Protection Potpourri

½ cup Juniper berries, whole
½ cup Basil, whole
2 Tbsp. Frankincense, ground
2 Tbsp. Dill seeds, whole
2 Tbsp. Fennel seeds, whole
2 Tbsp. Cloves, whole
8 Bay leaves, torn to pieces

Psychic Potpourri

1 cup Lemongrass
½ cup Mugwort
¼ cup Star Anise (or regular Anise), whole
2 Tbsp. Thyme
2 Tbsp. Yarrow
1 tsp. Mace
Dash genuine Saffron (if available)

Road to Mandalay Potpourri

4 oz. Orange blossoms
2 oz. Ylang-Ylang blossoms
1 tsp. Nutmeg
½ tsp. Cinnamon
2 oz. Heliotrope blossoms
1 oz. Frankincense
1 tsp. Orange peel
1 tsp. Vanilla

Royal Indian Love Potpourri

1 pint Heliotrope blossoms
2 oz. Oleander‡ blossoms
4 oz. Garden Pinks

1 oz. powdered Myrrh
4 oz. Patchouli leaves
1 Tonka bean, crushed

Spice Mix Potpourri

You may use this mixture over any potpourri.
½ oz. broken Cloves
½ oz. crushed Gum Benzoin
½ oz. powdered Orris root
½ oz. powdered Allspice, with a few whole berries
½ oz. powdered Mace
½ oz. whole Coriander seeds
½ oz. Cinnamon stick, crushed or powdered

Lightly mix together the above ingredients. Choose a pretty jar with a lid to hold your potpourri. Into the jar, place a layer of dried flower petals, such as rose, lavender, lemon verbena, or tiny rose buds. Over each layer, sprinkle some of the spice mix. Continue layering and sprinkling until the jar is filled. To freshen a room, simply remove the jar's lid.

Victorian Pincushion Potpourri

4 oz. Rose petals
1 oz. granular Frankincense
2 oz. Rosemary
1 oz. Lavender flowers
1 broken Cinnamon stick

Use dried flowers. Many Victorian pincushions were stuffed with rough-cut potpourri; sometimes the mixture was wrapped in cotton to make it easier to insert the pins and needles.

Xanadu Potpourri

1 pint Wisteria blossom
1 oz. powdered Myrrh
1 tsp. Vanilla
4 oz. China rosebuds
1 Tbsp. Lemon peel

Yule Potpourri

4 oz. Peppermint leaves

1 oz. powdered Benzoin Gum

½ tsp. Cinnamon

2 oz. Rose petals

1 tsp. Vanilla

Simmering Potpourri

I absolutely adore the simmering potpourris. They can be carried about the house to further spread of their energies.

Arabian Knights Potpourri

2 oz. Rose petals

1 oz. Sandalwood shavings

1 Cinnamon stick (broken)

1 drop Lilac oil

2 oz. Cedar shavings

1 drop Jasmine oil

1 oz. Coffee blossoms

With your fingers, mix these ingredients in a small bowl, while visualizing your entire being and soul completely protected by their aroma.

French Potpourri

4 oz. Jasmine flowers

1 oz. Rue

1 Vanilla bean, crushed

2 oz. Violets

1 oz. cut Orris root

Mix and charge the herbs for love in a small bowl. Visualize as usual using the blue and white light of the Goddess and God to charge the mixture.

Japanese Potpourri

2 oz. Peony blossoms

2 oz. Chrysanthemum blossoms

1 oz. granular Benzoin Gum
2 oz. Camellia flowers
1 oz. Oleander‡ flowers

Mix and charge, for purification, protection, riches, and love. Simmer as usual.

Lavender Potpourri

2 oz. Lavender flowers
1 Cinnamon stick, broken
1 oz. granular Myrrh gum
1 oz. Rose petals
2 oz. Damiana leaves

To expand, broaden, or to introduce love into your life, simmer this mixture of herbs. Charge as you would any potpourri. This mixture can also be charged and used for protection.

Love Simmering Potpourri

3 Tbsp. Rose petals
2 Tbsp. Chamomile
1 Tbsp. Coriander
1 Tbsp. Lavender
1 tsp. Cinnamon
½ Vanilla bean, crushed or extract
1 Tbsp. Rosemary

To expand, broaden, or to introduce love into your life, simmer this mixture of herbs. This can also be used to strengthen a long-standing relationship, or to bring your own family closer together. Love begins within. Love yourself, then seek another with whom to share love. Mix in a small bowl and charge with loving energies. Simmer daily, while saying:

> *Love awakens*
> *In these rooms;*
> *Come by the power*
> *Of these blooms!*

Magic Power Potpourri

This is to be used before and/or during all forms of magical rites. This formula boosts your reserve of personal power.

4 Tbsp. dried Orange peel
3 Tbsp. Peppermint
4 Tbsp. whole Allspice
2 Tbsp. ground Ginger
2 whole Carnations (red)
1 Tbsp. ground Cloves
4 parts Orange oil
4 parts Carnation oil

Mix and charge the herbs and spices in a small mixing bowl. As you mix, say these or similar words:

> *Flowers and spices*
> *Charged by the sun;*
> *Help me ensure that magic is done.*
> *Open the path to my energy;*
> *This is my will, and*
> *So mote it be!*

Simmer and let the herbs' power fill the air as you do your magical workings. (Remember to turn off the stove after your ritual.) If using an electric po-pot, move it to your altar room or wherever your rites are to be held.

Money Simmering Potpourri

If money is a problem rather than a pleasure, when you're faced with unexpected financial obligations, when the money you earn doesn't seem to come in fast enough, brew one of these and set its money-attracting energies into motion.

Variation One
2 Tbsp. Hyssop
6 Tbsp. Orange peel
2 Tbsp. Cloves

1 tsp. Nutmeg
1 tsp Peppermint
4 parts Jasmine
4 parts Honeysuckle‡
2 Cinnamon sticks, crushed

Variation Two

2 Cinnamon sticks, crushed
14 Tbsp. whole Cardamom seeds
2 Tbsp. whole Cloves
1 tsp. ground Nutmeg
1 tsp. ground Ginger
2 Tbsp. ground Sage
1 Tbsp. Peppermint
4 Tbsp. Orange peel
4 parts Jasmine
4 parts Honeysuckle‡

With your fingers, mix these ingredients in a small bowl, while visualizing increasing prosperity. As you mix them, say these or similar words:

> *Money simmer in the air;*
> *Money shimmer everywhere!*

Use as previously directed.

Protection Potpourri

Simmer mixture at regular intervals (once a week or so) to drench your home with protective energy. This safeguards it from outside influences of all kinds—if it's performed with the proper intent.

4 Tbsp. Rosemary (whole)
3 Bay leaves (whole)
1 Tbsp. Basil (whole)
2 Tbsp. Cedar (whole)
1 Tbsp. Sage (whole)
1 Tbsp. Fennel (whole)
1 tsp. Dill seed (whole)
1 tsp. Juniper berries (whole)
1 pinch dried Garlic (optional)

Mix in small bowl with your hands, visualizing your home as a protected place. Charge the herbs with protective energies. Add to simmering water. When the scented steam rises, chant the following or similar words:

> *Air and water, work my will*
> *To guard this house with power bold;*
> *Earth and fire, work to still*
> *All dangers both untold and told.*

Use 1 cup of water in your po-pot to 2 to 3 teaspoons of po-mixture.

Psychic Potpourri

To link your conscious mind with your psychic abilities and awareness, to enhance your ability to use tarot cards, rune stones, or any other scrying tools to glimpse possible future events, create this blend and simmer to stimulate your psychic mind.

3 Tbsp. Galangal
1 Tbsp. Star Anise
1 Tbsp. Lemongrass
1 Tbsp. Thyme
1 Tbsp. Rose petals
Pinch Mace
Pinch real Saffron

Mix and charge the herbs in a small bowl. Visualize your psychic awareness as under your control. Smell the fragrance rising from the herbs. Inhale the energies. Relax, chant the following words, and foretell.

> *Starlight swirls before my eyes;*
> *Twilight furls its wisdom wise;*
> *Moonlight curls within the skies:*
> *The time has come to prophesize.*

Purification Potpourri

To clear away the useless energies that exist within all homes, after household arguments, when a roommate moves out, whenever tension is in the air, simmer this mixture with at least one open window. (During winter, or rain, open the fireplace's damper, crack a window an inch, or otherwise ensure that there's a clear and easy path out of your home for the duration of the ritual.)

6 Tbsp. Peppermint

3 Tbsp. Arabic gum

1 Tbsp. Spearmint

1 Tbsp. Rosemary

1 Tbsp. dried Lemon peel

1 Tbsp. dried Orange peel

1 Tbsp. dried Lime peel

Mix, charge, and simmer as you say these or similar words:

> *Scented breeze, blow pure and clear*
> *Unwanted power far from here.*

Royal Indian Love Potpourri

1 pint Heliotrope blossoms

1 oz. Garden Pinks

4 oz. Patchouli leaves

2 oz. Oleander‡ blossoms

1 oz. powdered Myrrh gum

1 Tonka bean

Mix, charge, and simmer as usual.

CHAPTER NINE

Magical Inks

*As candles flickered in the crudely constructed hut casting
shadows of things to come, the crone dipped her quill into
the magically brewed ink and hastily inscribed a spell to
avert the misfortune foreseen in her crystal.*

S ince the beginning of recorded history, man has searched for the perfect
writing utensil. The first ink was probably made of charcoal; the first
pen, of a charred stick. These rudimentary writing implements can, of
course, still be used today. Ink has long been used in magic. Its most useful
application lies in its ability to transform the symbols and images of our magical goals into written and visible form. During magical rituals, these forms are
used to concentrate or focus intent, thereby helping to raise energy, program
it, and manifest it so it can be utilized in spell work. Therefore, ink can be considered a magical tool of the Craft of the Old and Wise.

During the Middle Ages and Renaissance, many a secret magical manuscript
was transcribed into a form that was (at that time) thought to be suitable.
Some of these manuscripts had sections on inks and their purification.

These inks were originally intended to invoke or banish potentially dangerous
beings from the physical plane. It was believed that it was necessary to purify
inks properly prior to their use in invocations or banishings. To this day, we
still purify and concentrate our inks, whether for invoking, banishing, or any
other magical use.

In modern times, it is very rare for witches to make their own inks. However,
it is my opinion that those who don't hamper their productivity, because the
inks of today are not magical and do not lend any energy to the spell or workings. The magical uses of inks have mostly been forgotten, and with them, a

total involvement in the magical arts, energies, and rituals. Many of us make our own incenses, oils, ointments and salves. So why don't we make our inks as well, and thereby benefit from the added power and energy that true witches find in magical inks?

Making Magical Ink

There are several things to remember when making magical inks: Lamp black is lighter than air. If it gets on anything, it is there permanently. It will not come out. So please wear appropriate clothing when working with these ink recipes. *CAUTION: Some of these herbs are poisonous and should be treated with great respect. The baneful herbs are listed in appendix 3 and are marked with a ‡ in recipes. If you have any doubts about whether to treat an herb as baneful or poisonous, please refer to this list. If you have allergies, please wear gloves and protective clothing, such as long-sleeved shirts or long pants.*

Never use metal when making magical inks; always use glass, pyrex, or a double-boiler made of stainless steel or enamel. And be sure never to use aluminum. It will taint the herbs and may poison the individual working with the herbs or inks.

Always use natural thickening agents, such as gum, in the inks. This will thicken the ink naturally and not taint its vibrational level. Inks can be difficult to work with and handle, but, in the long run, the magical energy and power gained from making your own inks pays off in increased power for your magical workings. It is satisfying to know that all that is magically possible has been done.

To prepare an ink, simply burn a stick or branch until its end is reduced to charcoal—not ash. When cool, use the stick as a natural charcoal pencil for recording your magical goal, making ritualistic signs, or conducting rituals. A new charcoal pencil should be made for each ritual. As the charcoal pencil burns, and as you draw or write, visualize your magical goal. To properly charge and purify your magical inks, use the oil-charging ritual given in chapter 2. This primordial rite may be enough to spark your ability to move and direct your personal power.

When writing with magical ink, use only sharpened quills or dip pens. The latter are usually available at stationary and office supply stores. Practice using the dip pen before using it for magic.

Using Magical Ink

There are many ways to use magical ink. Below are just a few:

- On appropriately colored paper, place an image of your magical goal. As you write the letters or images, visualize them shimmering with power and energy.

- On appropriately colored paper, write your goal. Next, anoint the paper with the appropriate true essential oil for your goal. Then burn the paper to ashes, while visualizing your goal. As it burns, see the energy you've poured into it streaming out to manifest your goal.

- To create a low-cost scrying tool, burn a psychism incense at night. Add several drops of black ink to a small, round bowl of water. When the water is totally darkened, turn off the lights, light a yellow candle, and gaze into the water. Relax your conscious, doubting mind and allow yourself to contact your psychic mind. Open yourself to receive information relating to possible future trends and possibilities.

CAUTION: Never take ink internally. Some older spells call for inks to be consumed. Most inks, however, are poisonous, so you should ignore this instruction.

Invisible Ink

Use milk and lemon juice. Write your goal on white paper and let dry. To make the writing appear, just hold over the flame of a candle. Be careful not to hold the paper too close, lest it catch on fire!

Ritualistic Example of Invisible Ink

With invisible ink, write or draw the goal or image of your magical purpose. Do this with intention, power, and visualization. When the ink has completely dried, look at the paper. You will see nothing. The blank paper represents your life without your goal being met. Now hold the paper near the candle flame. As the image slowly appears, send energy to it, knowing that what you need will manifest in your life as well.

Ink Recipes

If you're creating an ink for general magic, use a white candle; for money, use a green candle; for love, use a pink candle; for psychic powers, use a yellow candle. Use the lists in chapter 14 as a reference for determining the appropriate color.

To begin, light a candle of the proper color. Hold the back of a spoon's bowl in the flame of your candle, barely touching the wick, for approximately 30 to 45 seconds. Remove the spoon. You will have a coating of lampblack on the back of the spoon. Hold the spoon over a small bowl and scrape the lampblack off with a small piece of cardboard or cardstock. Remember—lampblack is lighter than air. If you are not careful, it will float away and get on anything in its path. And it won't come out! Repeat this process for about an hour, in order to accumulate enough lampblack for your ink. Be sure to visualize your magical goal at all times during the processing of the ink. By the time you finish gathering the lampblack, your hands will be dirty. If you are lucky, the handle of your spoon will not be too hot. I deliberately avoid giving measurements here, because it is impossible to measure lampblack. The more you accumulate, however, the more ink you can make.

Lampblack Ink Recipe
Lampblack
Distilled water
Gum Arabic

One drop at a time, add hot distilled water to the bowl of lampblack. Stop adding water before you think you should. If you accidentally get too much water, add more lampblack. Mix with your finger, until the water is an inky black. This is time-consuming because lampblack floats and is difficult to dissolve.

Once the water is inky black, add a small amount of gum arabic, and mix until the gum has been dissolved in the warm liquid. Any of these homemade inks should be the same consistency as commercially prepared ink. Store the ink in a small bottle for future use.

To prepare the following ink recipes, crush and strain the ingredients and add a small amount of gum arabic to thicken, if necessary.

Beet Juice Magical Ink
The juice of a beet will make a red ink. Add gum arabic to thicken if necessary.

Blackberry Magical Ink
The juice of a blackberry will make a dark black ink. Add gum arabic to thicken if necessary.

Boysenberry Magical Ink

The juice of a boysenberry will make a good ink. Add gum arabic to thicken if necessary.

Grape Juice Ink

Use real grape juice for this one. It won't work otherwise. Add gum arabic to thicken if necessary.

Pokeberry Magical Ink ‡

These berries produce a purple ink when crushed. *CAUTION: The seeds are poisonous, so keep this ink out of your mouth.*

Saffron Magical Ink

Saffron essences make a wonderful magical ink.

CHAPTER TEN

Magical Foods

The following recipes have come from all over the world. I don't even remember the origin of some of them. Most of these recipes I like very well. I have collected them over the years. Some come from my family, some from friends, some from the Goddess only knows where. I hope you enjoy them as much as I do. Feel free to experiment and change them around. I certainly have.

Breads and Baked Goods

Acorn Cookies

1¾ cups flour
½ tsp. salt
½ tsp. baking soda
1 tsp. baking powder
1 tsp. Cinnamon
1 tsp. Nutmeg
¼ pound butter
1 tsp. Vanilla
1 cup sugar
2 eggs
1 cup raisins
1½ cup chopped Acorns

Sift together the flour, salt, baking soda, baking powder, cinnamon, and nutmeg. Set aside. In a large bowl, cream the butter. Add the vanilla and sugar, and beat well. Add the eggs and beat until smooth. Gradually add the sifted dry ingredients, beating until thoroughly mixed. Stir in the raisins and acorns. Place well-rounded teaspoonfuls of dough two inches apart on a foil-covered cookie sheet. Bake in a preheated 400°F oven for 12 to15 minutes.

Anise Seed Cookies

Start off with your own favorite sugar cookie recipe or a box of cookie mix. This recipe is Greek in origin.

1 batch sugar cookie dough or large box of cookie
  mix
1 Tbsp. Anise seed
1 Tbsp. Sesame seed
2 tsp. grated Orange peel
2 tsp. grated Lemon peel
1 Tbsp. ground Cinnamon

For the cinnamon sugar, mix the following completely:

1 Tbsp. ground Cinnamon
2 Tbsp. sugar

Prepare the dough or mix according to directions. Knead in the anise seed, sesame seed, lemon peel, orange peel, and cinnamon. Roll out on lightly floured board to ¼ inch thick. Cut with a cookie cutter (Moon circles or crescents are nice) and place on cookie sheets. Sprinkle with cinnamon sugar mixture and bake according to the mix or recipe instructions.

Brown Danish Cookies

1 cup butter
1 cup sugar
4 cups all-purpose flour
1 tsp. baking powder
½ tsp. Ginger
1 Tbsp. grated Orange rind
½ cup molasses
¼ tsp. Cinnamon
Blanched Almonds for decoration

Cream butter and sugar. Add the rest of the ingredients. Knead together. Form into two rolls and chill. Slice cookies very thin and decorate with half an almond. Bake at 325°F for 8 to10 minutes. Can be frozen to store.

Cranberry Muffins

4 Tbsp. softened butter
2 cups fresh Cranberries
2¾ cups flour
¾ cup sugar
4 tsp. baking powder
½ tsp. salt
1 cup milk
2 lightly beaten eggs
1 small pkg. cream cheese

Preheat oven to 400°F. Combine the dry ingredients in one deep mixing bowl. Sift dry ingredients together. Stirring constantly with a big spoon, pour in the milk. Stir in the egg, butter, and cream cheese. Add the cranberries and continue to stir until all of the ingredients are well combined. Ladle batter in buttered muffin-tin cups, filling each about ⅔ full. Bake for 30 minutes, or until the muffins are brown and a toothpick inserted in the center comes out clean. Use this chant while cooking anything made of grain:

I invoke thee,
beloved Spirit of the Grain.
Be present in this sacred loaf.

Crescent Cakes

1 cup finely ground Almonds
1¼ cups flour
½ cup confectioner's sugar
½ cup butter, softened
2 egg yolks
¼ tsp. Almond extract

Mix almonds, flour, sugar, and extract until thoroughly blended. With your hands, work in the butter and egg yolks until well blended. Chill dough. Preheat oven to 325°F. Pinch off pieces of dough about the size of walnuts and shape into crescents. Place on greased sheets and bake for about 20 minutes. Serve during the Simple Feast, especially at Esbats. These are wonderful cookies. Try them; you will not be disappointed.

Herb-Frosted Currant Rolls

These are much like Hot Cross Buns, which date back further than the Christian tradition that has popularized them. Makes 6 dozen. You may use your own bun recipe or use a packaged mix.

1 13¾ oz. hot roll mix
6 Tbsp. sugar
½ cup currants or raisins
1 egg, well beaten
¾ cup confectioners sugar
½ tsp. Anise seed
1 Tbsp. Lemon juice

Prepare the roll mix according to the directions on the package, but add the sugar, currants, and egg. Cover with dishtowel or cheesecloth and let rise in a warm place until light and double in size (about 30 to 45 minutes). Roll out dough to a 1" thickness on a floured board. Cut with a floured biscuit cutter or the rim of a large glass. Place the rolls on a well-greased baking sheet. Cover and let rise again until doubled in size.

Bake at 375°F for 20 to 30 minutes. Combine the confectioners sugar, anise seed, and lemon juice. Beat until smooth. Spread on warm rolls.

Killarney Scones (Ireland)

2 cups sifted all-purpose flour
½ tsp. salt
1 Tbsp. sugar
4 tsp. baking powder
4 Tbsp. shortening
⅓ to ½ cup milk
1 egg, well-beaten
½ cup raisins or currants
Melted butter
Sugar

Sift dry ingredients together and cut in the shortening. Add the milk to the egg and then add this to the flour mixture. Add the raisins. Knead lightly and roll the dough to ½ inch thickness. Cut into small wedges and place on a no-stick cookie sheet. Brush with melted butter and sprinkle with sugar. Bake at 400°F for 15 minutes. Makes 15 scones.

Magic Pumpkin Squares

½ cup butter
1½ cups honey
2 eggs
1 cup buttermilk
2 cups mashed Pumpkin
2 cup whole wheat flour
½ tsp. salt
1 tsp. baking soda
2 tsp. Cinnamon
1 tsp. Nutmeg
1 tsp. Cloves
½ tsp. Allspice
2 cups uncooked Oats
1 cup quartered Dates
½ cup crushed Walnuts

Beat butter, eggs, honey, buttermilk, and pumpkin. Add flour, salt, baking soda, spices, and oats. Mix well. Add the dates and nuts and stir together. Grease a 9x9-inch pan and spread batter evenly. Bake in a preheated 375°F oven for 35 to 40 minutes, or until done. Remove from pan, cool, and cut into small squares.

Mandelformer (Swedish Tarts)

Use fluted tartlet pans; these are generally available in boxed sets in any shop that sells kitchen supplies. If unable to find these pans, tiny muffin tins can be used.

1 cup sweet butter or margarine
¾ cup white sugar
1 whole egg
2⅓ cup white enriched flour

1 cup ground, sweet roasted Almonds
Few sliced Almonds

Mix together the butter, sugar, egg, and flour; blend in the ground almonds. Carefully coat the tartlet pans with butter. Press the dough into the buttered tins until evenly and thinly coated. Bake at 350°F until lightly brown. Since the pans are quite small, you may find it necessary to arrange them on a cookie sheet for baking. When the tarts are done, remove the pans to a wire rack to cool. When cool, carefully remove the tarts from the pans. This confection is so delicate that any rough treatment will cause them to crumble. Fill with pudding, jam or jelly, cooked mincemeat, freshly sliced strawberries or other fruits, or pie fillings. They may be garnished with whipped cream and sliced almonds.

Sabbat Cakes
1½ cups rolled Oats
1½ cups flour
4 Tbsp. sugar
5 Tbsp. dark brown sugar
½ tsp. baking soda
½ tsp. salt
12 Tbsp. butter, cut into ½" bits
2 Tbsp. Vanilla extract
4 to 6 Tbsp. cold water

Blend together all dry ingredients and sift into a deep mixing bowl. Drop in the butter bits and stir the oat and flour mixture together with the butter until it looks like flakes of coarse meal. Pour the vanilla extract and four tablespoons of cold water over the mixture, toss together lightly and gather the dough into a ball. (Add up to two more tablespoons of cold water, drop by drop, if the dough begins to crumble.) Wrap the dough in waxed paper and refrigerate for at least 30 minutes. On a lightly floured surface, roll the dough out into a rough rectangle about ⅛ inch thick. With a stick and a sharp knife, cut the dough into two-inch triangles. Arrange the Sabbat cakes about an inch apart on a large buttered baking sheet and bake in a preheated 350°F oven for 20 minutes, until they are golden brown and firm. Cool on wire racks before serving. This recipe makes 40 two-inch triangular cakes.

Salem Brown Bread

2 cups buttermilk
¾ cup dark molasses
1 cup raisins
1 cup rye flour
1 cup whole wheat flour
1 cup yellow corn meal
¾ tsp. baking soda
1 tsp. salt
1 Tbsp. softened butter

Beat the buttermilk and molasses together vigorously, in a deep bowl. Stir in the raisins. Combine the flours, corn meal, baking soda, and salt, and sift them into the buttermilk mixture one cup at a time, stirring well after each addition. Butter the bottom and sides of two 2 ½-cup tin cans. Pour the batter into the cans, dividing it evenly between them. The batter should fill each can to within about one inch of the top. Cover each can loosely with a circle of buttered waxed paper, and then with a larger circle of aluminum foil. The foil should be puffed like the top of a French chef's hat, allowing an inch of space above the top edge of the cans so the batter can rise as it is steamed. Tie the waxed paper and foil in place with string. Stand the cans on a rack in a large pot and pour in enough boiling water to come about ¾ of the way up the sides of the cans. Bring the water to a boil. Cover the pot tightly and reduce the heat. Steam the bread for 2¼ hours. Remove the foil and paper from the cans at once, and turn the bread out.

Savory Corn Muffins

These are great on a snowy, cold day, served with a soup or stew and sweetened with honey drizzled all over them. Serves 8.

One 8 ½-oz. package corn muffin mix (about 1⅔ cups)
⅓ cup milk

1 egg
¼ tsp. dried summer Savory, crumbled
½ cup grated Longhorn cheese (optional)

Combine the corn muffin mix, milk, egg, cheese, and savory. Mix the dry ingredients until just moistened. Spoon into greased muffin tins, filling each half full. Bake at 400°F for 20 minutes. Some of the recipes use mixes for fast preparation. You can substitute your own favorite muffin recipe for the mix if you choose to.

Scottish Shortbread

1½ cups sifted all-purpose flour
1½ cups sifted powdered sugar
1 cup (2 sticks) butter

Sift the flour and powdered sugar into a medium-sized bowl; cut in the butter until the mixture is crumbly. Work the dough into a ball with your hands and knead about 10 minutes. Pat the dough into a ¼-inch thick rectangle, 14x12 inches, on a large ungreased cookie sheet. Cut into 2-inch squares or diamonds with a sharp knife. Decorate with colored candies, if desired. Bake at 300°F for 45 minutes, or until firm and lightly browned. Recut the shortbread at the marks and separate very carefully. Handle with extreme care! Remove from the pan to a wire rack. Store with waxed paper between the layers in a container with a tight-fitting lid. If stored for a few weeks, this shortbread mellows to a delicate delicious taste. (I recommend letting it age.)

Wiccan Handfasting Cake

1 cup butter
1 cup sugar
½ cup honey
5 eggs
2 cups flour
2 Tbsp. grated Lemon rind
2½ tsp. Lemon juice
1 tsp. Rosewater
Pinch of Basil
6 fresh Rose Geranium leaves

Cream butter and sugar until fluffy and light. Add the honey and mix well. Add the eggs, one at a time, beating well after each addition. Gradually add the flour and blend thoroughly with a large wooden spoon following each addition. Stir in the lemon rind, lemon juice, rose water, and a pinch of basil—the herb of love. Line the bottom of a greased 9x5x3-inch loaf pan with the rose geranium leaves and then pour in the batter. Bake in a 350°F oven for 1¼ hours. Remove from the oven when done and let cake stand on a rack for 20 minutes before unmolding. Sprinkle powdered sugar on top just before serving.

Wild Berry Bread

6 Tbsp. softened butter, cut into ½-inch cubes
2 cups flour
½ cup Raspberries
½ cup Blackberries
1 cup Blueberries
1 cup sugar
1½ tsp. baking powder
½ tsp. baking soda
½ tsp. salt
1 egg, slightly beaten
2 Tbsp. grated Orange peel
½ cup Orange juice

You may use fresh or frozen berries, depending on whether they are in season. Wash the berries under cold running water and pat them dry with paper towels. Crush the berries and set aside. Combine the flour, sugar, baking powder, baking soda, and salt, and sift into a deep bowl. Add the butter bits and, with your fingertips, rub the butter and dry ingredients together until they become like flakes of coarse meal. Mix in the egg, orange peel, and orange juice, and add the berries, while continuing to stir until all of the ingredients are thoroughly combined. Spoon the batter into a buttered 9x5-inch loaf pan, spreading it and smoothing the top with a spatula. Bake in a preheated 350°F oven for 1½ hours, or until the top is golden brown and a toothpick inserted in the center of the loaf comes out clean. Turn the loaf out onto a wire rack to cool.

Witches' Honey Bread

1½ cups buttermilk

1 cup honey

¼ cup molasses

2 tsp. baking soda

1 tsp. salt

1½ cups whole wheat flour

1 cup white flour

½ cup raisins

Combine the buttermilk, honey, molasses, baking soda, and salt. Mix the 2 flours together in a separate bowl and add to the buttermilk mixture. Stir in the raisins and pour the batter into a greased 9x5-inch loaf pan. Bake the bread for one hour in a 350°F oven. Turn the loaf out, inverted, on a wire rack to cool.

Beverages

In addition to the beverages listed below, any commercial brand of sparkling water can be used as a ritual beverage.

Beer and Ale

The beverages most often mentioned in Tameran/Egyptian writings are water, milk, beer, and wine. The following recipes for beer and ale are from an ancient text.

Almost any grain can be made into beer. As far as we know, grain was traditionally first sprouted in the same way we make sprouts for salads and sandwiches. The sprouts and some water were ground into a moist dough and formed into cakes. (One on-line source mentions the addition of yeast.) These cakes were lightly cooked, then broken up into water. After a day or two, when the mixture had fermented enough to be alcoholic, it was strained and served. The mixture would keep for only a day or so before it became undrinkable. If you prefer not to ferment your own ales or beers, any malt liquor will serve just as well as a symbolic beverage.

Red Beer: Red beer is mentioned in both legend and literature. Its red color may be attributable to the grain used, or to an additive. One legend regarding an aspect of the Goddess mentions beer as colored either with pomegranate juice or ochre. There is a beer available today that is "red." You may honor Sekhmet by having this beer at your gathering. I don't believe it is wise to mention the name of this product, but I will give you a hint—its name is Irish.

Mead: In ancient records, there is mention of the ancient Tamerans/Egyptians drinking beer sweetened with honey. This mixture resembled mead. And remember, the Tamerans did have honey. The bees, and therefore the honey they created, were sacred to Min, God of Fertility. The Nile valley is very hot and arid. Water mixed with honey, or honey itself just sitting around in jars, could easily have fermented.

Alcoholic Mead

1 quart honey
3 quarts distilled water

Mix the honey and water and boil for 5 minutes. (If you wish to include herbs and spices, add them while it cooks.) Cool the mixture to just above body temperature. Add a package of yeast and mix. Put in a large container. Cover with plastic wrap or plastic bags, and allowing for expansion. Put in a dark place and let sit for seven days. Refrigerate until the sediment settles (two or three days). Strain and bottle. Keep in a cool dark place. This is now drinkable, but I'm told that it is even better when aged for several months. Be careful, this is no lightweight drink. It is about 60 proof!

Non-Alcoholic Mead

1 quart honey
3 quarts distilled water
½ cup Lemon juice
1 sliced Lemon
½ tsp. Nutmeg
Pinch of salt

Boil five minutes, cool, and bottle immediately. Keep refrigerated to prevent fermentation.

Nettle Ale

2 gallons young Nettles
2½ gallons water
¾ oz. bruised Ginger root
4 oz. Sarsasparilla
4 lbs. malt
2 oz. hops

1½ lbs. sugar

1 oz. yeast

Wash the nettles and place them in a large pot. Add 2½ gallons of well water or pure spring water, the ginger root, sarsasparilla, malt, and hops. Boil for 15 to 20 minutes. Remove from heat and strain over 1½ lbs. of sugar. Stir well until the sugar dissolves and then add the yeast. Bottle the ale when it begins to ferment. Bubbles will form and start coming to the surface. Seal the bottles with corks and tie down with string. Nettle ale does not need to be aged.

Egyptian Wines

The following are wines made from grape stock that originally came from Egypt.

Malmsley—Madeira Dessert Wine

Rainwater Madeira

Nebbilio

Amarone

Nebbilio D'Alba

Est Est Est

Pino Grigio

Wines Related to Egyptian Wines

Sauvignon Blanc—similar to Delta Wines

L'Tour Blanc (has a picture of Asar on its label)

Isian Beverages

Lychee liqueur

Ouzo or other plain, clear liqueur

Clear Creme de Menthe (another good lunar beverage, as it hints of the "cold Moon fire," with its cool taste

Miscellaneous Drinks

Milk of Isis

1 quart milk (4 cups)

6 Tbsp. Almond syrup (recipe follows)
Several large strawberries (or a red fruit juice)

To prepare the almond syrup, dissolve 1 cup sugar in 1 cup water and bring to a boil, stirring occasionally, until the syrup begins to thicken. Add 2 tablespoons almond extract and stir. Milk of Isis can also be made with vanilla syrup. Just substitute 1 tablespoon of vanilla extract for the 2 tablespoons of almond extract. Add the syrup to the milk, stirring well (you may also use a blender). Squeeze several large strawberries into the milk for a light pink color, or use another red fruit juice of your choice. Serve chilled.

Non-Alcoholic Sabbat Beverages

Apple juice, grape juice, grapefruit juice, orange juice, pineapple juice, black tea, soft mead, guava nectar, cinnamon coffee, ginger tea, and hibiscus tea can all be used as non-alcoholic Sabbat beverages as well.

Dandelion Wine

3 quarts open Dandelion flowers
2 gallons spring water
7 lbs. sugar
3 Oranges
3 Lemons
¼ box seedless raisins
1 yeast (pkg. or cake)

Cover tightly packed dandelions in a crock with boiling water. Let it stand three days. Strain through a colander and discard dandelions. Add the seven pounds of sugar to the liquid. Slice the oranges and lemons, leaving the peels, but removing the seeds. Add the fruits to the liquid. Next, add the raisins and stir thoroughly. Boil for 20 minutes and then remove from the heat. Let it stand for another 24 hours. Add the yeast, dissolved in six table-spoons of hot water. Stir, then strain the mixture through a piece of wet muslin or clean dishtowel into wine bottles, filling them to the brim. Tie pieces of muslin over the bottle tops or seal with corks. Do not cap bottles too tightly. Small amounts of gas may form and must be allowed to escape. The wine is ready to drink after fermentation has stopped and no more bubbles appear in the bottles. Store in a dark cool place for up to six months.

Divination Wine

Follow the instructions for Dandelion Wine, using one quart each of cowslip flowers, dogwood blossoms, and rose hips instead of the three quarts of dandelions. Omit the raisins from the recipe.

Hot Mulled Punch

This is great for large gatherings. Add 1½ quarts of cranberry juice to 1 quart of apple juice. Put in a 36- to 40-cup coffee maker. Place ½ cup brown sugar, 1½ teaspoons of whole cloves and 4 to 5 cinnamon sticks in the basket of the coffee maker. When the brewing cycle is done, remove the basket containing the spices and serve hot. Very festive and delicious.

Mandrake‡ Wine

Remove the stems, skins, and seeds from 13 medium apples. Boil the apples for about 20 minutes. Drain and mash together with the full, ripe, oval lemon-colored fruit of one mandrake‡ (American variety) also known as the mayapple. *CAUTION: Do not use any other part of the mandrake. The fully ripe fruit is edible, but the rest of the plant is very poisonous.* Follow the instructions for Dandelion Wine, using three quarts mashed apples and mandrake‡ fruit in place of the dandelions. Omit the raisins from the recipe.

Merry May Punch

2 cups sweet Woodruff (leaves and blossoms)
1 quart sweet wine
1 pint wild Strawberries
½ cup sugar
Grated peel and juice of 1 Lime

Steep the sweet woodruff (leaves and blossoms) in the wine for three hours on low heat. Cool. Wash and hull the strawberries. Crush and combine them with the wine, sugar, grated lime peel, and lime juice. Cover and chill for several hours. Strain liquid and discard the pulp. Fill a large punch bowl with crushed ice and pour the punch over the ice. Add some sweet woodruff blossoms to the punch just before serving.

Mulled Herb Wine

1 cup boiling water
⅛ tsp. Rosemary leaves, crushed
¼ tsp. Mint, crushed
4-5 whole Cloves
1 cup grape juice
1 cup dry cocktail sherry or wine
1 stick of Cinnamon

Pour the boiling water over the rosemary and mint; steep for 15 minutes. Add the cloves and continue to steep the mixture for another 15 minutes. Strain; mix this liquid with the grape juice and sherry or wine in a pan. Place over low heat until hot. Strain, add the cinnamon stick, and serve hot.

Nectar of the Gods

2 cups Apricot nectar
1½ cups fruit salad
1 cup sliced Bananas
1 cup Pineapple juice
1 cup chopped Pineapple
1 cup maraschino Cherry juice
2 oz. rum

Mix all ingredients together in a large punch bowl. Chill for several hours and add crushed ice just before serving.

Non-Alcoholic Herb Punch

This is a good drink to serve at pagan gatherings or for any get-together. Even children can enjoy this one.

1 large handful Lemon balm
2 large handfuls Borage

1 large handful Mint
1 cup Pineapple or any other fruit juice
6 Lemons, juiced
2 Oranges, juiced
1 quart strong tea
Syrup made of 1 cup sugar, boiled with ½ cup water
3 quarts ginger ale

Pour 1½ quarts boiling water over the lemon balm and let steep for 20 minutes. Strain the liquid onto the borage and mint. Add the fruit juices, tea, and syrup. Refrigerate at least 8 hours. Strain into a punch bowl. Add ice, some extra mint, and ginger ale.

Rose Hip Wine

After cleaning them thoroughly, crush 5 pounds of rose-hips. Place in 2 quarts of water and allow to sit overnight. Add 1 oz. yeast and 1¾ pounds of sugar. Let ferment for 7 days. Strain well. Add 2 quarts water, and an additional 1¾ pounds of sugar. Allow to ferment for another 7 days. This is a good heart tonic and is absolutely delicious.

Sage Wine

1 cup fresh Sage
½ cup claret or Burgundy wine

Place the fresh sage and the wine in an electric blender and run it on high speed for a few minutes, until the sage leaves are pulverized. Return the wine to its original bottle and chill well before serving.

Sandalwood Drink

1½ quarts water
5 Cloves
5 green Cardamom pods
1 cup honey
4 drops Sandalwood, or 4 tsp. Sandalwood water
1 Lemon, juiced
1 cup plain low-fat yogurt
1 quart tonic water or plain soda water

Boil the water, cloves, and cardamom for 5 to 6 minutes. Add the honey and sandalwood; boil until the syrup is thick. Remove from heat, stir in lemon juice, and let cool. Put the yogurt and cooled syrup into a blender. Puree until liquid is frothy. Pour into a bowl and mix with soda water. Serve cold.

Sharbatee Bulab Drink

This Indian drink is excellent when made in June, for the roses will be blooming. Serves 6–8. *CAUTION: Be sure to use blossoms that have not been treated with pesticides.*

5 large fragrant Roses in full bloom or 10 Wild Roses
2 quarts cold water
1⅓ cups sugar
¼ cup Lemon juice
3 cups crushed Pineapple (fresh or canned)
Finely crushed ice
Extra Rose petals

Wash the roses and shake off the excess water. Carefully take off the petals and put them in a large bowl. Pour the cold water over them and let stand in a dark, but not refrigerated, place for about 4 hours. Strain out the petals, saving the water. Dissolve the sugar in the lemon juice and add this to the rose water. Stir in the pineapple. When ready to serve, pour over crushed ice and top with a rose petal in each glass.

Sweet Tomato Wine

Remove the stalks from 3 quarts of ripe red tomatoes. Cut the tomatoes into small pieces and then mash them well. Drain through a hair-sieve. Season the tomato juice to taste with salt and sugar. Pour into jars and tie pieces of muslin over the tops. Let stand until the fermentation process has ended and there are no more bubbles. Pour off the clear liquid into wine bottles and cork tightly.

Allow the wine to age at least three months in a cellar or other cool, dark place before drinking.

Sweetened Condensed Milk

Mix together ⅔ cup sugar, 1 cup powdered coffee creamer, ½ cup boiling water, and 3 tablespoons of margarine. Blend in a blender until smooth. Use in any recipe that calls for sweetened condensed milk. This is better than the canned version.

Yogurt Drink

This drink came from India and is rather like an exotic milk shake, minus the fat and cholesterol.

1 quart plain low-fat yogurt
2 Tbsp. Rose water or 4 drops Rose essence
6 Tbsp. honey or light brown sugar
6 ice cubes

Put the yogurt, rose water, and honey in a blender and puree. Add the ice cubes and blend until the yogurt is whipped. Serve in tall glasses.

Teas

Apple Tea

Wash and core several apples and slice, do not peel. Put the apples on a greased, wax paper-lined cookie sheet. Place in an oven on low heat, with door cracked open. Turn over to ensure they dry completely. When the apple slices are dry, close the oven door and roast until lightly browned. Cool and store in a tightly closed container. Place several slices in your teapot and fill with boiling water. Steep about 10 minutes. Add honey as needed for sweetener.

Gypsy Tea
2 Oranges
3 Lemons
13 Cloves
1 Tbsp. ground Allspice

½ Cinnamon stick
3 Tbsp. black tea
2 quarts boiling water
1¼ cups sugar

Squeeze juice from oranges and lemons; set juice aside. Remove rinds and put in a large container. Add cloves, allspice, cinnamon stick, and tea. Pour boiling water over the tea mixture and let it stand for about 10 minutes. Strain and then return liquid to container. Stir in the orange juice, lemon juice, and sugar. Gypsy tea may be served either hot or cold, over crushed ice.

Indian Spiced Tea

The people of India like spices in their tea, because the spices taste wonderful and also create extra body heat in cold weather. Milk is also a favorite to put in the tea. If you wish to be authentic, add 1 cup low-fat milk during the last simmering process. This is especially good for the cold ritual months. Serves 6.

7 cups cold water
6 green Cardamom pods
1 Cinnamon stick
6 Cloves
1¼-inch piece fresh Ginger root, peeled and chopped
¼ cup light brown sugar or honey
2 Tbsp. black tea leaves

In a large pot, bring the water to a boil. Stir in the spices and brown sugar. Boil gently for five minutes. Turn off the heat, cover the pot with a lid, and let the mixture steep for ten minutes. Add the tea leaves and bring to a boil. Lower the heat, cover the pot, and simmer for another five minutes. Strain the tea and serve.

Lemon Balm Tea

Use 20 sprigs of fresh lemon balm, 4 tablespoons honey, 10 whole cloves, and the juice of ½ lemon. Pour 1 quart of boiling water over the lemon balm, then add the other ingredients. (If dried herb is used, use half the amount normally used.) Let steep 10 minutes. Strain and serve.

Rose Hip Tea

Gather and clean the rose hips. Be sure no pesticides have been used on the roses or you may poison yourself. Chop in the blender. Air-dry them before storing in a tightly closed container. To make the tea, pour 1 cup boiling water over ½ teaspoon of the crushed rose hips. Steep 5 minutes until color is bright pink. Add sugar or honey to taste. Try with cloves, or use cinnamon sticks to stir the tea.

Russian Tea

1 pot hot tea
⅛ tsp. each Cloves and Nutmeg
1 whole Cinnamon stick
Rum or Vodka (optional)
Sprigs of fresh Mint

Steep cloves, nutmeg, and cinnamon in the tea for several minutes. When ready to serve, add rum or vodka. Top each with a sprig of mint. This recipe came from a Russian foreign exchange student who grew up in a Wiccan home.

Hot Chocolates

Hot Chocolate

Combine 2 cups powdered milk, 1 cup powdered sugar, ¼ cup cocoa, 1 cup powdered coffee creamer, and a dash of salt, and mix together in a blender until finely chopped. If you like, add 2 tablespoons malted-milk powder. To use, add 4 tablespoons of mixture to 1 cup of boiling water.

Hot Chocolate Topping

Make up 1 pint of whipping cream as usual, but add a sweet liqueur (of your choice) into the cream while whipping. It may be necessary to add another pint of whipping cream, depending on how thick you want the topping to be.

Mexican Hot Chocolate

4 to 6 oz. semisweet dark chocolate, broken into small
  pieces, or cocoa powder
1 quart milk
Dash Cloves
1 tsp. ground Cinnamon
Dash Almond extract or Vanilla extract
Sugar to taste

Gently heat the chocolate with the milk, cloves, cinnamon, almond or vanilla extract, and sugar. Stir constantly until the chocolate is melted. Whip to a froth with
a whisk. Serve immediately.

Minted Hot Chocolate

Prepare your hot chocolate. Stir it with a peppermint
candy stick or add a round peppermint candy.

Coffees

Cafe Vienna

Combine ½ cup instant coffee, ½ teaspoon cinnamon, a
pinch of baking soda, ⅔ cup powdered milk, and ⅔ cup
sugar. Blend until finely ground in a blender. Use 2
rounded teaspoons for each cup of boiling water.

Cafe Cappuccino

Combine 1 cup powdered milk, ¾ cup sugar, ½ cup
instant coffee, ¼ teaspoon dried or powdered orange
peel, and ⅛ teaspoon baking soda. Mix in a blender. Add
2 rounded teaspoons to each cup of boiling water.

Coffee Substitutes

1. Use either dandelion or chicory root. Wash the roots
   carefully and spread in a large flat pan. Place in an
   oven at 180 to 200°F for up to 4 hours. Turn to
   ensure even drying, or use a dehydrator. When the

roots are completely dry and cool, you may store them as roots to grind fresh, or you can grind them before placing them in a tightly closed container. Use as you would coffee, or mix half-and-half with commercial coffee.

2. Mix and grind together 1 cup of ginseng root, ½ cup licorice root, 1 cup sarsasparilla root, 1 cup Irish moss, 2 cups holy thistle, ½ cup dried orange peel, and 5 cups roasted chicory or dandelion root. Use powdered malt in place of licorice root if desired.

International Coffee

Mix together 1 cup instant coffee, 2 cups powdered coffee creamer, 1 teaspoon cinnamon, 1 cup sugar, and 2 cups of powdered milk. Place in a blender and mix until very finely ground. Use 2 or more teaspoons to each cup of boiling water.

Swiss Mocha

Mix together ½ cup of instant coffee, 2 tablespoons cocoa, ⅓ teaspoon baking soda, 1 cup sugar, and 1 cup dried milk. Blend in a blender until very finely ground. Place 2 teaspoons of mixture in 1 cup boiling water.

Honey

Honey helps restore energy and has a general calming effect. It also helps to dissolve mucus. Applied externally to the skin, it disinfects and heals minor wounds, cuts, and abrasions.

The Components of Honey

The principal ingredients of honey are glucose, simple sugars, and fructose. Other ingredients are water, organic acids, various proteins, pollen, and enzymes. The glucose and fructose in honey have been predigested by the bees that produced it. These simple sugars are quickly and easily absorbed into the digestive track, and they have an overall soothing effect on the body. They can also provide a healthful energy boost. Honey is a healthy treat, but take care when using it as a sweetener. Just 1 tablespoon of honey has 64 calories, compared to 46 calories in granulated sugar.

Tips for Purchasing Honey

There are many kinds of honey. Its consistency, fragrance, and taste depend on the types of flowers from which bees collect the nectar. Look for honey that has been produced by beekeepers who do not feed their bees refined sugar or use harmful pesticides. *CAUTION: Do not give unpasteurized honey to infants. It contains a type of bacteria that, although harmless to older children and adults, can be very dangerous to those younger than a year old.*

Honey Recipes

Honey Bath

2 oz. honey
1 eight oz. glass water
5 drops true essential Lavender oil

Mix all ingredients in a glass, stir clockwise with a glass stick, and charge as usual. Place 1 or 2 tablespoons of the mixture into your bath water to help you relax and combat insomnia.

Wounds Dressing

Apply externally to the wound to promote healing by drawing excess water from the tissues and reducing swelling. In addition, honey contains a germ-killing substance called inhibine that helps prevent infections. Spread the honey directly on the wound and cover with a sterile bandage. Charge as usual for healing.

Anti-Hay Fever

Honey contains grains of pollen that, over time, may have a desensitizing effect, making it useful for the relief of allergies. Hay fever sufferers are advised to eat honey that has been harvested locally. Charge as usual for healing.

Asthma, Bronchitis, and Respiratory Ailments

Honey is an outstanding household remedy that can be used in combination with various medicinal herbs for relief of coughs and wheezing associated with bronchitis, whooping cough or other minor respiratory ailments.

1 tsp. finely chopped fresh Thyme
honey

Mix both ingredients together and take the mixture orally as needed to soothe inflamed lungs and airways. Charge for healing as usual.

Honey Cakes

An old custom among witches is to bake special cakes and cookies in honor of the Goddess. The sweets are then used in coven circles or left outdoors at sites that are sacred to the Goddess and her consort.

⅔ cup shortening
1 cup sugar
2 eggs
2 tsp. honey
2 tsp. Vanilla
1 tsp. white wine
1 tsp. of herbs or spice for your intention
2½ cups flour
1 tsp. baking powder
1 tsp. salt
2 Tbsp. Oats

Cream shortening, sugar, eggs, honey, vanilla, and wine. Then add the herbs or spices. Blend in baking powder, flour, salt, and oats. Mix together. Spoon batter onto cookie sheet, or roll out and cut in the shape of a crescent Moon. Bake at 350°F for 9 to 10 minutes.

Honey Zucchini Bread

3 eggs, beaten
1 cup honey
2 cups grated zucchini
1 Tbsp. Vanilla
1 cup vegetable oil
3 cups all-purpose flour
1 tsp. baking soda
½ tsp. baking powder
1 Tbsp. Cinnamon

1 tsp. salt
1 cup finely chopped nuts

Mix the beaten eggs, honey, zucchini, vanilla, and oil. In a separate bowl, mix the flour, baking soda, baking powder, cinnamon, and salt. Add the egg mixture to the dry mixture, stirring only enough to moisten. Add the nuts, and pour into two well-greased loaf pans. Bake at 325°F for one hour, or until bread tests done.

Dressings and Condiments

Celery Seed Dressing

Combine 1 tablespoon of salt, 1 tablespoon celery seed, 1 to 1½ tablespoons dry mustard, ¾ teaspoon paprika, ¾ cup vinegar, 1 cup sugar, and ½ of a small onion. Place in a blender and mix well, then add 2¼ cups vegetable oil in a steady stream to the mixture. Refrigerate.

Chili Sauce

Peel and chop 1 gallon tomatoes, add ½ cup of chopped onion, ½ cup chopped sweet peppers, ½ cup chopped red peppers, 5 teaspoons salt, ½ cup brown sugar, ½ teaspoon cayenne pepper, 1 teaspoon nutmeg, 2 teaspoons ginger, 1 teaspoon cinnamon, 1 tablespoon mustard. Mix well. Add 1 quart of vinegar and cook to desired consistency. Pour into sterile jars and seal.

French Dressing

Combine ¼ cup of water, ½ cup of vinegar, 1½ cups salad oil, 1 cup catsup, 2 teaspoons Worcestershire sauce, ½ cup sugar, 1 teaspoon salt, 1 teaspoon pepper, a teaspoon of table mustard, and ½ teaspoon powdered garlic in a quart jar and shake well.

International Mustards

To make your own flavors of mustard, start with mustard flour. To get an English flavor, add vinegar. For Chinese flavor, use beer. You may also use white wine, horseradish, sage, oregano, paprika, basil, garlic, onion, chervil, cloves, lovage, turmeric, rosemary, marjoram, chili powder, cumin, allspice, cinnamon, thyme, tarragon, parsley, dill, Tabasco, curry, savory, nutmeg, or chives to flavor the mustard flour. Mix the spices and mustard flour in any combination before adding any liquid. Thin with milk or mayonnaise to make a smooth paste. Allow to stand until the flavors are well blended. Mix in small batches for greater pungency. These mustards last a long time and make excellent gifts.

Mayonnaise

Combine 1 egg in blender with ¾ teaspoon salt, ¼ teaspoon paprika, ¼ teaspoon dry mustard, 1 tablespoon vinegar, and 1 tablespoon lemon juice. Add ¼ cup vegetable oil and start the blender. Then add ¾ cup vegetable oil in a small steady stream to the mixture, blending until smooth.

Russian Dressing

Mix together 3 rounded tablespoons of mayonnaise, 2 tablespoons catsup, 1 teaspoon horseradish, ¼ teaspoon Worcester-shire sauce, 1 tablespoon relish. Mix well and chill before serving.

Tartar Sauce

Mix together 3 heaping tablespoons mayonnaise, 1 finely chopped hard-boiled egg, 1 tablespoon relish, 1 teaspoon chopped onion, 1 teaspoon powdered garlic, a few drops lemon juice.

Thousand Island Dressing #1

Mix together ½ cup mayonnaise with 2 tablespoons cat-sup, 1 chopped hard-boiled egg, 1 tablespoon chopped sweet pepper, and 1 tablespoon relish. Mix well and chill thoroughly.

Thousand Island Dressing #2

Combine 1 cup mayonnaise, ¼ cup catsup, 1 chopped hard-boiled egg, 1 finely chopped onion, ⅓ cup chopped olives, 1 tsp. table mustard, ¼ cup chopped sweet pepper, and ½ cup finely chopped celery. Mix well and chill.

Seasonings

Chicken Soup Seasoning Mix

Mix ¼ cup each chives, tarragon, marjoram, basil, savory, and 3 teaspoons of sage. Add 1 to 2 teaspoons of the spice mix to your chicken soup. Put the mixture in a pepper mill to make it easy to add the amount wanted for flavor. Keep in a tightly closed jar.

Curry Powder

Mix together 2 teaspoons coriander seeds, 4 teaspoons powdered cinnamon, 2 teaspoons ginger, and 2 teaspoons ground turmeric. Mix together well and you have your own curry powder.

Pickling Spice

Mix together 2 tablespoons coriander seed, 2 tablespoons allspice, 1 tablespoon mustard seed, 2 bay leaves, and about 1 inch of a ginger root finely chopped.

Poultry Seasoning

Mix together 3 tablespoons each of marjoram and thyme, and 1 tablespoon each of sage, savory, and rosemary. Add 2 teaspoons celery seeds, ½ teaspoon each of pepper, oregano, and allspice. Store in a tightly closed container and use in sauces, dressing, or any recipe in which you would use poultry seasoning. Also good in meatloaf.

Pumpkin or Apple Pie Spice

Mix 3 teaspoons powdered allspice, 3 teaspoons nutmeg, 2 teaspoons ground cloves, 2 tablespoons cinnamon, and 2 tablespoons ground ginger. Store in a jar with a tight lid.

Rice Pilaf Mix

Mix 3 tablespoons each of garlic powder and thyme, 2 teaspoons each of allspice and coriander, 1 tablespoon black pepper, 5 tablespoons oregano, and ¾ cup basil. Use 2 tablespoons of mixture for each cup of rice. Store in a tightly capped jar.

Scalloped Potato Mix

Mix 16 tablespoons each of flour, cornstarch, and dried milk. Add 8 teaspoons of salt, 6 teaspoons onion powder, and 1 teaspoon of pepper. Sprinkle 6 tablespoons of mix over 3 cups of dehydrated potatoes. Dot with 3 tablespoons of butter, mix in 2⅓ cups of boiling water, and ⅔ cup milk. Bake in a 350°F oven for 50 to 55 minutes. Store in a tightly capped jar.

Taco

Mix 3 tablespoons each of oregano and corn starch, 2 tablespoons each of basil, crushed pepper flakes, and garlic powder. Add 5 tablespoons of chili pepper and ½ cup of minced onion flakes. Store in a tightly closed container. Use 1½ tablespoons of spice mix for each pound of meat. If making a meatless recipe, use 1½ tablespoons of taco mix for every 2 cups of whatever you're using.

Syrups and Jellies

Dandelion Jelly

Pick 1½ quarts of dandelion blossoms. Take the stems off and rinse the blossoms well. Add 3 cups water and boil for 3 minutes. Drain and add 1 teaspoon lemon extract and ½ teaspoon orange extract to 2⅔ cups of the liquid. Mix in a box of pectin and bring to a rolling boil. Add 4½ cups sugar all at once to the mixture. Bring to a boil again and boil for 3 minutes, stirring constantly. Remove from heat and skim off top. Put in sterile jars immediately and seal. If you choose, you can then put them into a water bath to make sure they seal properly.

Maple Syrup

Stir together 4 cups white sugar, ½ cup brown sugar, and 2 cups cold water. Add 2 tablespoons corn syrup if you have it. Cover and simmer for 10 minutes. Remove from heat and add 1 teaspoon vanilla and 2 teaspoons maple flavoring. This syrup keeps well.

Mayapple‡ Marmalade

In late summer or early fall, pick ½ gallon of ripe mayapples‡. *CAUTION: Remove the stem ends, as they are poisonous.* Cut in quarters and put in a kettle. Add 1 cup of water and simmer 15 minutes, stirring occasionally. When tender enough to mash, put through a colander to remove the skins and seeds. To 4 cups of pulp, add 1 box of pectin and bring to a boil. As soon as the mixture comes to a boil, add 5 cups of sugar. Stir constantly. Let it come to a hard boil and boil for 1 minute more. Remove from heat and skim off foam. Put into sterile jars immediately and seal. *CAUTION: This plant is poisonous. Do not eat any of the leaves or stems from the plant. Collect mayapples only when they are fully ripe. The American Indians used young shoots from this plant to commit suicide!*

Rose Apple Conserve
2 quarts chopped tart Apples (Winesap, Macintosh, etc.)
1 pint red Raspberries
3½ cups sugar
1 pint powdered Rose petals of a fragrant variety
1 tsp. Cinnamon

2 Tbsp. Lemon juice
¼ cup chopped English walnuts
1 pkg. fruit pectin

Follow the cooking instructions for jams on the package of fruit pectin. You can substitute fresh rose petals for powdered ones. Use only flowers that have not been treated with pesticides (therefore, not from a florist). Makes about 9 cups.

Rose Hip Marmalade

Pick and remove stem ends from 3 pounds of rose hips. Crush hips in a blender. Place in pan, cover with 4 cups of boiling water, and simmer 30 minutes. Rub through a sieve to remove seeds and hulls. This should yield about 5 cups of pulp.

Squeeze 2 large oranges and 1 lemon. Add the juices to the pulp. Put the rind of 1 orange through a grinder; add that to the pulp. Add 6 cups of sugar to the pulp mix. Boil about 20 minutes. Remove from heat, skim, and pour immediately in sterile jars and seal.

Rose Syrup

Boil 1 cup water and 1 cup sugar for 15 minutes. Add 1 cup fragrant red rose petals—petals only, please. Steep until cool. Strain if desired. Use on pancakes, waffles, or ice cream for a wonderful treat.

Miscellaneous Recipes

Beltane Marigold Custard
2 cups milk
1 cup unsprayed Marigold petals
¼ tsp. salt
3 Tbsp. sugar
1 to 2-inch piece Vanilla bean
3 egg yolks, slightly beaten
⅛ tsp. Allspice
⅛ tsp. Nutmeg

½ tsp. Rose water
Whipped cream

Crush marigold petals with a spoon or clean mortar and pestle reserved for cooking. Mix the salt, sugar, and spices together. Scald milk with the marigolds and the vanilla bean. Remove the vanilla bean and add the slightly beaten yolks and dry ingredients. Cook on low heat in a double boiler. When the mixture coats a spoon, add the rose water and cool. *CAUTION: Do not cook this mixture in an aluminum pan. Top with whipped cream, garnish with fresh marigold petals.*

Bourbon Balls

This recipe makes about 30 one-inch candies, but be warned that they won't last long.

1 6-oz. pkg. semi-sweet chocolate pieces
3 Tbsp. light corn syrup
¼ cup Bourbon
½ cup sugar
1¼ cups crushed Vanilla wafers (about 36)
1 cup finely chopped Pecans

In a double boiler, melt the chocolate pieces, stirring constantly. Remove pan from the heat. Blend in the corn syrup and bourbon; stir in the sugar, vanilla wafers, and pecans until well blended. Allow to cool slightly. Pat about 1 teaspoon of the mixture into a ball with your hands. Roll each ball in the remaining sugar and place on a cookie sheet. Cover and chill several hours. To store, put in a wide-mouthed jar with a tight-fitting lid.

Cheese Log

2 3-oz. pkg. cream cheese
1 5-oz. jar smoky cheese spread
1 5-oz. jar Roquefort cheese spread
1 5-oz. jar sharp Cheddar cheese spread
½ tsp. grated or dried onion
½ tsp. Worcestershire sauce
¼ cup undiluted evaporated milk
½ cup finely chopped Pecans or Walnuts

Let the four cheeses stand at room temperature for an hour or so. Put them in a bowl with the onion and Worcestershire sauce. Mix with a fork until smooth and well blended (I usually use my hands). Stir in milk, a little at a time, until blended in thoroughly. Cover and chill until firm—overnight, or about 4 hours. Shape into long rolls about 2" thick. Roll each cheese-roll in the chopped nuts. Wrap in waxed paper or plastic wrap and chill until ready to serve with crackers.

Dehydrated Potatoes

Peel and slice potatoes. Blanch for 10 seconds and immediately place in cold water. Chill for 15 minutes. Dry off completely. Spray cookie sheet with a vegetable-oil cooking spray and place the sliced potatoes on the cookie sheets. Bake in 150°F oven, propping the oven door open slightly. After about an hour, turn the slices over. Dry for approximately 3 hours. Potatoes will be brittle when done. Cool and store in a tightly closed container. Carrots can be dried in the same manner.

Irish Trifle

1 day-old pound cake
1 cup sherry or fruit juice
2 cups strawberries, sliced
2 cups nuts (Almonds or Walnuts)
1 6-oz. pkg. strawberry gelatin
1 cup cooked custard or whipping cream, or both

Put a layer of torn cake pieces into the bottom of a 10" pan. Pour part of the sherry or juice over the cake. Add half of the strawberries and nuts. Make a second layer of these ingredients. Prepare the gelatin using only 2 cups of water; pour over the layers. When the mixture is slightly set, top it with cooled custard and/or whipping cream. Refrigerate overnight.

May Day Pudding

4 Tbsp. plus 1 tsp. softened butter
2 eggs

6 cups milk
1½ tsp. Tansy
4 finely chopped sweet Cicely leaves
½ cup dark molasses
¼ cup sugar
¼ tsp. baking soda
¼ tsp. salt
1 cup yellow corn meal

Preheat oven to 350°F. With a pastry brush, spread one teaspoon of butter over the bottom and sides of a two-quart baking dish. Set aside. In a four- to five-quart saucepan, beat the eggs with a wire whisk until they are well mixed. Stirring constantly with the whisk, add four cups of the milk, tansy, sweet cicely leaves, molasses, sugar, baking soda, and salt. Simmer over medium heat, stirring until the molasses and sugar dissolve. Pour in the corn meal very slowly, stirring constantly to keep the mixture smooth. Cook uncovered, stirring occasionally, until the pudding is thick. Beat in the four tablespoons of butter and remove from heat. Pour in the remaining two cups of milk, beating constantly. Pour the pudding into the buttered baking dish and bake for one hour. Reduce the oven temperature to 300°F and continue to bake for about four more hours, until the May Day pudding is firm.

Mushroom Bites

This is a simplified recipe originally from ancient Greece. If you want to be authentic, wrap the mixture in phyllo pastry sheets.

3 pounds fresh mushrooms
½ cup minced onion
1 stick margarine, plus melted margarine for brushing tops
½ cup grated Parmesan cheese
Salt and pepper to taste
¾ cup bread crumbs
1 pound phyllo pastry or tubes of prepared dinner rolls.

Clean and chop the mushrooms finely. Sauté the onion in one stick of margarine until golden brown. Add mushrooms and cook until all the liquid is absorbed. Remove from the heat and add cheese, salt, pepper, and bread crumbs.

Separate dinner rolls. Roll each piece out into a very thin circle. Use about 1 teaspoon of the filling in the center of each roll. Fold over to make a half-circle and seal the edges with a fork. Take care not to tear the dough. Place on a nonstick cookie sheet. Brush the tops with the melted margarine and bake in a 375°F oven for 15 to 20 minutes, or until golden brown. Best served warm. (If using phyllo sheets, carefully lay out one sheet at a time and fill; fold into a triangular shape.)

Rose Hip Soup

Cover 2 cups of rose hips with 2 cups of water and simmer 2 hours, until the rose hips are tender. In a separate bowl, mix ½ cup of sugar with 2 tablespoons of cornstarch. Add this to the rose hip soup to thicken it. Boil briskly for 3 minutes, stirring constantly. Add ½ cup of white wine before serving. If served cold, top with whipped cream and lemon slices.

Sauerkraut

Place a one-inch thick layer of shredded cabbage in a crock. Sprinkle with 1 teaspoon of salt. Continue to layer the cabbage and the salt until the crock is full. Place a plate over the kraut and weigh it down with something heavy. Let it sit overnight and remove the scum that will be on it the next day. Stir the cabbage thoroughly. Do this daily until the fermentation has stopped. Place in sterile jars and cover tightly.

Soup Mix

Mix 8 teaspoons instant bouillon (chicken or beef), 2 tablespoons dried onion, and 1 teaspoon dried parsley. Add 2 tablespoons of the mix to 4 cups of water. Add other dried vegetables, such as carrots or mushrooms. Add as much rice or noodles as you desire. Simmer until rice or noodles are done. Add salt and pepper to taste. Store in a tightly capped container.

Witches' Granola

4 cups rolled wheat
1 cup rolled oats
½ cup bran
1 cup chopped nuts
1 cup hulled Sunflower seeds
1½ cups shredded Coconut
1 cup raisins
½ cup Sesame seeds
½ cup oil
1 cup honey
2 tsp. Vanilla extract

Mix together the rolled wheat, oats, bran, chopped nuts, sunflower seeds, coconut, raisins, and sesame seeds. Heat the oil, honey, and vanilla. Combine with the dry ingredients and mix. Bake on an oiled cookie sheet for 30 minutes in a 375°F oven, turning frequently.

CHAPTER ELEVEN

Magical Beauty Treatments

Beauty magic is as old as time itself. The art goes back to the Babylonians, Sumerians, Polynesians, ancient Egyptians, Chinese, Japanese, and African tribal peoples. Although it has been claimed that beauty is only skin deep, magic goes to the very center of our being. When the two are blended, we have the perfect combination for attracting love and all that we desire for ourselves and our loved ones.

Beauty products are very important for our mental and physical health. The commercial products produced today are full of artificial chemicals that penetrate the pores of your skin. Every time you apply them, you put chemicals into your body—chemicals you would never dream of eating!

The natural recipes that follow are simple to make and magically charged, thus providing the best of both the ancient and modern worlds. Just keep in mind that, if you have allergies, you should test the herbs and/or oils used in each recipe to prevent any bad reactions. Not all people know that they are allergic to certain herbs or oils. All people have different needs and requirements, so please keep this in mind as you make your magical beauty products.

The use of colors affects your behavior and emotional disposition. The tradition of outlining the eyes to honor the Goddess of Love and making the eyes more radiant and mysterious is a time-honored custom all over the globe. Green, rose, or copper eye shadow or eyeliner draw in energy from Venus, the planet of love and romance. Pink eye shadow, blush, or lipstick strengthen self-esteem. Glitter refracts and reflects light and sends out light and love to others.

Wearing jewelry on your face or body is also very powerful. Pay particular attention to how you adorn your forehead, as this is where your third eye is located. East Indians wear a red dot over this chakra point; Ancient Druids wore a crown with a band of jewels in the center of the forehead; the African Berbers use black makeup to tattoo their faces with stars, Moons, and other magical symbols. I personally wear a quartz crystal across my third eye—a practice that can be particularly powerful.

Remember, there is beauty and majesty in natural simplicity. And always charge your makeup, jewelry, and body paint before you use them, catalyzing them with the specific intention of your magical or spell goal.

Magical Scents

The scientific community has shown that scent plays a greater role in sexual attraction among humans than previously thought. It has been shown that the sense of smell is indeed linked to the brain's limbic system—which affects sexual behavior, emotion, and even memory—and that scents can trigger different responses in different people. The animal kingdom has always been stimulated by the scent of potential mates. The latest scientific research indicates that men and women also respond strongly to scent. The way to a lover's heart may, in fact, be through his or her nose! Perhaps those Madison Avenue advertisements, alluring as they may be, do have a scientific basis!

Most witches, however, prefer to make their own scents, because they then know that the ingredients have been magically collected and charged to do their bidding—that is, to get what is good and correct for them. It is, unfortunately, true that manufactured scents may get you a partner—but they may get you the wrong one! If you choose to create your own personal fragrance, find out the fragrance family or category of aroma to which most of your favorite scents belong. You can do this by testing different oils. Floral fragrances tend to be popular among women, but Oriental fruity, spicy, green, and citrus scents provide other aromatic options.

Application

A perfume should always be applied to clean, dry skin to prevent it from mixing with any other scent or scents. Dab a little of the perfume on your pulse points: wrists, throat, nape of the neck, between the breasts, earlobes, bend in the elbows, and behind the knees. These areas of the body have excellent circulation, allowing the scent to develop more fully and even helping it to last longer.

Making Your Own Magical Scents

Here are some scents for you to try. If you don't find one that suits you, feel free to experiment and create an original scent of your own.

Base oil (Jojoba): This golden, medium-weight oil is a liquid plant wax. Produced from cold-pressed jojoba seeds, it makes an excellent carrier base for natural perfumes, since it has a very long shelf life, is easily absorbed by the skin, and is non-greasy.

Jasmine oil, for intense richness: Used to make many fine perfumes, jasmine flowers are picked before dawn to prevent any of the soft and sensuous oil from evaporating.

Geranium oil, for harmony and balance: This delicate, rosy fragrance is very effective in treating stress, fatigue, and anxiety. It is an inexpensive alternative to genuine rose oil.

Ylang-Ylang oil, for relaxation: Possibly the most erotic aroma on Earth, this sweet, tropical scent is reportedly an aphrodisiac. It calms the senses and relaxes the muscles.

Patchouli oil, for prolonging a fragrance: This oil acts as a fixative, slowing evaporation and prolonging the scent.

You can enhance your body lotions and bath oils with homemade perfume by adding 1½ to 2 teaspoons of perfume to ½ cup of lotion or oil. As fragrance evaporates, it rises, so be sure to apply lotion behind your knees and ankles so you can fully enjoy the scent.

Pour the jojoba, or whatever you are using as a base oil, into a dark glass bottle with a glass rod applicator or glass stirring rod. Add the true essential oils drop by drop and rotate in a clockwise direction, stirring with glass rod to mix the oils. You can vary the proportions of the true essential oils according to personal preference, but note that the geranium oil is what gives this blend its floral flavor.

Perfume Components

There are three scent levels to every perfume. These are "notes" that support each other and create the overall scent. Essential oils—classified as either top, middle, or base notes—give each perfume its own special harmony and character. Here are some of the characteristics of these "notes."

Top note: This is the scent you notice first, but it doesn't last long, because it evaporates the fastest. Top notes are a small portion of the final blend and include fresh, light, citrus scents. They are found in oils like bergamot, neroli, lemon, lime, rosemary, orange, or mint. *CAUTION: Too much bergamot oil can irritate the skin and should not be used by pregnant women or epileptics.*

Middle note: This links the base and top scents and determines the fragrance family. Middle notes include flowery essential oils like rose, geranium, and ylang-ylang.

Base note, or fixative: This scent lasts the longest. It adds fullness to and carries the other scents. Derived from balsams, roots, resins, and wood, bases include oils like sandalwood, vetivert, and patchouli. Be careful: too much patchouli oil will easily overwhelm the scent. Base notes tend to be dark, heavy, and sweet.

Perfume Recipes

Ancient Indian Cologne

¼ pt. everclear
1 oz. glycerin
1 oz. sandalwood powder
1 drop oleander oil
1 pt. distilled water
1 tsp. tonka bean extract
¼ tsp. cinnamon
1 drop lemon oil

To make the tonka bean extract follow the tincture directions in chapter 3. Mix, charge for love, spirituality, protection, and healing, pour into a pretty bottle and store out of sunlight.

Bewitching Organic Perfume

Simmer any three of the following in 1 cup of spring water, along with 1 tablespoon of sea salt.

Apples
Cloves
Cinnamon
Lovage-root powder
Yarrow flower
Strawberry oil
Patchouli oil
Synthetic Musk oil (Harm none!)

Let the aroma permeate your home or add a small quantity to your favorite cologne or perfume. To enhance its effect, place a few drops on your lover's desk, pillow, car, doorknob, or clothes. Even though the scent will fade, the magic stays and will work for the traditional four days.

China Forest Cologne

¼ pint Everclear
1 oz. Glycerin
2 tsp. Sandalwood powder
1 drop Rose oil
1 pint distilled water
1 drop Pine needle oil
1 drop Cedar oil
1 drop Bergamot Mint bouquet

Mix, charge for protection, healing, or prosperity. Pour into a pretty bottle and store out of sunlight.

European Rose Cologne

¼ pint Everclear
1 oz. Glycerin
2 drops Rose oil
1 pint distilled water
1 drop Lemon oil
1 drop Bergamot Mint bouquet

Mix, charge for love, pour into a pretty bottle, and store out of sunlight.

Far Eastern Cologne

¼ pint Everclear
1 oz. Glycerin
1 drop Rose oil
1 drop synthetic Musk oil (Harm none!)
1 pint distilled water
1 drop Wisteria oil
1 drop Bergamot Mint bouquet

Mix, charge for prosperity or protection, pour into a pretty bottle, and store out of sunlight.

Florentine Nights Love Potion #1

2 Tbsp. Jojoba oil or base oil
3 drops Bergamot oil
2 drops Neroli oil

8 drops Jasmine oil
12 drops Geranium oil
8 drops Ylang-Ylang oil
4 drops Patchouli oil

This is a reliable and good love potion to add to commercial perfumes.

Florentine Nights Love Potion #2

Use equal parts of the following:

Patchouli oil
Benzoin oil
Lotus bouquet
Heliotrope oil
Orris oil
Olive oil

Mix and charge the two recipes above for love. Add a few drops of number two to your favorite perfume or cologne to improve your chances of bringing your true magical mate into your life.

India Cologne

1 pint distilled water
1 oz. Sandalwood powder
1 Tbsp. powdered Myrrh
1 drop Patchouli oil
¼ tsp. Nutmeg
4 oz. Everclear
1 oz. glycerin
1 Tbsp. powdered Frankincense
1 drop Tonka bean bouquet
½ tsp. Cinnamon

To make the tonka bean bouquet, use the oil recipe on page 12. Mix and charge for protection, exorcism, or spirituality. Pour into a pretty bottle and store out of sunlight.

India Mystery Cologne

1 pint distilled water
1 oz. glycerin

1 oz. powdered Frankincense
1 drop Lemon oil
¼ pint Everclear
1 tsp. Nutmeg
1 tsp. Cinnamon
1 drop Tonka bean bouquet

To make the tonka bean bouquet, use the oil recipe on page 12. Mix and charge for protection or love. Pour into a pretty bottle and store out of sunlight.

Jasmine Cologne

1 part distilled water
4 oz. Everclear
1/4 tsp. Cinnamon
1 drop Bergamot bouquet
1 oz. glycerin
1 tsp. Vanilla
2 drops Jasmine oil

Mix and charge for love or lust. Pour into a pretty bottle and store out of sunlight.

Money Perfume

Dab the following perfume on your wrist, forehead, solar plexus, bank deposit slips, job applications, and any correspondence that deals with money.

2 cups spring water
⅛ oz. Heliotrope oil
Heather herb or Heather oil
Cinnamon sticks
Solid gold jewelry (not gold plate or silver)
2 Tbsp. sea salt
Chamomile tea bag (so leaves can stay filtered)
Red Clover (in unbleached muslin bag)

Place all the charged ingredients into a glass or enamel pan and mix them together. Bring the mixture to a slow simmer, then turn off the stove. (If possible, use a gas or wood stove; electrical stoves can interfere with the energy.) If you have a large-denomination bill, such as $100, place it on the stove next to the pan, but don't let it catch on fire! Etch the word "money" or "wealth" on the side of a gold, yellow, or bright blue candle and, as the potion is warming, hold the burning candle over the bill. Or place the candle in a holder and pile money around it. When you finish, you will have a potion that can be dabbed on wrists, forehead, and solar plexus. Wipe the jewelry clean and wear it as usual. The jewelry helps to charge the potion and, in turn, is infused with the energy of the money spell. Wearing it will bring prosperity. You can also pour the potion, once it has cooled, over a charged crystal. Seal the potion in a jar and place it on your altar, or, if you have made the potion for someone else's use, give it to him or her as a gift.

Orient Mysterious Cologne

¼ part Everclear
1 oz. glycerin
1 drop Rose oil
1 tsp. Vanilla
1 pint distilled water
1 drop Wisteria oil
1 drop Lemon oil

Mix and charge for love, lust, or psychic powers. Pour into a pretty bottle and store out of sunlight.

Rose Cologne

1 part distilled water
1 oz. glycerin
1 drop Rose oil
4 oz. rubbing alcohol
1 drop Rose Geranium oil
1 drop Bergamot Mint bouquet

Mix and charge for love. Pour into a pretty bottle and store out of sunlight.

Royal Japanese Cologne

1 part distilled water
1 oz. glycerin

1 drop Carnation

1 drop Rose oil

1 drop synthetic Musk oil (Harm none!)

¼ part Everclear

1 drop Cherry oil

1 drop Oleander‡ oil

1 tsp. Vanilla

Mix and charge for passion or love. Pour into a pretty bottle and store out of sunlight.

Spanish Love Cologne

1 part distilled water

4 oz. Everclear

1 drop Lemon oil

1 oz. glycerin

2 drops Orange oil

Mix and charge for love. Pour into a pretty bottle and store out of sunlight. To change the scent slightly, try adding one or two drops of bergamot mint bouquet.

Tibetan Cologne

1/4 pint Everclear

1 oz. glycerin

1 drop Bergamont Mint bouquet

1 pint distilled water

1 drop Patchouli oil

1 drop synthetic Musk oil (Harm none!)

Mix, charge for money, prosperity, or lust, pour into a pretty bottle and store out of sunlight.

Magical Dress

Anyone seeking a lover should pay attention to how he or she dresses. Not that you have to dress to the hilt every day, but other people do evaluate you, at least initially, on your clothes. While clothes may not make either the woman or the man, they are the first indications we get of who the person inside those clothes might be. As you become more self-confident about your personal identity and know your strengths and weaknesses, you should dress to send out the right signals. Clothes and fashions project your persona. If you feel drawn to 1930s fashions or hippie garb from the 1960s, wear them; but know why. Know what it is about you that enjoys dressing in this way. Whether you dress according to *Vogue* or delight in rejecting society's trends and setting your own, you express and use your magical power when you do so.

Colors are also important; they can highlight your best features or tone down unflattering ones. Design and pattern play similar roles. By your dress, you make statements about yourself. You cast spells. You announce what you want by announcing who you are—if even just for the night.

Please do not overlook the power of talismans such as feathers, beads, ribbons, or headbands and armbands that can be inscribed with runes, magic words, or love symbols. Braid feathers or ribbons into your hair, charging them for whatever love intention or other purpose you require. Wear a special piece of jewelry for your intentions and spells.

Magical Robes

Ritual clothing can be as complicated or as simple as you care to make it. This very simple robe is easy to make and will serve you well. It is based on the galabayah worn presently in Egypt and can be used by both men and women.

When cutting the fabric for this garment, measure from the top of your shoulder to the floor. This will give you enough fabric to hem your garment. Don't forget that the fabric must be folded in the middle to form both the front and the back of the garment. Thus, if your garment length is 54 inches, you need to multiply that by 2 for the total length of fabric you will need. Use 54- to 60-inch wide material.

First, measure the person who will wear the robe. Place the edge of a tape measure at the top of his or her shoulder and have them hold it. Take the fabric and fold it in half. Cut a half-circle through the doubled layers of fabric to make a hole for the head. Slit this down the center about 6 inches on the front side of the fabric. This forms a small V shape and allows a little more room in the neck and throat area.

Measure down 12 inches from the top fold on each side of the robe. From your measuring point, cut in about 12 inches, then cut down at an angle. Sew a ⅝-inch seam along these lines. Sew along all rough edges, turning a small hem about ¼ inch from the edge of the fabric. Turn the garment right side out and press. Run zigzag stitching around all raw edges to preven unraveling. Once complete, wear the garment a few times before you decide if you want to decorate it and how.

Face and Body Care

Since time immemorial, we human beings have endeavored to improve our physical appearance in order to increase our self-esteem and sensuality and uplift our emotions. When we feel good about ourselves, everything else seems to go better for us. Try the following recipes to enhance yourself and your life.

Emergency Skin Eruption Cream

This is good for teenagers. Steep 2 papaya mint tea bags in ½ cup boiling water. Let sit until tea is very strong. Heat to a degree that is bearable to the skin and apply as a compress to the eruption. This does help. I know, because many of my younger friends have tried it with success.

Basic Cleansing Cream

2 Tbsp. Beeswax
2 oz. Lanolin
2 Tbsp. herbal infusion (see list below)
⅜ cup Olive oil
⅛ oz. essential oil

Melt lanolin and beeswax in a double boiler over low heat. When melted, add the olive oil. Remove from heat and stir in essential oil. Stir continuously until cool. It will thicken and become creamy. Store in a screw-top jar. Use this cream to cleanse your face. Apply a small amount and massage into your face. Place a hot cloth over your face. As the cloth cools, rinse it in hot water to heat it up again. Do this several times. Remove all traces of cleanser with a clean tissue. Use an herbal infusion as a skin toner.

Herbs for Facial Herbal Infusion

This is a list of herbs that can be added to the recipe above. You can use them individually or combine several together depending on your individual needs.

Chamomile: Tones up relaxed muscles.

Fennel: An infusion of the leaves and seeds clears up spots.

Lemon balm: Smooths wrinkles.

Mints: All mints are excellent astringents.

Rosemary: Tightens sagging skin.

Comfrey: Mix with witch hazel as an excellent tonic to smooth wrinkles.

Thyme: Excellent astringent, it helps to clear acne.

You will notice the effects on the first application. Use daily. Prepare the mixture in a china or earthenware container. Steep for 30 minutes and strain. Bottle the mixture in a screw-top container and refrigerate. It keeps for about a week. Use cold. This infusion has many beneficial effects, depending on the herb used.

Lip Care

2 cups white wine
Small piece Gum Benzoin

Bring the two ingredients to a slow boil for 30 minutes. Put 15 drops of this in a glass of water. It will turn milky and have a very good smell. Apply the liquid to your lips. The preparation will bring the blood to the surface and make your lips a natural red. This can also be used as a splash for the face. Splash on and allow to dry. It gives color and a nice clear complexion. It's also good for freckles, pimples, and skin eruptions.

Lip Balm

½ cup Almond oil
¼ cup Cocoa butter
¼ cup Coconut oil

Melt the above ingredients over a low fire. Stir in 1 table-spoon honey and 2 oz. beeswax. After the beeswax is melted, add 1½ teaspoons of any natural flavoring: vanilla, cherry, lemon, orange, or coconut. In fact, any of the flavorings you have in your cooking supplies will do nicely. Mix completely and test for firmness. It needs to be firm, so you may have to add more melted beeswax to get the desired consistency.

Eye Makeup Remover

Safflower oil works well for this. Remove your eye makeup daily to prevent eye infections. This is nonallergenic, so people with allergies should have no problem with it.

Miscellaneous Remedies

Nail Care

3 Tbsp. Almond oil
3 Tbsp. raw Linseed oil
3 Tbsp. honey

To soften cuticles and strengthen the nails, massage this into your nails and cuticles.

For Splitting Nails

Eating plenty of cucumber or drinking the juice of cucumbers seems to help correct this problem.

Stimulating Aftershave

1 part Peppermint
1 part Yarrow flowers
1 part Lavender flowers
3 parts Sage

Place ingredients in a large jar and cover with rubbing alcohol. Let steep for 2 weeks. Strain and add 1 cup of water. If your skin is dry, add 2 tablespoons of glycerin or almond oil. This also makes a wonderful massage for aching muscles.

Styptic Lotion

¼ cup water
½ tsp. Alum
⅛ tsp. glycerin

Shake well every time you use the lotion. Apply to nicks after shaving to stop the bleeding.

After Bath Splash

1 quart Witch Hazel
½ cup Mint
½ cup Lemon balm
½ cup Rosemary
½ cup Lavender

Mix the herbs of your choice to make this bath splash. Let steep in the Sun for 2 weeks, shaking every day. It will turn a nice herbal green. Strain, place in a tightly closed container, and label. Use as a fragrant rub after bathing.

After Bath Splash for Men

Equal parts lavender and pine needles

Boil and steep for 15 minutes. Strain and add to bath water. Lavender, verbena, nutmeg, geranium, lemon balm, and thyme are all good to add for a manly scent. If desired, you may add 1 tablespoon (or more) of this herb mixture to enhance the scent.

Bath Powder #1

1 oz. Orris root
½ Tbsp. powdered Cloves
1 oz. powdered Sage
2 oz. corn starch

Mix well. To make different scents, simply add the herb of your choice. Use powdered herbs if possible, otherwise grind the herbs as finely as possible. Keep tightly closed to retain the scent.

Bath Powder #2

Simply add a few drops of essential oil to cornstarch or arrowroot. Apply after bath. Add the same scent that you use to make your perfumes.

Aphrodisiac

Orange blossoms

Rose petals
Chamomile
Bee balm
Fennel
Licorice
Ginseng
Mints (any of them)

This is a good tea to drink after you've thoroughly relaxed with your love bath. To use, put 1 teaspoon of any of the herbs (or mixture of them) in 1 cup boiling water. Let steep 15 minutes. Strain and sweeten with honey. Ginger and lemon may be added to the tea to your taste.

CHAPTER TWELVE

Magical Pets and Spellcraft

There has always been a natural kinship between animals and practitioners of the magical arts. The familiar, or magical pet, has long been the mediator between the witch or magician and the forces of nature. Through living and working together in ritual, the witch and the familiar form an unusual bond that is often utilized in magic. Animals are closer to Mother Earth and all of her powers and nuances. They hear the music of the infinite and powerful cosmos, and experience both the known and the unknown.

Witches that are adept in magic, like animals, live in complete rhythm with the pulses of Mother Nature and the cosmos. Before we can change any part of the cosmos, we as individuals must attune to it and be with it. Developing a close relationship with finned, furred, or feathered creatures is a wonderful start. To form a direct link with Mother Earth and the cosmos, all we have to do is share our homes with these creatures, leave them food and water, and let them enjoy their freedom. In so doing, we create psychic bonds between human and animal.

Your animals should be magically guarded. There are a variety of charms for protecting them against accidents, disease, and theft. The following will give you some examples that can be adapted for just about any need or situation.

Protective Symbols and Objects

Engrave protective symbols and signs such as pentagrams on the back of your pet's tags and licenses. If you choose, make a round metal tag of your own, scratch or carve magical words or symbols on it, and hang it with your pet's other tags.

If your animal must live in a cage or tank, attach some protective object to its home: Holed stones, quartz crystals, seashells, or even tiny pieces of paper on which you've inscribed a spell of protection that you wrote yourself. You can also encircle the cage or tank with pure white wool yarn or a cord containing nine knots.

To protect your pet from the evil eye and to enhance the love you share, simply place a necklace of seashells either on the animal or around its home. A small, rounded seashell attached to the animal's collar works well also.

Alternatively, you can purchase a small bell of any type and use it to protect your animal. The bell must have an audible ring to it. Suspend this from your pet's collar, visualizing the ring guarding the pet. The ringing bell will automatically banish negativity as the pet moves. A bell can also be hung from your pet's cage or placed on its bed, as long as it is placed so that it is still able to ring.

Attuning Your Animal to You

To attune your animal to your vibrations, simply allow it to eat from your dinner plate when you've finished your meal. The few crumbs your pet eats will strengthen its relationship with you.

Pet Spells

I have created these spells out my own personal needs over the years. Please feel free to experiment and add to them or come up with new ones of your own. Blessed be.

Won't Leave Home Spell

While whether to leave home or not should be the animal's decision, you don't want it to leave before it has gotten to know you. Hold your pet up before a mirror. If it seems to notice its reflection, it will remain at home. Or, if you have a fireplace, have the animal look up the chimney. Such spells are best performed on the day the animal arrives.

Cat Return Home Spell

These spells are specifically designed to remind a cat to return home after its nocturnal escapades. First, attune yourself to your pet; stroke or cuddle it, or simply gaze at it. Align your breathing. Visualize as you perform any of the following spells.

Putting a small dab of sugar in your cat's mouth at 9 o'clock on a Friday morning is also said to be quite effective. You also might try buttering its paws. If your cat does run away but is recovered, hold it and very gently swing the animal thrice through the air. This will attach your pet to your home.

Dog Return Home Spell

Placing a few hairs from your dog's tail under the steps of your house's entrance can keep your dog from straying. One ancient rite involves putting a piece of cheese in your boot heel!

The most logical and powerful spell known to man is simply to feed your pet properly, and give it love and attention. This weaves a magic spell that is powerful enough to guarantee your pet's continued presence in your loving home.

Listless, Out-of-Sorts, Antisickness Spell

If your pet seems out of sorts, but has no medical problem, try one of these. Set the animal on the floor and sprinkle salt in an unbroken circle (going counterclockwise) around it. If you can do this before the pet moves from the circle, it should be cured. (Sprinkle salt around the cage if the animal lives in one.) Or try feeding your pet the core of a quince. If it won't eat one, try to get it to walk (fly, swim, crawl, or slither) in a counterclockwise circle three times. If this can be accomplished, the bewitchment of your pet will be totally destroyed.

Spells to Protect Your Pet from Theft

I have had good luck with these antitheft spells. You might wish to consider them for your own pets.

1. At sunrise, have your pet sit quietly and, naked (how private is your backyard?), run thrice around your pet, saying at every turn:

    Thief, your eyes shall never shine

On this animal of mine!
Thief, your hands shall never find
This guarded animal of mine!

2. Take the animal you want to protect to a crossroads at midnight. Let a few hairs (feathers, etc.) fall from the animal on the ground and say:

Crossroads,
Pathways, attend to me:
This beast shall not be pulled on thee!

3. Take a few hairs, feathers, or some other part of the animal (or, failing this, draw as exact a likeness of the creature as your talent allows). Place this with protective herbs (such as juniper, basil, bay, rosemary, vervain, St. John's wort, dill, etc.) into a small box. Permanently seal the box and tie it shut with nine white cords. Bury it as close to your home as possible. Your pet should be safe from thieves.

Magical Animal Attributes

The following list contains the magical correspondences of many of our animal companions. By understanding their natural abilities, we can better understand both the animals themselves and our relationships with them.

Canary: Promotes harmony, love, happiness, good fortune.

Chameleon: Changes color, influences weather, invisibility.

Fish: Abundance, prosperity, children, harmony, divination, fertility, bringing a companion into your life.

Frog: Initiation and transformation, destruction of negativities and distractions, rebirth.

House bird: Divination, increased memory and mental powers, travel.

House cat: Strong protector, independent and self-assured, searching for hidden information, seeing spirits.

House dog: Tracking, companionship, keen hearing, loyalty, willingness to follow through, protection.

Lizard: Dreams, understanding dreams, mental creations.

Lovebirds: Love, companionship, marriage.

Parrot: Imitation, mockery, unintelligent repetition.

Snakes: Psychic energy, creative power, immortality, wisdom, understanding, connection with spirit.

Spiders: Wisdom, creativity, new life.

Turtle or tortoise: Patience, long life, perseverance.

CHAPTER THIRTEEN

Magical Substitutions

Many flowers, herbs, spices, and true essential oils can be found locally in gardens, plant nurseries, wild herb shops, health food stores, supermarkets, or gourmet food markets. Any store that carries kitchen herbs and spices is a good place to start looking for your magical ingredients.

The lists in this chapter can be used for reference when you don't have one of the ingredients you need for a recipe and need to identify a substitute. Always remember that the Craft is forever changing and substitutions are often necessary. And above all, don't be afraid to experiment!

Following are some general rules to follow in finding substitutions for magical herbs and oils.

1. Rosemary can safely be used for any other herb.
2. Rose can be substituted for any flower.
3. Frankincense or copal can take the place of any gum resin.
4. Tobacco‡ can be used in place of any poisonous herb.

See "Bouquets" on page 9 for other substitution ideas.

Herb and Plant Substitutions

All listings here refer to plant materials, not oils, unless otherwise stated. *CAUTION: All illegal or poisonous herb and plant substitutions are marked with a ‡.*

Acacia, Gum: Gum Arabic

Aconite‡: Tobacco‡

Arabic, Gum: Frankincense, Gum Mastic, Tragacanth (for binding wet ingredients, not for incense use)

Ammoniac, Gum: Asafoetida‡

Asafoetida‡: Tobacco‡, Valerian Root

Balm Of Gilead: Rose Buds, Gum Mastic

Bay Laurel Leaves or Laurel Leaves: Bay Leaves

Bdellium, Gum: Copal, Pine resin, Dragon's Blood

Belladonna‡: Tobacco‡

Benzoin: Gum Arabic, Gum Mastic

Cachana: Angelica Root

Camphor‡ oil: Eucalyptus oil, Lavender oil

Carnation: Rose petals anointed with few drops Clove oil

Cardamom: Use substitutions from Lust or Love magical goals, or Venus in the planetary substitution section

Cassia: Cinnamon

Castor Bean: A few drops of Castor oil

Cedar: Sandalwood

Cinquefoil: Clover, Trefoil

Citron: Equal parts Orange peel and Lemon peel

Clove: Mace, Nutmeg

Clover: Cinquefoil

Copal: Frankincense, Cedar

Coriander: Cilantro

Cowbane‡: Tobacco‡

Cypress: Juniper, Pine needles

Deerstongue: Tonka Bean (not for internal use), Woodruff, Vanilla

Dittany Of Crete: Gum Mastic

Dragon's Blood: Equal parts Frankincense and Red Sandalwood

Eucalyptus oil: Camphor‡ oil, Lavender oil

Euphorbium: Tobacco‡

Frankincense: Copal, Pine resin

Galangal: Ginger root

Grains Of Paradise: Black Pepper

Gum Ammoniac: Asafoetida‡

Gum Bdellium: Copal, Pine resin, Dragon's Blood

Hellebore‡: Tobacco‡, Nettle

Hemlock‡: Tobacco‡

Hemp‡: Nutmeg, Damiana, Star Anise, Bay, Tobacco‡

Henbane‡: Tobacco‡

Hyssop: Lavender

Ivy: Cinquefoil

Jasmine: Rose

Juniper: Pine

Lavender: Rose

Lemongrass: Lemon peel

Lemon peel: Lemongrass

Lemon Verbena: Lemongrass, Lemon Peel

Mace: Nutmeg

Mandrake‡: Or American variety of the mayapple‡

Mastic, Gum: Gum Arabic, Frankincense, Benzoin

Mint (any type): Sage

Mistletoe‡: Mint, Sage

Mugwort: Wormwood‡

Neroli: Orange oil

Niaouli: Equal parts Lemon oil, Orange oil, and Lime oil

Nightshade‡: Tobacco‡

Nutmeg: Mace, Cinnamon

Oakmoss: Patchouli

Orange: Tangerine peel

Orange Flowers: Orange peel

Palmarosa: Half Rose oil and Half Lemon oil

Pansy: Heartsease is the same plant

Patchouli: Oakmoss

Peppermint: Spearmint

Pepperwort: Rue, Grains of Paradise, Black Pepper

Pine: Juniper

Pine Resin: Frankincense, Copal

Red Sandalwood: Sandalwood mixed with a pinch of Dragon's Blood

Rose: Yarrow

Rose Geranium: Rose

Rue: Rosemary mixed with a pinch of Black Pepper

Saffron: Orange peel

Sandalwood: Cedar

Sarsasparilla: Sassafras

Soapwort: Wild Sweet William

Solomon Seal: Use substitutions from protection and exorcism goals

Smallage: Parsely

Snakehead: Snakeroot

Sassafras: Sarsasparilla

Soapweed: Yucca is the same plant

Spearmint: Peppermint

Storax: Benzoin

Sulfur: Tobacco‡, Club Moss, Asafoetida‡

Thyme: Rosemary

Tobacco‡: Bay

Tonka Bean: Deerstongue, Woodruff, Vanilla

Trefoil: 3-Leaf Clover

Wormwood‡: Mugwort

Yarrow: Rose

Yew‡: Tobacco‡

Magical Goal Correspondences

Use these lists for mixing your own blends and concoctions or when substituting. Use the following key to identify the type of substance referenced.

H = Herb, gum, flower, bark, root, leaf, fruit, seed

O = Essential oil, absolute oil

B = Bouquet

S = Synthetic

T = Tincture

Astral Projections

Benzoin: H, O, T

Dittany Of Crete: H

Cinnamon: H, O, T

Jasmine: H, O

Poplar: H

Sandalwood: H, O, T

Courage

Allspice: H

Black Pepper: H, O

Dragon's Blood: H

Frankincense: H, O, T

Geranium: H, O, T

Rose Geranium: H, O, T

Sweet Pea: H, B

Tonka: H, B

Thyme: H

Divination

Anise: H

Camphor‡: H, O, T

Clove: H, O, T

Hibiscus: H

Meadowsweet: H

Orange: H, O

Orris: H

Exorcism

Angelica: H

Basil: H, O

Brimstone: H

Clove: H, O, T

Copal: H, O, T

Cumin: H

Dragon's Blood: H

Frankincense: H, O, T

Garlic: H

Heliotrope: H

Horehound: H

Juniper: H, O

Lilac: H

Mallow: H

Mistletoe‡: H

Myrrh: H, O, T

Pepper, Cayenne: H

Peppermint: H, O

Pine: H, O

Rosemary: H, O, T

Sagebrush: H

Solomon's Seal: H, O

Sandalwood: H, O, T

Snapdragon: H

Thistle: H

Vetivert: H, O

Yarrow: H, O

Happiness

Apple Blossom: H

Catnip: H

Hyacinth: H

Lavender: H, O, T

Marjoram: H

Meadowsweet: H

Sesame: H

St. John's Wort: H

Healing, Health

Allspice: H

Angelica: H

Bay: H, O

Clamus: H

Carnation: H

Cedarwood: H, O

Cinnamon: H, O, T

Citron: H

Coriander: O

Eucalyptus: H, O

Fennel: H

Gardenia: H

Heliotrope: H

Honeysuckle‡: H

Juniper: H, O

Lemon balm: H, O

Lime: H, O, T

Mugwort: H

Niaouli: H, O

Palmarose: O

Pepper, Cayenne: H

Peppermint: H, O, T

Pine: H, O

Poppy Seed: H

Rose: H, O

Rosemary: H, O, T

Saffron: H

Sandalwood: H, O, T

Sassafras: H

Spearmint: H, O

Spikenard: H

Thyme: H

Violet: H

Willow: H

Wintergreen: H

Yerba Santa: H

Love

Apple Blossom: H, B

Apricot: O (no scent)

Basil: H, O

Chamomile: H, O

Catnip: H

Chickweed: H

Cinnamon: H, O, T

Civet: S

Clove: H, O, T

Copal: H, O, T

Coriander: H, O

Cumin: H

Dill: H

Dragon's Blood: H

Gardenia: H

Geranium (Rose): H, O

Ginger: H, O

Hibiscus: H

Jasmine: H, O

Juniper: H, O

Lavender: H, O, T

Lemon: H, O, T

Lemon balm: H, O

Lemon Verbena: H, O

Lime: H, O, T

Lotus: B

Marjoram: H

Mastic: H

Mimosa: H

Myrtle: H

Neroli: O

Orange: H, O

Orchid: H

Orris: H

Palmarosa: O

Peppermint: H, O, T

Plumeria: H

Rose: H, O

Rosemary: H, O, T

Sarsasparilla: H

Stephanotis: H

Sweet Pea: B

Thyme: H

Tonka: H, B,T

Tuberose: H, B

Vanilla: H,T

Vervain: H

Vetivert: H, O

Violet: H

Yarrow: H, O

Ylang-Ylang: O

Luck

Allspice: H

Calamus: H

Fern: H

Grains of Paradise: H

Hazel: H

Heather: H

Irish Moss: H

Nutmeg: H, O,T

Orange: H, O

Poppy Seed: H

Rose: H, O

Spikenard: H

Star Anise: H,T

Tonka: H, B,T

Vetivert: H, O

Violet: H

Lust

Ambergris: S

Caraway: H

Cardamom: H, O

Cinnamon: H, O,T

Civet: S

Clove: H, O, T

Deerstongue: H, T

Ginger: H

Grains of Paradise: H

Hibiscus: H

Lemongrass: H, O

Nettle: H

Olive: H, O

Parsley: H

Patchouli: H, O, T

Peppermint: H, O, T

Rosemary: H, O, T

Saffron: H

Sesame: H

Stephanotis: H

Tuberose: H, B, T

Vanilla: H

Yerba Mate: H

Money And Riches

Allspice: H

Almond: H

Basil: H, O

Bergamot Mint: H, B

Calamus: H

Cedarwood: H, O, T

Cinnamon: H, O, T

Cinquefoil: H

Clove: H, O, T

Clover: H

Dill: H

Elder: H

Galangal: H, T

Ginger: H, O

Heliotrope: H

Honeysuckle‡: H

Hyssop: H

Jasmine: H, O

Myrtle: H

Nutmeg: H, O, T

Oakmoss: H, B

Orange: H, O

Patchouli: H, O, T

Peppermint: H, O, T

Pine: H, O, T

Sage: H, T

Sassafras: H

Tonka: H, B, T

Vervain: H

Wood Aloe: H, O, T

Woodruff: H

Peace

Cumin: H

Gardenia: H, B

Lavender: H, O, T

Lily: H

Magnolia: B

Meadowsweet: H

Narcissus: H

Pennyroyal: H

Tuberose: H, B

Violet: H

Power, Magical

Allspice: H

Carnation: H

Dragon's Blood: H

Ginger: H, O

Gum Mastic: H

Tangerine: H, O

Vanilla: H,T

Protection

Angelica: H

Anise: H, O

Arabic, Gum: H

Asafoetida‡: H

Balm of Gilead: H

Basil: H, O

Bay: H, O

Bergamot Mint: H, B

Black Pepper: H, O

Calamus: H

Caraway: H

Carnation: H

Cedarwood: H, O

Cinnamon: H, O,T

Cinquefoil: H

Clove: H, O,T

Clover: H

Copal: H, O,T

Cumin: H

Cypress: H, O

Dill: H

Dragon's Blood: H

Eucalyptus: H, O

Fennel: H

Fern: H

Flax: H

Frankincense: H, O,T

Galangal: H,T

Geranium (Rose): H, O

Heather: H

Honeysuckle‡: H

Hyacinth: H

Hyssop: H

Juniper: H, O

Lavender: H, O,T

Lilac: H

Lime: H, O,T

Lotus: B

Mandrake‡: H

Marigold: H

Mimosa: H

Mistletoe‡: H

Mugwort: H

Myrrh: H, O,T

Niaouli: O

Orris: H

Patchouli: H, O,T

Pennyroyal: H

Peony: H

Peppermint: H, O,T

Petitgrain: O

Pine: H, O

Rose: H, O

Rose Geranium: H, O

Rue: H

Sage: H,T

St. John's Wort: H,T

Sandalwood: H, O,T

Solomon's Seal: H, O,T

Thistle: H

Valerian: H

Vervain: H

Vetivert: H, O

Violet: H

Wood Aloe: H,T

Woodruff: H

Wormwood‡: H

Psychic Awareness

Acacia, Gum: H

Anise: H

Bay: H, O

Camphor‡: H, O,T

Cassia: H, O

Cinnamon: H, O

Citron: H

Clove: H, O,T

Flax: H

Galangal: H,T

Gardenia: H

Heliotrope: H

Honeysuckle‡: H

Lemongrass: H, O

Lilac: H

Mace: H, O

Marigold: H

Mastic, Gum: H

Mugwort: H

Nutmeg: H, O,T

Orange: H, O

Orris: H

Peppermint: H, O,T

Rose: H, O

Saffron: H

Star Anise: H,T

Thyme: H

Tuberose: H, B

Wormwood‡: H

Yarrow: H, O

Psychic (Prophetic) Dreams

Camphor‡: H, O,T

Cinquefoil: H

Heliotrope: H

Jasmine: H, O

Marigold: H

Mimosa: H

Rose: H, O

Purification

Anise: H

Arabic, Gum: H

Bay: H, O

Benzoin: H, O,T

Calamus: H

Chamomile: H, O

Camphor‡: H, O

Cinnamon: H, O,T

Copal: H,T

Eucalyptus: H, O

Fennel: H

Frankincense: H, O,T

Hyssop: H

Lavender: H, O,T

Lemon: H, O,T

Lemon Verbena: H, O

Lime: H, O,T

Mimosa: H

Musk: S

Myrrh: H, O,T

Parsley: H

Peppermint: H, O,T

Pine: H, O

Rosemary: H, O

Sandalwood: H, O,T

Thyme: H

Tobacco‡: H

Valerian: H

Vervain: H

Spirituality

Arabic, Gum: H

Cassia: H, O,T

Cinnamon: H, O,T

Copal: H, O,T

Frankincense: H, O,T

Gardenia: H

Heliotrope: H

Jasmine: H, O

Lotus: B

Myrrh: H, O,T

Pine: H, O

Sage: H

Sandalwood: H, O,T

Wisteria: H

Wood Aloe: H,T

Planetary Substitutions

The following lists are useful when you need to substitute ingredients or when compounding your own planetary blend.

Sun

Acacia: H

Arabic, Gum: H

Bay: H, O

Benzoin: H, O,T

Carnation: H, O

Cedarwood: H, O

Chicory and Chicory root: H,T

Cinnamon: H, O, T

Citron: H

Copal: H, O, T

Eyebright: H, T

Frankincense: H, O, T

Juniper: H, O

Mastic, Gum: H

Mistletoe‡: H

Oak: H

Orange: H, O

Rosemary: H, O, T

Sandalwood: H, O, T

Tangerine: H, O

Wood Aloe: H, T

These herbs promote healing, protection, success, illumination, magical power, physical energy, and settlement of legal matters.

Moon

Calamus: H

Camphor‡: H, O, T

Coconut: H

Gardenia: H

Grape: H

Jasmine: H, O

Lemon: H, O, T

Lemon balm: H, O

Lotus: B

Myrrh: H, O, T

Poppy seed: H

Sandalwood: H, O, T

Willow: H

These herbs promote sleep, prophetic (psychic) dreams, psychic awareness, gardening, love, healing, fertility, peace, compassion, and spirituality. They are also useful in blends concerned with the family.

Mercury

Almond: H

Bergamot Mint: H, B

Caraway: H

Dill: H

Fennel: H

Lavender: H, O, T

Lemongrass: H, O

Lemon Verbena: H, O

Peppermint: H, O, T

Thyme: H

These herbs promote intelligence, eloquence, divination, study, self-improvement. They also overcome addictions and break negative habits, and encourage travel, communication, and wisdom.

Venus

Apple Blossom: H

Cardamom: H, O

Crocus: H

Daisy: H

Geranium (Rose): H, O

Heather: H

Hyacinth: H

Iris: H

Licorice: H

Lilac: H

Magnolia: H, B

Myrtle: H

Orchid: H

Orris: H

Plumeria: H

Rose: H, O

Spearmint: H, O, T

Stephanotis: H

Sweet Pea: B

Tansy: H

Thyme: H

Tonka: H, B

Tuberose: H

Vanilla: H,T

Violet: H

Willow: H

Ylang-Ylang: O

These herbs promote fidelity, love interchanges, reconciliation, youth, joy, beauty, happiness, pleasure, luck, friendship, meditation, and compassion.

Mars

Allspice: H

Asafoetida‡: H

Basil: H, O

Broom: H

Coriander: H, O

Cumin: H

Deerstongue: H,T

Dragon's Blood: H

Galangal: H,T

Ginger: H, O

Nettle: H

Peppermint: H, O,T

Pine: H, O

Tobacco‡: H

Woodruff: H

Wormwood‡: H

These herbs promote courage, aggression, politics, exorcism, healing after surgery, physical strength, sexual energy, defensive magic, and protection.

Jupiter

Anise: H

Cinquefoil: H

Clove: H, O,T

Honeysuckle‡: H, O

Hyssop: H

Maple: H

Nutmeg: H, O,T

Oakmoss: H, B

Sage: H,T

Sarsasparilla: H

Sassafras: H

Star Anise: H,T

Ti: H

These herbs promote money, prosperity, meditation, spirituality, and the settlement of legal problems.

Saturn

Amaranth: H

Bistort: H

Comfrey: H

Cypress: H, O

Mimosa: H

Pansy: H

Patchouli: H, O

Tamarisk: H

Solomon's Seal: H, O

Elemental Substitutions

Earth, air, fire, and water are the basic components of the cosmos. All that will exist in the future or has existed in the past is made up of one or more of these four elements. The elements are much more than physical substances, they are the energies behind the manifest or unmanifest nature of all things.

For best results and effects, attune with an element before using one of its herbal products. Elemental magic is not the easiest forms of magic to master, because the elements are active all around us.

Earth

Bistort: H

Cypress: H, O

Fern: H

Honeysuckle‡: H

Horehound: H

Magnolia: H, B

Mugwort: H

Narcissus: H

Oakmoss: H, B

Patchouli: H, O,T

Primrose: H

Rhubarb: H

Vervain: H

Vetivert: H, O

These herbs promote business success, money, fertility, peace, stability, growth (as in gardens), employment, etc.

Air

Acacia: H

Arabic, Gum: H

Almond: H

Anise: H

Benzoin: H, O,T

Bergamot Mint: H, B

Citron: H

Lavender: H, O,T

Lemongrass: H, O

Lemon Verbena: H, O

Mace: H, O

Marjoram: H

Mastic, Gum: H

Parsley: H

Peppermint: H, O,T

Sage: H,T

Star Anise: H,T

These herbs promote communication, travel, intellect, eloquence, divination, freedom, and wisdom.

Fire

Allspice: H

Angelica: H

Asafoetida‡: H

Basil: H, O

Bay: H, O

Carnation: H, O

Cedarwood: H, O

Cinnamon: H, O,T

Clove: H, O,T

Copal: H,T

Coriander: H, O

Deerstongue: H,T

Dill: H

Dragon's Blood: H

Fennel: H

Frankincense: H, O,T

Galangal: H, O,T

Garlic: H

Grains of Paradise: H

Heliotrope: H

Juniper: H, O

Lime: H, O

Marigold: H

Nutmeg: H, O,T

Orange: H, O

Peppermint: H, O

Rosemary: H, O,T

Rose Geranium: H, O

Sassafras: H

Tangerine: H, O

Tobacco‡: H

Woodruff: H

These herbs promote communication, defensive magic, physical strength, willpower, courage, magical power, and purification.

Water

Apple Blossom: H

Lemon balm: H, O

Calamus: H

Chamomile: H. O

Camphor‡: H, O,T

Cardamom: H, O

Catnip: H

Cherry: H

Coconut: H

Comfrey: H

Elder: H

Eucalyptus: H, O

Gardenia: H

Heather: H

Hyacinth: H

Iris: H

Jasmine: H, O

Lemon: H, O,T

Licorice: H

Lilac: H

Lily: H

Lotus: B

Myrrh: H, O,T

Orchid: H

Orris: H

Passion Flower: H

Peach: H

Plumeria: H

Rose: H, O

Sandalwood: H, O,T

Spearmint: H, O,T

Stephanotis: H

Sweet Pea: B

Solomon's Seal: H, O

Tansy: H

Thyme: H

Tonka: H, B, T

Vanilla: H, T

Violet: H

Ylang-Ylang: O

These herbs promote love, healing, peace, reconciliation, compassion, destressing, sleep, friendship, dreams, and psychism.

Astrological Substitutions

Create your own blends with these herbs, or use them as substitutes. If one of these herbs is unavailable, look to the signs ruling the planet for further suggestions.

Aries (ruled by Mars)

Allspice: H

Carnation: H, O

Cedarwood: H, O

Cinnamon: H, O, T

Clove: H, O, T

Copal: H, O, T

Cumin: H

Deerstongue: H, T

Dragon's Blood: H

Fennel: H

Frankincense: H, O, T

Galangal: H

Juniper: H, O

Musk: S

Peppermint: H, O

Pine: H, O

Taurus (ruled by Venus)

Apple Blossom: H

Cardamom: H, O

Daisy: H

Honeysuckle‡: H, O

Lilac: J

Magnolia: H, B

Oakmoss: H, B

Orchid: H

Patchouli: H, O

Plumeria: H

Rose: H, O

Thyme: H

Tonka: H, B, T

Vanilla: H

Violet: H

Gemini (ruled by Mercury)

Almond: H

Anise: H

Bergamot Mint: H, B

Citron: H

Clover: H, T

Dill: H

Horehound: H

Lavender: H, O, T

Lemongrass: H, O

Lily: H

Mace: H, O

Mastic, Gum: H

Parsley: H

Peppermint: H, O, T

Cancer (Moonchildren—ruled by the Moon)

Ambergris: S

Calamus: H

Eucalyptus: H, O

Gardenia: H, B

Jasmine: H, O

Lemon: H, O, T

Lemon balm: H, O

Lilac: H

Lotus: B

Myrrh: H, O, T

Rose: H, O

Sandalwood: H, O, T

Violet: H

Leo (ruled by the Sun)

Acacia: H

Benzoin: H, O, T

Cinnamon: H, O, T

Copal: H, O, T

Frankincense: H, O, T

Heliotrope: H

Juniper: H, O

Musk: S

Nutmeg: H, O, T

Orange: H, O

Rosemary: H, O, T

Sandalwood: H, O, T

Virgo (ruled by Mercury)

Almond: H

Bergamot Mint: H, B

Cypress: H, O

Dill: H

Fennel: H

Honeysuckle‡: H, O

Lavender: H, O, T

Lily: H, O

Mace: H, O

Moss: H

Patchouli: H, O

Peppermint: H, O, T

Libra (ruled by Venus)

Apple Blossom: H

Catnip: H

Lilac: H

Magnolia: H, B

Marjoram: H

Mugwort: H

Orchid: H

Plumeria: H

Rose: H, O

Spearmint: H, O,T

Sweet Pea: S

Thyme: H

Vanilla: H,T

Violet: H

Scorpio (ruled by Mars, Pluto)

Allspice: H

Ambergris: S

Basil: H, O

Clove: H, O,T

Cumin: H

Deerstongue: H,T

Galangal: H,T

Gardenia: H

Ginger: H, O

Myrrh: H, O,T

Pine: H, O

Vanilla: H,T

Violet: H

Sagittarius (ruled by Jupiter)

Anise: H

Carnation: H

Cedarwood: H, O

Clove: H, O, T

Copal: H, O, T

Deerstongue: H, T

Dragon's Blood: H

Frankincense: H, O, T

Ginger: H, O

Honeysuckle‡: H

Nutmeg: H, O, T

Orange: H, O

Rose: H, O

Sage: H, T

Sassafras: H

Star Anise: H, T

Capricorn (ruled by Saturn)

Cypress: H, O

Honeysuckle‡: H

Magnolia: H, B

Mimosa: H

Oakmoss: H, B

Patchouli: H, O

Vervain: H

Vetivert: H, O

Aquarius (ruled by Saturn and Uranus)

Acacia: H

Almond: H

Benzoin: H, O, T

Citron: H

Cypress: H, O

Lavender: H, O, T

Mace: H, O

Mastic, Gum: H

Mimosa: H

Patchouli: H, O

Peppermint: H, O,T
Pine: H, O

Pisces (Ruled by Jupiter and Neptune)

Anise: H

Calamus: H

Catnip: H

Clove: H, O,T

Eucalyptus: H, O

Gardenia: H

Honeysuckle‡: H, O

Jasmine: H, O

Lemon: H, O,T

Mimosa: H

Nutmeg: H, O,T

Orris: H

Sage: H,T

Sandalwood: H, O,T

Sarsasparilla: H, O

Star Anise: H,T

Sweet Pea: B

CHAPTER FOURTEEN

Magical Correspondences

I have included the following tables and lists for easy referencing and research. Because many of them are almost impossible to find elsewhere, I have placed them here in an effort to make them accessible to everyone.

Dream-Magic Herbs

Adder's Tongue

Agrimony

Camphor‡

Cleandine (lesser)

Cinnamon

Daisy

Holly‡

Hops

Ivy

Lemon Verbena

Mandrake‡ root

Marigold

Mistletoe‡

Mugwort

Onion

Peppermint

Spearmint

Purslane

Rose

St. John's Wort

Verbena

Vervain

Wormwood‡

Yarrow

Flowers and Herbs of the Celebrant

Spring and Summer Rites: Crowns or chaplets of wild or purchased flowers.

Winter Rites: Pine or Oak, and necklaces of herbs and seeds (such as Tonka beans, whole Nutmegs, Star Anise, Acorns), and nuts strung on a natural fiber. Pine cones may also be used.

Full Moon Rituals: Wear night-blooming, fragrant flowers to energize yourself with lunar energies.

Cardinal Points and Herbs

North: Corn, Cypress, Fern, Honeysuckle‡, Wheat, Vervain

East: Acacia, Bergamot, Clover, Dandelion, Lavender, Lemon Grass, Mint, Mistletoe‡, Parsley, Pine

South: Basil, Carnation, Cedar, Chrysanthemum, Dill, Ginger, Heliotrope, Holly‡, Juniper, Marigold, Peppermint

West: Apple Blossoms, Lemon Balm, Camellia, Catnip, Daffodil, Elder, Gardenia, Grape, Heather, Hibiscus, Jasmine, Orchid

Herbs Of The Goddesses and Gods

Acacia: Al-Ozza, Buddha, Neith, and Osiris

Aconite‡: Hecate and Medea

Agave: Mayauel

All Heal: Hercules

Anemone: Adonis, Aphrodite, and Venus

Angelica: Atlantis and Michael

Anise: Apollo and Mercury

Aster: All pagan goddesses and gods

Azalea: Hecate

Barley: Odin

Basil: Erzulie, Krishna, Lakshmi, and Vishnu

Belladonna‡: Atropos, Bellona, Circe, and Hecate

Benzoin: Aphrodite, Mut, and Venus

Blackthorn:Triple Goddess in her dark and protective aspect

Blessed Thistle: Pan

Broom: Blodeuwedd

Campion: Aphrodite and Venus

Catnip: Bast and Sekhmet

Centaury:The centaur Chiron

Chamomile: Karnayna

Chaste Tree: Ceres

Coltsfoot: Epona

Cornflower: Flora, and associated with the myths of Cyanus and Chiron

Cowslip: Freya

Crocus: Aphrodite and Venus

Daffodil: Proserpina

Daisy: Aphrodite, Artemis, Belides, Freya, Thor, Venus, Zeus, and associated
   with Mary Magdalene, Saint John, and Saint Margaret Of Antioch

Dandelion: Brigit

Dittany: Diana, Osiris, and Persephone

Dogwood: Consus

Elecampane: Helen

Eyebright: Euphrosyne

Fennel: Adonis

Fenugreek: Apollo

Ferns: Kupala

Flax: Hulda

Garlic: Hecate and Mars

Hawthorn: Hymen

Heather: Isis and Venus Erycina

Heliotrope: Apollo, Helios, Ra, Sol, and All Sun Gods

Holly‡: Hel, Mother Holle, and the Horned God in his waning year aspects

Horehound: Horus

Houseleek: Jupiter and Thor

Hyacinth: Apollo, Artemis, and Hacinthus

Iris: Hera, Horus, Iris, and Isis

Ivy: Attis, Bacchus, Dionysus, Dusares, and Osiris

Jasmine: Diana

Jimsonweed: Apollo, Chingichnich, and Kwawar

Lady's Mantle: Various Earth goddesses, and associated with the Virgin Mary of the Christian mythos

Lavender: Hecate, Saturn, and Vesta

Lettuce: Adonis

Lily: Astarte, Hera, Juno, Lilith, and Ostara

Loosestrife: Kupala

Lotus: Brahma, Buddha, Cunti, Hermes, Horus, Isis, Juno, Juan-Yin, Lakshmi, Osiris, Padma, Tara, and associated with the myth of Lotis and Priapus

Maidenhair Fern: Dis, Kupala, and Venus

Mandrake‡: Aphrodite, Diana, Hecate, Saturn, and associated with Circe and the legendary Teutonic sorceress, the Alrauna Maiden

Marigold: Xochiquetzal

Marjoram: Aphrodite and Venus

Meadowsweet: Blodeuwedd

Mints: Dis, Hecate, Mintha, and associated with the classical legend of the nymph Menthe

Mistletoe‡: Jupiter, Odin, Zeus, and associated with the myths of Balder and Aeneas

Monkshood‡: Hecate, and associated with Cerberus

Moonwort: Aah, Artemis, Diana, Hina, Selene, Sin, Thoth, and all lunar deities

Mosses: Tapio

Motherwort: Various Mother-goddess figures

Mugwort: Artemis, Diana, and associated with the legend of John the Baptist

Mulberry Bush: Minerva, and associated with the classical legend of the Babylonian lovers, Pyramus and Thisbe

Mullein: Circe and Ulysses

Narcissus: Dis, Hades, Narcissus, Persephone, and Venus

Orchid: Bacchus and Orchis

Orris Root: Aphrodite, Hera, Iris, Isis, and Osiris

Osiers: Hecate

Parsley: Aphrodite, Persephone, Venus, and associated with death and the devil of the Christian mythos

Peony: associated with the legend of Peon

Pennyroyal: Demeter

Peppermint: Zeus

Periwinkle: Aphrodite

Plantain: Venus

Poppy: Ceres, Diana, and Persephone

Primrose: Freya and Paralysio

Purslane: Hermes

Raspberry: Venus

Reeds: Inanna and Pan

Rose: Aphrodite, Aurora, Chloris, Cupid, Demeter, Erato, Eros, Flora, Freya, Hathor, Holda, Isis, Venus, and associated with the Virgin Mary of the Christian mythos

Rue: Mars

Rushes: Acis

Rye: Ceres

Sage: Consus and Zeus

Sandalwood: Venus

Saxifrage: Kupala

Shamrock: Trefuilngid Rte-Eochair

Solomon's Seal: Vor, and associated with the legendary King Solomon of Israel

Strawberry: Freya, Frigga, Venus, and associated with the Virgin Mary of the Christian mythos

Sugar Cane: Cupid, Eros, and Kama

Sunflower: Apollo and Demeter

Tansy: associated with the Virgin Mary and the classic legend of Ganymede

Tarragon: Lilith

Thistle: Thor, and associated with the Virgin Mary of the Christian mythos

Ti Plant: Pele

Trefoil: Olwen

Verbena: Diana and Hermes

Vervain: Aradia, Cerridwen, Demeter, Diana, Hermes, Isis, Juno, Jupiter, Mars, Mercury, Persephone, Thor, and Venus

Violet: Aphrodite, Attis, Io, Venus, Zeus, associated with the Virgin Mary of the Christian mythos

Water Lily: Surya and all water nymphs

Wood Sorrel: all triple goddesses, and associated with Saint Patrick

Wormwood‡: Artemis, Diana, the Great Mother, and all pagan nymphs of Russia

Yarrow: The Horned God of the Wiccans, and associated with the Greek hero Achilles

Plants Of The Home Circle

If you have to work indoors, choose an odd-numbered selection of sacred plants and grow them in your altar room or area. If they need more sunlight, simply move them outside until it is time for your ritual. Give them love, energy, and tenderness and they will empower you in your worship and magic.

African Violets

Cacti (all types)

Ferns (all types)

Holly‡

Hyssop

Palms (all types)

Red Geraniums

Rose

Rose Geranium

Rosemary

Ti (green only) (cordyline terminalis)

Wax Plant (Hoya carnosa)

Trees and Their Planetary Rulers and Astrological Influences

Alder: Venus, Cancer (Black Alder), and Pisces

Almond: Sun

Apple Tree: Venus, Libra, and Taurus

Apricot Tree: Venus and Neptune

Ash: Sun

Aspen: Mercury

Avocado: Venus

Balsam: Mercury

Banana Tree: Moon, Scorpio

Banyan: Jupiter

Bay: Sun, Leo

Bayberry: Mercury

Bay Laurel: (See Bay)

Beech: Saturn, Sagittarius

Bergamot: Venus

Birch: Venus

Bo Tree: Jupiter

Box: Saturn

Breadfruit Tree: Venus

Cashew Tree: Mars, Scorpio

Cedar: Mercury

Cherry Tree: Venus, Libra

Chestnut: Jupiter

Coconut Tree: Venus

Coffee Tree: Mercury and Uranus

Cypress: Saturn, Capricorn

Dogwood: Venus and Neptune

Elder: Venus

Elm: Saturn, Sagittarius

Eucalyptus: Pluto

Fig Tree: Jupiter

Fir: Jupiter

Hawthorn: Mars

Hazel: Mercury

Hemlock‡: Saturn, Capricorn

Holly‡ Oak: (See Ilex)

Holm Oak: (See Ilex)

Ilex: Saturn, Capricorn

Juniper: Sun and Mars

Kola: Uranus

Laurel: Sun, Leo

Lime Tree: Jupiter

Magnolia: Jupiter

Mango Tree: Moon

Maple: Jupiter

Mastic: Mars

Medlar: Saturn

Mountain Ash: Moon

Mulberry Tree: Mercury and Jupiter

Myrrh: Jupiter, Aquarius

Myrtle: Venus

Nutmeg: Jupiter and Uranus

Oak: Jupiter, Sagittarius

Olive Tree: Sun and Jupiter

Orange Tree: Venus and Neptune, Leo

Palm: Sun, Scorpio

Peach Tree: Venus and Neptune, Leo

Pear Tree: Venus and Neptune

Peepul: Jupiter

Pine: Saturn

Pipal: (See Peepul)

Plane Tree: Venus and Jupiter

Plum Tree: Venus

Pomegranate: Venus, Mercury, and Uranus

Poplar: Saturn

Quince: Saturn

Rowan: Moon

Service Tree: Saturn

Storax: Sun

Sumac: Jupiter

Sycamore: Venus and Jupiter

Tamarind: Saturn

Walnut: Sun

Willow: Moon

Yew‡: Saturn, Capricorn

Trees of Pagan Deities, Heroes, and Nymphs

Alder: Bran

Almond: Artemis, Attis, Chandra, Hecate, Jupiter, Phyllis, and Zeus

Apple Tree: Aphrodite, Flora, Hercules, the Hesperides, Frey, Idhunn, Pomona, and all love goddesses

Apricot Tree:Venus

Ash: Akka, Mars, Odin, Poseidon

Aspen: Gaia (Mother Earth),The Maruts, Nunu, and Zeus

Avocado: Flora and Pomona

Banana Tree: Kanaloa

Banyan: Hina, Shu, Shiva,Vishnu, and Zeus

Bay Laurel: Apollo, Adonis, Buddha, Ra, Artemis, Gaia (Mother Earth), Mars Helios, Aesculapius, and Daphne

Beech: Bacchus, Diana, Dionysus, and Hercules

Birch:Thor, Kupula, and Lady of the Woods

Bo Tree: Buddha

Breadfruit Tree: Pukuha Kana and Opimea

Cedar: Artemis, Ea, and Wotan

Cherry Tree: Flora, Pomona, Maya, the virgin mother of Buddha

Coconut Tree: Ganymede and Tamaa

Cypress: Ahura Mazda, Apollo, Artemis, Astarte, Beroth, Cupid, Dis, the 3 Fates, the Furies, Hades, Hercules, Jove, Melcarth, Mithra, Ohrmazd, Pluto, Saturn, and Zoroaster

Dogwood: Apollo, Consus, and Mars

Elder: Dyrads, Ellewoman, Holda, Freya, Hylde-Moer, Venus, and all mother-goddess figures

Elm:The Devas, Embla, Ut, and Vertumnus

Ficus: Romulus and Remus

Fig: Bacchus, Brahma, Dionysus, Flora, Jesus Christ, Juno Caprotina, Mars, Mohammed, Pluto, Pomona, Zeus, and the Indo-Iranian Great Mother

Fir: Bacchus, Dionysus,Tapio, Byblos, Athene, Pan, Cybele, Artemis, Diana, and other lunar goddesses

Hawthorn: Cardea and Hymen

Hazel:Thor and Chandra

Ilex: Faunus

Mango Tree: Pattini

Maple: Nanabozho

Mulberry: Flora, Minerva, Pomona, and San Ku Fu Jen

Myrrh: Adonis, Aphrodite, Cybele, Demeter, Hecate, Juno, Mara, Myrrha, Ra Rhea, and Saturn

Myrtle: Alcina, Aphrodite, Artemis, Astarte, Dionysus, Hathor, Myrsine, Myrtelus, and Venus

Oak: Allah, Ares, Balder, Glodeuwedd, Brahma, Ceres, Dagda, Demeter, Diana, Dianus, the Dryads, Hades, Har Hou, Hera, Hercules, Hours, Janicot, Jehova, Jumala, Jupiter, Kashiwas-No-Kami, Mars, Odin, Perkunas, Perun, Pluto, Taara, Thor, Zeus, and all thunder gods

Olive Tree: Amen-Ra, Apollo, Aristaeus, Athena, Brahma, Flora, Ganymede, Indra, Jupiter, Minerva, Pomona, Poseidon, Wotan, Zeus, and all Sun gods

Orange Tree: Hera and Zeus

Palm: Aphrodite, Apollo, Astarte, Baal-Peor, Chango, Hanuman, Hermes, Mercury, and Saravati

Peach Tree: Flora, Pomona, Shou-Hsing, and Wang Mu

Pear Tree: Flora, Hera, and Pomona

Pine: Attis, Cybele, Dionysus, Poseidon, Pan, Rhea, Silvanus, and Shou-Hsing

Plane Tree: Helen

Plum Tree: Flora and Pomona

Pomegranate: Du'uzu, Hera, Kubaba, Mercury, Persephone, Saturn, and Uranus

Poplar: Brahma, Dis, The Heliades, Hercules, Phaeton, Persephone, Pluto, and Zeus

Quince: Aphrodite and Venus

Rowan: All Moon goddesses

Storax: Loki, Mercury, and Thoth

Sycamore: All Egyptian gods and goddesses

Tamarisk: Apollo

Walnut: Dionysus

Willow: Artemis, Beli, Brigid, Circe, Hecate, Helice, Hera, Hermes, Orpheus, Osiris, Persephone, and all death aspects of the triple Moon goddess

Yew‡: Hecate and Saturn

Woods Of The Balefire

If you build a fire for an outdoor ritual, it can be made up of a combination of any or all of the following woods. If these are not available, use native woods. Rites done on a lakeshore or seashore can be illuminated with balefires of dried driftwood collected prior to the rite.

Apple

Cedar

Dogwood

Juniper

Mesquite

Oak

Pine

Poplar

Rowan

Dates and Times

This section contains lists and tables of information you can use to cast spells and work magic using dates, planets, goals, and astrological signs.

4 Major Sabbats

Candlemas: February 2
Beltane: May 1
Lammas: August 1
Samhain: October 31

4 Lesser Esbats

Vernal Equinox: March 20
Summer Solstice: June 24
Autumnal Equinox: September 23
Winter Solstice/Yule: December 21

Days, Planets, Colors, and Goals

Day	Planet	Correspondence	Color	Incense
Sunday	Sun	Exorcism, Healing, Prosperity	Orange, White, Yellow	Lemon, Frankincense
Monday	Moon	Agriculture, Animals, Female Fertility, Messages, Reconciliations, Theft, Voyages	Silver, White, Grey	African Violet, Honeysuckle‡, Myrtle, Willow, Wormwood‡
Tuesday	Mars	Courage, Physical Strength, Revenge, Military Honors, Surgery, Breaking Negative Spells	Red, Orange	Dragon's Blood, Patchouli
Wednesday	Mercury	Knowledge, Communication, Divination, Writing, Business Transactions	Yellow, Gray, Violet, all opalescent hues	Jasmine, Lavender, Sweet Pea

Days, Planets, Colors, and Goals, continued

Day	Planet	Correspondence	Color	Incense
Thursday	Jupiter	Luck, Health, Happiness, Legal Matters, Male Fertility, Treasure, Wealth, Employment	Purple, Indigo	Cinnamon, Musk, Nutmeg, Sage
Friday	Venus	Love, Romance, Marriage, Sexual Matters, Physical Beauty, Friendships, Partnerships	Pink, Green, Aqua, Chartreuse	Strawberry, Rose, Sandalwood, Saffron, Vanilla
Saturday	Saturn	Spirit, Communication, Meditation, Psychic Attack or Defense, Locating Lost or Missing Persons	Black, Grey, Indigo	Black Poppy Seeds, Myrrh

Sun Sign Correspondences

Birth Date	Sun Sign	Lucky and Protective Stones and Minerals	Color
March 21 to April 19	Aries	Diamond, Amethyst, Topaz, Garnet, Iron, Steel	Red
April 19 to May 20	Taurus	Coral, Sapphire, Emerald, Turquoise, Agate, Zircon, Copper	Azure
May 20 to June 21	Gemini	Aquamarine, Agate, Amber, Emerald, Topaz, Aluminum	Electric Blue
June 21 to July 22	Cancer	Opal, Pearl, Emerald, Moonstone, Silver	Pearl, Rose
July 22 to August 22	Leo	Diamond, Ruby, Gold, Sardonyx, Chrysoberyl	Orange
August 22 to September 23	Virgo	Jade, Rhodonite, Sapphire, Carnelian, Aluminum	Gray Blue
September 23 to October 23	Libra	Opal, Sapphire, Jade, Quartz, Turquoise, Copper	Pale Orange
October 23 to November 22	Scorpio	Bloodstone, Topaz, Aquamarine, Jasper, Silver	Dark Red
November 22 to December 21	Sagittarius	Lapis Lazuli, Topaz, Turquoise, Coral, Tin	Purple

Sun Sign Correspondences, continued

Birth Date	Sun Sign	Lucky and Protective Stones and Minerals	Color
December 21 to January 20	Capricorn	Onyx, Jet, Ruby, Lead, Malachite	Brown
January 20 to February 19	Aquarius	Aquamarine, Jade, Flourspar, Sapphire, Zircon, Aluminum	Green
February 19 to March 21	Pisces	Amethyst, Alexandrite, Bloodstone, Stitchite, Silver	Ocean Blue

Lucky and Unlucky Dates

Month	Lucky Dates	Unlucky Dates
January	3, 10, 27, 31	12, 23
February	7, 8, 18	2, 10, 17, 22
March	3, 9, 12, 14, 16	13, 19, 23, 28
April	5, 17	18, 20, 29, 30
May	1, 2, 4, 6, 9, 14	10, 17, 20
June	3, 5, 7, 9, 13, 23	4, 20
July	2, 6, 10, 23, 30	5, 13, 27
August	5, 7, 10, 14	2, 13, 27, 31
September	6, 10, 13, 18, 30	13, 16, 18
October	13, 16, 25, 31	3, 9, 27
November	1, 13, 23, 30	6, 25
December	10, 20, 29	15, 26

Nightly Planetary Hours

Hour		Sun.	Mon.	Tue.	Wed.	Thur.	Fri.	Sat.
1	6/7 P.M.	Jupiter	Venus	Saturn	Sun	Moon	Mars	Mercury
2	7/8 P.M.	Mars	Mercury	Jupiter	Venus	Saturn	Sun	Moon
3	8/9 P.M.	Sun	Moon	Mars	Mercury	Jupiter	Venus	Saturn
4	9/10 P.M.	Venus	Saturn	Sun	Moon	Mars	Mercury	Jupiter
5	10/11 P.M.	Mercury	Jupiter	Venus	Saturn	Sun	Moon	Mars
6	11/12 P.M.	Moon	Mars	Mercury	Jupiter	Venus	Saturn	Sun
7	12/1 A.M.	Saturn	Sun	Moon	Mars	Mercury	Jupiter	Venus

Nightly Planetary Hours, continued

Hour		Sun.	Mon.	Tue.	Wed.	Thur.	Fri.	Sat.
8	1/2 A.M.	Jupiter	Venus	Saturn	Sun	Moon	Mars	Mercury
9	2/3 A.M.	Mars	Mercury	Jupiter	Venus	Saturn	Sun	Moon
10	3/4 A.M.	Sun	Moon	Mars	Mercury	Jupiter	Venus	Saturn
11	4/5 A.M.	Venus	Saturn	Sun	Moon	Mars	Mercury	Jupiter
12	5/6 A.M.	Mercury	Jupiter	Venus	Saturn	Sun	Moon	Mars

Daily Planetary Hours

Hour		Sun.	Mon.	Tue.	Wed.	Thur.	Fri.	Sat.
1	6/7 A.M.	Sun	Moon	Mars	Mercury	Jupiter	Venus	Saturn
2	7/8 A.M.	Venus	Saturn	Sun	Moon	Mars	Mercury	Jupiter
3	8/9 A.M.	Mercury	Jupiter	Venus	Saturn	Sun	Moon	Mars
4	9/10 A.M.	Moon	Mars	Mercury	Jupiter	Venus	Saturn	Sun
5	10/11 A.M.	Saturn	Sun	Moon	Mars	Mercury	Jupiter	Venus
6	11/12 A.M.	Jupiter	Venus	Saturn	Sun	Moon	Mars	Mercury
7	12/1 P.M.	Mars	Mercury	Jupiter	Venus	Saturn	Sun	Moon
8	1/2 P.M.	Sun	Moon	Mars	Mercury	Jupiter	Venus	Saturn
9	2/3 P.M.	Venus	Saturn	Sun	Moon	Mars	Mercury	Jupiter
10	3/4 P.M.	Mercury	Jupiter	Venus	Saturn	Sun	Moon	Mars
11	4/5 P.M.	Moon	Mars	Mercury	Jupiter	Venus	Saturn	Sun
12	5/6 P.M.	Saturn	Sun	Moon	Mars	Mercury	Jupiter	Venus

Colors

This list can be useful when choosing candles for magical ritual or spells, tinting bath salts, or designing entire rituals around herbal products. Some differences of opinion do exist and color is a magical system within itself. Use your instinct when working with color.

Magic and Color

White: Protection, purification, peace, truth, binding, sincerity, chastity, happiness, exorcism, spirituality, tranquillity

Red: Protection, strength, health, energy, vigor, lust, sex, passion, courage, exorcism, love, power

Black: Absorbing and destroying negativity, healing severe diseases, banishing, attracting money

Light Blue: Understanding, tranquillity, healing, patience, happiness, overcoming depression

Dark Blue: Change, flexibility, subconscious mind, psychic perception, healing

Green: Finances, money, fertility, prosperity, growth, good luck, employment, beauty, youth, success in gardening

Gray: Neutrality, cancellation, stalemate

Yellow or Gold: Intellect, charm, attraction, study, persuasion, confidence, divination, good fortune, psychic power, wisdom, vision, sleep

Brown: Working magic for animals, healing animals, the home

Pink: Love, honor, fidelity, morality, friendship

Orange: Adaptability, stimulation, attraction, encouragement, all legal matters

Purple: Power, healing severe disease, spirituality, medication, exorcism, ambition, business progress, tension relief

Numbers

Since the beginning of time, numbers have been viewed as signs with mystical significance. The following is based on the ancient Pythagorean system (on which modern-day numerology is based). If any number keeps appearing for you in various forms, pay attention to the associated meanings for that number. *CAUTION: Do not ignore the secret language of number signs.*

One: Independence, new beginnings, self-development, oneness with life, individuality, progress and creativity

Two: A balance of the yin and yang energies (the polarities) of the universe, self-surrender, putting others first, a dynamic attraction one to another, knowledge that comes from the balance and marriage of the two opposites

Three: Trinity, mind-body-spirit, threefold nature of divinity, expansion, expression, communication, fun, self-expression, giving outwardly, openness and optimism. This number relates to the Wiccan 3-by-3 law—whatever you send out, you will receive threefold

Four: Security, foundations, four elements and the four sacred directions, self-discipline through work and service, productivity, organization, and wholeness

Five: Feeling free, self-emancipation, active, physical, impulsive, energetic, changing, adventuresome, resourceful, travel, curiosity, free soul, excitement and change

Six: Self-harmony, compassion, love, service, social responsibility, beauty, the arts, generosity, concern, caring, children, balance, community service

Seven: Inner life and inner wisdom, mystical number symbolizing wisdom, seven chakras and seven heavens, birth and rebirth, religious strength, sacred vows, path of solitude, analysis, contemplation

Eight: Infinity, material prosperity, self-power, abundance, cosmic consciousness, reward, authority, leadership

Nine: Humanitarianism, selflessness, dedication of your life to others, completion, endings, universal compassion, tolerance, and wisdom

Master Numbers

In the Pythagorean tradition, master numbers were thought to have a special power and significance of their own.

Eleven: Developing intuition, clairvoyance, spiritual healing, other metaphysical faculties

Twenty-two: Unlimited potential of mastery in any area—spiritual, physical, emotional, and mental

Thirty-three: All things possible

God and Spirit Correspondences

The following lists and tables contain information on magical goals and their related deities.

Deities and Their Purposes

Agriculture: Adonis, Amon, Aristaeus, Baldur, Bonus Eventus, Ceres, Consus, Dagon, Demeter, Dumuzi, Esus, Gahanan, Inari, Osiris, Saturn, Tammuz, Thor, Triptolemus, Vertumnus, Zochipilli, Yumcaa

Arts: Ea, Hathor, Odin, Thene, Thor

Astrology: Albion

Cats: Bast, Freya

Childbirth: Althea, Bes, Camenta, Cihuatcoatl, Cuchavira, Isis, Juan Yin, Laima, Lucina Meshkent

Communications: Hermes, Janus, Hermod, Mercury

Courage: Tyr

Dreams: Geshtinanna, Morpheus, Nanshe

Earth: Asia, Consus, Daghda, Enlil, Frigga, Frija, Gaea, Ge, Geb, Kronos, Ninhursag, Ops, Prithivi, Rhea, Saturn, Sif, Tellus

Fertility: Amun, Anaitis, Apollo, Arrianrhod, Asherali, Astarte, Attis, Baal, Bacchus, Bast, Bona Dea, Boucca, Centeotle, Cernunnos, Cerridwen, Cybele, Daghda, Demeter, Dew, Dionysus, Eostre, Frey, Freya, Frigga, Indra, Ishtar, Ishwara, Isis, Kronos, Ono, Lulpercus, Min, Mut, Mylitta, Ningirsu, Ops, Osiris, Ostara, Oya, Pan, Pomona, Quetzalcoatl, Rhea, Rhiannon,

Saturn, Selkhet, Sida, Tane, Telepinu, Telluno, Tellus Mater, Thunor, Tlazolteotl, Yarilo, Zarpanitu

Good Luck and Fortune: Bonus Eventus, Daikoku, Fortuna, Ganesa, Jorojin, Laima, Tyche

Healing: Apollo, Asclepius, Bast, Brigid Eira, Gula, Ixtlilton, Khnos, Paeon

Journeys: Echua, Janus

Law, Truth, and Justice: Astraea, Maat, Misharu, Themis

Love: Aizen Myo-O, Alpan, Angus, Aphrodite, Asera, Astarte, Asthoreth, Belili, Creirwy, Cupid, Dzydzilelya, Rao, Eros, Erzulie, Esmeralda, Februa, Freya, Frigga, Habondia, Hathor, Inanna, Ishtar, Kades, Kama, Kivan-Non, Kubaba, Melusine, Menu, Minne, Nanaja, Odudua, Olwen, Oshun, Prenda, Sauska, Tlazoletotl, Turan, Venus, Xochipilli, Zochiquetzal

Lunar Magic: Aah, Artemis, Asherali, Astarte, Baiame, Bendis, Diana, Gou, Hathor, Hecate, Ilmaqah, Ishtar, Isis, Jacy, Kabul, Khons, Kilya, Lucina, Luna, Mah, Mama Quilla, Mani, Menu, Metzli, Myestaa, Nanna, Pah, Selene, Sin, Soma, Taukiyomi, Thoh, Varuna, Yarikh, Yerak, Zamna

Marriage: Airyaman, Aphrodite, Aryan, Bes, Bah, Ceres, Errata, Frigga, Hathor, Hera, Hymen, Juno, Patina, Saluki, Svarog, Thalassa, Tutunis, Vor, Xochipilli

Music and/or Poetry: Apollo, Benten, Bragi, Brigid, Hathor, Orpheus, Odin, Thoth, Vainemuine, Woden, Xochipilli

Prophecy, Divination, and the Magical Arts: Anubis, Apollo, Brigid, Carmenta, Ea, Exu, Hecate, Isis, Odin, Set, Shamash, Simbi, Tages, Thoth, Untunktahe, Woden, Xolotl

Reincarnation: Hera, Khensu, Ra

Sea: Amphitrite, Benten, Dylan, Ea, Enoil, Glaucus, Leucothea, Manannan Mac Lir, Neptune, Nereus, Njord, Paldemon, Phorcys, Pontus, Poseidon, Proteus, Shoney, Yamm

Sky: Aditi, Anshar, Anu, Dyaus, Frigg, Hathor, Horus, Joch-Huva, Jupiter, Kumarbis, Nut, Obatala, Rangi, Svarog, Tane, Thor, Tiwaz, Ukko, Uranus, Varuna, Zeus

Shapeshifting: Freya, Volkh, Xolotl

Sleep: Hypnos (also see the list of deities who rule over dreams)

Solar Magic: Amaterasu, Apollo, Atum, Baldur, Bochica, Dazhbog, Helios, Hiruku, Horus, Hyperion, Inti, Legba, Lugh, Mandulis, Mao, Marduk, Maui, Melkart, Mithra, Orunjan, Paiva Perun, Phoebus, Ra, Sabazius, Samas, Sams, Shamash, Sol, Surya, Tezcatlipoca, Tonatiuh, Torushompek, Utto, Vishnu, Yhi

Vengeance: Nemesis

Wealth and Prosperity: Daikoku, Jambhala, Kuber, Plutus, Thor

Weatherworking: Adad, Aeolus, Agni, Amen, Baal, Bragi, Buriash, Catequil, Chac-Mool, Chernobog, Donar, Fomagata, Ilyapa, Indra, Jove, Jupiter, Kami-Nari, Koza, Lei-Kung, Marduk, Nyame, Perkunas, Pillan, Pulug, Quiateot, Raiden, Rammon, Rudra, Shango, Sobo, Summanus, Taki-Tsu-Hilo, Tawhaaki, Tawhiri, Tefnut, Thor, Thunor, Tilo, Tinia, Typhoeus, Typhon, Yu-Tzu, Zeus, Zu

Wisdom: Aruna, Athena, Atri, Galdur, Brigid, Dainichi, Ea, Enki, Fudo-Myoo, Fugen Bosatsu, Fukurokuju, Ganesa, Minerva, Nebo, Nimir, Oannes, Odin, Oghma, Quetzalxoatl, Sia, Sin, Thoth, Vohumano, Zeus

Magical Intentions

Banishing: Saturn, Fire

Beauty: Venus, Water

Courage: Mars, Fire

Divination: Mercury, Air

Employment: Sun, Jupiter

Energy: Sun, Mars, Fire

Exorcism: Sun, Fire

Fertility: Moon, Earth

Friendships: Venus, Water

Happiness: Venus, Moon, Water

Healing, Health: Moon, Mars (to burn away disease), Fire (the same), Water

Home: Saturn, Earth, Water

Joy, Happiness: Venus, Water

Love: Venus, Water

Money, Wealth: Jupiter, Earth

Peace: Moon, Venus

Power: Sun, Mars, Fire

Protection: Sun, Mars, Fire

Psychism: Moon, Water

Purification: Saturn, Fire

Sex: Mars, Venus, Fire

Sleep: Moon, Water

Spirituality: Sun, Moon

Success: Sun, Fire

Travel: Mercury

Wisdom, Intelligence: Mercury, Air

Elemental Dragons

Element	Cardinal Points	Dragon Name	Color
Earth: Land and Moon Beams	North	Grael	Clear Dark Green
Water: Oceans and Rivers	West	Naelyan	Blue
Air: Breezes and Wind	East	Sairys	Yellow
Fire: Sunbeams	South	Fafnir	Pure Red
Light Side of the Soul: Mother	NA	NA	White
Dark Side of the Soul: Father	NA	NA	Black

Elemental Spirits

Element	Spirit Name	Leader	Attracted By	Rulers Of
Earth	Gnomes or Trolls	Gob	Salts and Powders	Riches and Treasure
Water	Nymphs or Undines	Neckna	Washes and Solutions	Plants and Healing
Air	Sylphs or Zephyrs	Paralda	Oils and Incense	Knowledge and Inspiration
Fire	Salamanders	Djin	Fire and Incense	Freedom and Change

Gods of the Ancients

Correspondence	Germanic	Roman	Greek	Egyptian	Babylonian
Supreme God	Woden Frigg	Jupiter Juno	Zeus Hera	Ra	Marduk
Creator				Ptah	Anu
Sky	Frigg	Jupiter	Uranua Zeus	Nut	Anu Anshar
Sun		Apollo	Helios	Ra	Shamash
Moon		Diana	Artemis	Thoth	Sin
Earth	Sif	Tellus	Gaea	Geb	Enlil
Air					Enlil
Fire	Hoenir	Vulcan	Hephaestus		Girru
Sea	Niord	Neptune	Poseidon		

Gods of the Ancients, continued

Correspondence	Germanic	Roman	Greek	Egyptian	Babylonian
Water and Rain	Thor	Jupiter	Zeus	Tefnut	Ea
Light	Balder	Apollo	Apollo		
Thunder	Thor	Jupiter	Zeus		
Wind			Aeolus	Amen	Markuk
Storm		Jupiter	Zeus		Adad
Dawn		Aurora	Eos		
Mother Goddess	Nerthus	Venus	Aphrodite	Isis	Ishtar
Fertility	Frey	Bona Dea	Rhea	Osiris	
Harvest	Balder	Saturn	Cronos		
Vegetation	Balder	Ceres	Adonis	Osiris	Tammuz
Death	Hel	Pluto	Hades	Osiris	Nergal
Music and Poetry	Bragi		Apollo	Thoth	
Wisdom and Learning	Nimir	Minerva	Athena	Thoth	Nebo
War	Tiu	Mars Bellona	Ares Athena		
Love	Freya	Cupid	Eros		
Messenger	Hermod	Mercury	Hermes		
Healing	Eira	Apollo	Apollo		Gula
Hunting	Uller	Diana	Artemis		
Wine		Liber	Dionysus		
Divine Smith and Artificer	Mimir	Vulcan	Hephaestus		

Herbs and Their Folk Names

A

Aaron's Rod: Goldenrod, Mullein

Absinthe: Wormwood‡

Achillea: Yarrow

Aconite‡: Wolfsbane‡

Adder's Mouth: Adder's Tongue

African Pepper: Grains of Paradise

Agave: Maguey

Ague Grass: Ague Root

Agueweed: Boneset

Ahuactol: Avocado

Ajo: Garlic

Alantwurzel: Elecampane

Albahaca: Basil

Alehoof: Ground Ivy

Alhuren: Elder

Alison: Alyssum

All Heal: Mistletoe‡, Valerian

Alligator Pear: Avocado

Alraun: Mandrake‡

Alycompaine: Elecampane

Amantilla: Valerian

Amber: St. John's Wort

American Adder's Tongue: Adder's Tongue

American Dittany: Basil

American Mandrake‡: Mayapple‡

Aneton: Dill

Anneys: Anise

Aniseseed: Anise

Anthropomorphon: Mandrake‡

Appleringie: Southernwood

Aquifolius: Holly‡

Arabic: Arabic, Gum

Arberry: Uva Ursa

Archangel: Angelica

Arched Fig: Banyan

Armstrong: Knotweed

Arrowroot: Yarrow

Artemis Herb: Mugwort

Artemesia: Mugwort

Artetyke: Cowslip

Arthritica: Cowslip

Asphodel: Daffodil

Assaranaccara: Avens

Assear: Comfrey

Ass's Foot: Coltsfoot

Assyfetida: Asafoetida‡

Asthma Weed: Lobelia‡

Aunee: Elecampane

Autumn Crocus: Saffron

Ava: Kava-Kava

Ava Root: Kava-Kava

B

Baaras: Mandrake‡

Bad Man's Plaything: Yarrow

Bairnwort: Daisy

Baie: Bay

Balessan: Balm of Gilead

Balsam: Balm of Gilead

Balsumodendron Gileadenis: Balm of Gilead

Bamboo Briar: Sarsaparilla

Banal: Broom

Banewort: Belladonna‡, Pansy

Banwort: Pansy

Bardana: Burdock

Basam: Broom

Bashoush: Rue

Bat's Wing: Holly‡

Battree: Elder

Bay Laurel: Bay

Bay Tree: Bay

Bearberry: Uva Ursa

Bear's Foot: Lady's Mantle

Baear's Grape: Uva Ursa

Bear Weed: Yerba Santa

Beaver Poison: Hemlock‡

Bee Balm: Balm, Lemon

Beechwheat: Buckwheat

Beer Flower: Hops

Beggar's Buttons: Burdock

Beggarweed: Dodder

Beggery: Fumitory

Beithe: Birch

Ben: Benzoin

Bejamen: Benzoin

Bennet: Avens

Bereza: Birch

Bergamot: Bergamot, Orange

Berke: Birch

Beth: Birch, Trillium

Beth Root: Trillium

Bilberry: Blueberry

Bindweed: Morning Glory

Birdlime: Mistletoe‡

Bird's Eye: Pansy

Bird's Foot: Fenugreek

Bird's Nest: Carrot

Bishopwort: Betony, Wood

Bisom: Broom

Biscuits: Tormentil

Bitter Grass: Ague root

Bitter Root: Gentian

Bizzon: Broom

Black Cherry: Belladonna‡

Black Cohosh: Cohosh, Black

Black Nightshade‡: Henbane‡

Black Pepper: Pepper

Blackroot: Ague root

Black Sampson: Echinacea

Black Snake Root: Cohosh, Black

Black Tea: Tea

Blackthorn: Sloe

Black Wort: Comfrey

Bladder Fucus: Bladderwrack

Bladderpod: Liverwort

Blanket Leaf: Mullein

Blessed Herb: Avens, Pimpernel

Blessed Thistle: Thistle Holly‡

Blind Buff: Poppy

Blindeyes: Poppy

Blood: Dragon's Blood

Bloodroot: Tormentil

Bloody Butcher: Valerian

Blooming Sally: Loosestrife

Blowball: Dandelion

Blue Buttons: Periwinkle

Blue Eyes: Potato

Blue Gum Tree: Eucalyptus

Blue Magnolia: Magnolia

Blue Mountain Tea: Goldenrod

Blue Violet: Violet

Blume: Dragon's Blood

Bly: Blackberry

Blye Eyes: Potato

Box: Beech

Boke: Beech

Boneset: Comfrey

Bonewort: Pansy

Bookoo: Buchu

Bo Tree: Bodhi

Bottle Brush: Horsetail

Bouleau: Birch

Bouncing Bet: Pansy

Boure Tree: Elder

Boxwood: Dogwood

Boy's Love: Southernwood

Brain Thief: Mandrake‡

Bramble: Blackberry

Bramblekite: Blackberry

Brandy Mint: Peppermint

Brank: Buckwheat

Bras: Rice

Bread and Cheese Tree: Hawthorn

Bream: Broom

Bride of the Meadow: Meadowsweet

Bride of the Sun: Marigold

Bridewort: Meadowsweet

British Tobacco‡: Coltsfoot

Britannica: Vervain

Broom: Gorse

Broom Tops: Broom

Brown Mint: Spearmint

Bruisewort: Comfrey, Daisy

Brum: Broom

Buche: Beech

Buckeye: Horse Chestnut

Buckles: Cowslip

Bucco: Cuchu

Budwood: Dogwood

Buffalo Herb: Alfalfa

Bugbane: Cohosh, Black

Bugloss: Borage

Buke: Beech

Buku: Buche

Bull's Blood: Horehound

Bull's Foot: Coltsfoot

Bumble-Kite: Blackberry

Bumweed: Pilot Weed

Burning Bush‡: Wahoo‡

Burn Plant: Aloe

Burrage: Borage

Burrseed: Burdock

Butterbur: Coltsfoot

Butter Rose: Primrose

Buttons: Tansy

C

Caarobe: Carob

Calamus Draco: Dragon's Blood

Calendula: Marigold

Calf's Snout: Snapdragon

California Barberry: Oregon Grape

California Pepper Tree: Pepper tree

Camomyle: Chamomile

Candlewich Plant: Mullein

Can, Sugar: Sugar Cane

Cankerwort: Dandelion, Ragwort

Cape Gum: Acacia

Capon's Trailer: Valerian

Carageen: Irish Moss

Caroba: Carob

Carobinha: Carob

Carpenter's Weed: Yarrow

Carthage Apple: Pomegranate

Carya: Walnut

Cassilago: Henbane‡

Cassilate: Henbane‡

Cat: Catnip

Catmint: Catnip

Catnep: Catnip

Catrup: Catnip

Cat's Foot: Ground Ivy

Cat's Valerian: Valerian

Cat's Worts: Catnip

Caucasian Walnut: Walnut

Cechan: Balm of Gilead

Cedron: Lemon Verbena

Centinode: Knotweed

Centocchiio: Periwinkle

Ceylon Morning Glory: Wood Rose

Chafe Weed: Life Everlasting

Chamaimelon: Chamomile

Chameleon Star: Bromeliad

Chanvre: Hemp‡

Checkerberry: Wintergreen

Chelidonium: Celandine‡

Cherry Pie: Heliotrope

Chewing John: Galangal

China Aster: Aserr

China Root: Galangal

China Tea: Tea

Chinese Anise: Star Anise

Chinese Lovage: Lovage

Chinese Parsley: Coriander

Chocolate: Carob

Christ's Ladder: Centaury

Christ's Thorn: Holly‡

Church Steeples: Agrimony

Churnstaff: Toadflax

Cilantro: Coriander

Circeium: Mandrake‡

Cirocoea: Mandrake‡

Citrus Plant: Parosela

Cleavers: Bedstraw, Fragrant

Clot: Mullein

Clotbur: Burdock

Cloudberry: Blackberry

Clove Root: Avens

Coakum: Poke‡

Cocan: Poke‡

Cocklebur: Agrimony

Cockleburr: Burdock

Colewort: Avens

Colic Root: Galangal

Common Bamboo: Bamboo

Common Fig: Fig

Common Heather: Heather

Common Lilac: Lilac

Common Thyme: Thyme

Compass Point: Pilot Weed

Compass Weed: Rosemary

Coneflower: Echinacea

Consolida: Comfrey

Consumptive Weed: Yerba Santa

Convallaria: Lily of the Valley‡

Cornish Lovage: Lovage

Corona Solis: Sunflower

Couch Grass: Witch Grass

Coughwort: Coltsfoot

Coumaria Nut: Tonka

Cowcucumber: Cucumber

Cow-Flop: Foxglove‡

Cougars: Knotweed

Cramped: Cinquefoil

Crocus: Saffron

Crossword: Boneset

Crowbar: Poke‡

Crow Corn: Ague root

Crown for a King: Wormwood‡

Crown of Thorns: Euphorbia

Cuckoo's Bread: Plantain

Cuckowe's Meat: Sorrel, Wood

Cucumber Tree: Magnolia

Culantro: Coriander

Cumino: Cumin

Cuminoaigro: Cumin

Cupid's Car: Wolfsbane‡

Cutweed: Bladderwrack

Cuy: Cowslip

D

Daffy-Down-Dilly: Daffodil

Daphne: Bay

Date Palm: Palm, Date

Deadly Nightshade‡: Belladona‡

Deadmen's Bells: Foxglove‡

Death Angel: Agaric

Death Cap: Agaric

Death Flower: Yarrow

Death's Herb: Belladona‡

Delight of the Eye: Rowan

Delphinium: Larkspur

Delydoyne: Celandine‡

Desert Rue: Parosela

Deus Caballinus: Henbane‡

Devil's Apple: Datura

Devil's Cherries: Belladona‡

Devil's Dung: Asafoetida‡

Devil's Eye: Henbane‡, Periwinkle

Devil's Flower: Bachelor's Buttons

Devil's Fuge: Mistletoe‡

Devil's Guts: Dodder

Devil's Milk: Celadine

Devil's Nettle: Yarrow

Devil's Oatmeal: Parsley

Dewberry: Blackberry

Dew of the Sea: Rosemary

Dhan: Rice

Digitalis: Foxglove‡

Dill Weed: Dill

Dilly: Dill

Divale: Belladonna‡

Doffle: Mullein

Dog-Bur: Houndstongue

Doggies: Toadflax

Dog Grass: Witch Grass

Dog Standard: Ragwort

Dog's Tongue: Houndstongue

Dogtree: Dogwood

Dollor: Meadowsweet

Donnerbesen: Mistletoe‡

Draconia Resina: Dragon's Blood

Dragon Bushes: Toadflax

Dragon's Blood Palm: V's Blood

Dragonwort: Bistort

Drelip: Cowslip

Dropberry: Solomon's Seal

Drunkard: Marigold

Duck's Foot: Mayapple‡

Duir: Oak

Dumbledore's Delight: Wolfsbane‡

Dutch Honeysuckle‡: Honeysuckle‡

Dutch Rushes: Horsetail

Dwale: Belladonna‡

Dealeberry: Belladonna‡

Dwayberry: Belladonna‡

E

Earthbank: Tormentil

Earthsmoke: Fumitory

Earth Star: Bromeliad

Easter Giant: Bistort

East India Catarrh Root: Galangal

Edellebore: Liverwort

Eerie: Yarrow

Egyptian Gum: Arabic, Gum

Egyptian Thorn: Acacia

Eldrum: Elder

Elm, Slippery: Slippery Elm

Elven: Elm

Enchanter's Plant: Vervain

Enebro: Juniper

English Cowslip: Primrose

English Elm: Elm

Englishmans Foot: Plantain

English Serpentary: Bostort

English Valerian: Valerian

English Walnut: Walnut

Euphrosyne: Eyebright

European Aspen: Aspen

European Elm: Elm

European Mistletoe‡: Mistletoe‡

European Elm, Slippery: Elm, Slippery

Euryangium Musk Root: Sumbul

Everlasting: Life Everlasting

Ewe Daisy: Tormentil

Eye Balm: Golden Seal

Eyes: Daisy

F

Faggio: Beech

Fagos: Beech

Fairies' Horses: Ragwort

Fair Lady: Belladonna‡

Fairy Bells: Sorrel, Wood

Fairy Cup: Cowslip

Fairy Fingers: Foxglove‡

Fairy Eggs: Molukka

Fairy Thimbles: Foxglove‡

Fairy Weed: Foxglove‡

False Wintergreen: Pipsissewa

Faya: Beech

Featherfew: Feverfew

Febrigue Plant: Feverfew

Felon Herb: Mugwort

Feltwort: Mullein

Fenkel: Fennel

Feverwort: Boneset, Centaury

Field Balm: Catnip

Field Balsam: Life Everlasting

Field Daisy: Daisy

Field Hops: Yarrow

Finnochio: Fennel

Fireweed: Doddeer

Five Finger Blossom: Cinquefoil

Five Finger Grass: Cinquefoil

Five Fingers: Cinquefoil, Tormentil

Flag Lily‡: Blue Flag‡

Flannel Plant: Mullein

Flax Weed: Toadflax

Flesh and Blood: Tormentil

Fleur de Coucou: Daffodil

Fleur-de-Lis: Blue Flag‡

Floppy-Dock: Foxglove‡

Floptop: Foxglove‡

Florentine Iris: Orris

Fores De Cerveza: Hops

Florida Dogwood: Dogwood

Flower of Immortality: Amaranth

Flowering Cornel: Dogwood

Flowering Dogwood: Dogwood

Fluellin: Toadflax

Flukes: Potato

Flute Plant: Meadow Rue

Folk's Gloves: Foxglove‡

Food of the Gods: Asfoetida

Foxes Glofa: Foxglove‡

Fox Bells: Foxglove‡

Foxtail: Club Moss

Frangipangi: Plumeria

Fragrant Valerian: Valerian

Frauenschlussel: Cowslip

Frau Holle: Elder

French Wheat: Buckwheat

Frey: Gorse

Frozen Roses: Wood Rose

Fruit of the Gods: Apple

Fruit of the Underworld: Apple

Fuga Daemonum: St. John's Wort

Fumiterry: Fumitory

Furze: Gorse

Fyrs: Gorse

G

Gagroot: Lobelia‡

Galgenmannchen: Mandrake‡

Galingale: Galangal

Gallowgrass: Hemp‡

Gallows: Mandrake‡

Gallowort: Toadflax

Ganeb: Hemp‡

Ganja: Hemp‡

Garclive: Agrimony

Garden Celadine: Celadine

Garden Dill: Dill

Garden Heliotrope: Valerian

Garden Lettuce: Lettuce

Garden Mint: Mint, Spearmint

Garden Purslane: Purslane

Garden Rue: Rue

Garden Sage: Sage

Garden Thyme: Thyme

Garden Violet: Pansy

Garden Robe: Southernwood

Gargaut: Galangal

Garget: Poke‡

Gazels: Hawthorn

Gearwe: Yarrow

Gemeiner Wachholder: Juniper

Geneva: Juniper

Genista: Broom

German Rue: Rue

Ghost Flower: Datura

Gill-Go-over-the-Ground: Ground Ivy

Gillies: Carnation

Gilliflower: Carnation

Gin Berry: Juniper

Ginepro: Juniper

Gin Plant: Juniper

Giver of Life: Corn

Gladdon: Calamus

Goat's Leaf: Honeysuckle‡

Goat Weed: St. John's Wort

Golden Apple: Apricot

Golden Bough: Mistletoe‡

Golden Purlsane: Purslane

Golden Star: Avens

Goldes: Marigold

Goldy Star: Avens

Goldruthe: Goldenrod

Gonea Tea: Goldenrod

Good Luck Plant: Green Ti (Bad Luck Red Ti)

Goosegrass: Cinquefoil

Gorst: Gorse

Gort: Ivy

Goss: Gorse

Gout Root: Briony

Goutberry: Blackberry

Grandilla: Passion Flower

Grape, Oregon: Oregon Grape

Grass: Hemp‡

Gravelroot: Joe-Pye Weed

Gravel Root: Meadowsweet

Graveyard Dust: Mullein

Graveyard Flowers: Plumeria

Great Burdock: Burdock

Greater Celadine: Celandine‡

Greater Pimpernel: Pimpernel

Greater Scullcap: Scullcap

Great Herb, the: Foxglove

Great Morel: Belladonna‡

Grecian Laurel: Bay

Greek Hay-Seed: Genugreek

Green Broom: Broom

Green Mint: Spearmint

Green Osier: Bogwood

Green Spine: Spearmint

Grenadier: Pomegranate

Groats: Oats

Ground Apple: Chamomile

Goundbread: Cyclamen

Groundeswelge: Groundsel

Ground Holly‡: Pipsissewa

Ground Raspberry: Golden Seal

Grundy Swallow: Groundsel

Guardrobe: Rosemary

Guinea Grains: Grains of Paradise

Gum Arabic: Arabic, Gum

Gum Arabic Tree: Arabic, Gum

Gum Benzoin: Benzoin

Gum Bush: Yerba Santa

Gum Byrrh Tree: Myrrh

Gum Mastic: Masttic

Gum Plant: Comfrey

Gypsy Flower: Houndstongue

H

Hag's Tapers: Mullein

Hagthorn: Hawthorn

Hand of Power: Lucky Hand

Hanf: Hemp‡

Happy Major: Burdock

Haran: Horehound

Hardock: Burdock

Harebell: Bluebell

Harefoot: Avens

Haw: Hawthorn

Haya: Beech

Haymaids: Ground Ivy

Hazels: Hawthorn

Headache: Poppy

Head Waak: Poppy

Healing Herb: Comfrey

Heart Leaf: Liverwort

Heart's Ease: Pansy

Heath: Heather

Hebenon: Henbane‡

Hedge Taper: Mullein

Hedgemaids: Ground Ivy

Heermannchen: Camomile

Hellweed: Dodder

Helmet Flower: Scullcap

Helping Hand: Lucky Hand

Hempseed: Joe-Pye Weed

Hen and Chickens: Houseleek

Henbells: Henbane‡

Herba John: St. John's Wort

Herba Sacra: Vervain

Herb Bennet: Avens, Hemlock‡

Herb of Circe: Mandrake‡

Herb of Enchantment: Vervain

Herb of Gladness: Borage

Herb of Grace: Rue, Vervain

Herb of Mary: Pimpernel

Herb of the Cross: Vervain

Herb Peter: Cowslip

Herb Trinity: Liverwort

Herb Walter: Woodruff

Herbygrass: Rue

Hetre: Beech

Hexenmannchen: Mandrake‡

High Blackberry: Blackberry

Hildemoer: Elder

Hoarhound: Horehound

Hog Apple: Mayapple‡

Hogsbean: Henbane‡

Hogweed: Knotweed

Holigolds: Marigold

Hollunder: Elder

Holm: Holly‡

Holy Herb: Vervain, Yerba Santa

Holy Thistle: Thistle, Holly‡

Holy Tree: Holly‡

Holy Wood: Mistletoe‡

Honey: Clover

Honeystalks: Clover

Hoodwort: Scullcap

Horseheal: Elecampane

Horse Violet: Pansy

Hreow: Rue

Huath: Hawthorn

Huauhtli: Amaranth

Hulm: Holly‡

Hundred Leaved Grass: Yarrow

Huran: Horehound

Hurrburr: Burdock

Husbandman's Dial: Marigold

Hylder: Elder

Hyssop Herb: Hyssop

I

Incense: Frankincense

Incensier: Rosemary

Indian Arrow Wood: Wahoo‡

Indian Dye: Golden Seal

Indian Elm: Slippery Elm

Indian Fig Tree: Banyan

Indian God Tree: Indian

Indian Gum: Arabic, Gum

Indian Paint: Golden Seal

Indian Pony: Life Everlasting

Indian Root: Trillium

Indian Sage: Bonset

Indian Tobacco‡: Lobelia‡

India Root: Galangal

Inkberry‡: Poke‡

Intoxicating Pepper: Kava-Kava

Iris: Blue Flag‡

Irish Broom: Broom

Irish Tops: Broom

Isana: Henbane‡

Isopo: Hyssop

Italian Lovage: Lovage

Italian Parsley: Lovage

J

Jacob's Ladder: Lily of the Valley‡

Jalap: High John the Conqueror

Jatamansi: Sumbul

Jaundice Root: Golden Seal

Jessamine: Jasmine

Jimsonweed: Datura

Joe-Pie: Joe-Pye Weed

Johnny Jumper: Pansy

John's Wort: St. John's Wort

Jopi Weed: Joe-Pye Weed

Jove's Flower: Carnation

Jove's Nuts: Oak

Joy of the Mountain: Marjoram

Jupiter's Bean: Henbane‡

Joy on the Ground: Periwinkle

Juglans: Oak

Juno's Tears: Vervain

Jupiter's Staff: Mullein

Jusquiame: Henbane‡

K

Kaempferia Galanga: Galangal

Kaphnos: Fumitory

Karan: Myrrh

Karcom: Saffron

Heckies: Hemlock‡

Kelp: Bladderwrack

Kenning Wort: Celandine‡

Key Flower: Cowslip

Key of Heaven: Cowslip

Kex: Hemlock‡

Kharkady: Hibiscus

Khus-Khus: Vetivert

Ki: Ti

Kif: Hemp‡

King Root: Bloodroot

Kinnikinnick: Uva Ursa

Kiss-Me-at-the-Garden-Gate: Pansy

Klamath Weed: St. John's Wort

Knight's Mifoil: Yarrow

Knit Back: Comfrey

Knotgrass: Knotweed

Knotted Marjoram: Marjoram

Knyghten: Yarrow

Ko: Sugar Cane

Krokos: Saffron

Kunkuma: Saffron

L

Lacris: Licorice

Ladder to Heaven: Lily of the Valley

Lady's Foxglove‡: Mullein

Ladies Meat: Hawthorn

Ladies' Seal: Briony

Lad's Love: Southernwood

Lady Ellhorn: Elder

Ladykins: Mandrake‡

Lady of the Meadow: Meadowsweet

Lady of the Woods: Birch

Lady's Key: Cowslip

Lady's Laces: Dodder

Lady's Mantle: Yarrow

Lady's Seal: Solomon's Seal

Lady's Thistle: Thistle

Lama: Ebony

Lamb Mint: Spearmint

Lammint: Peppermint

Lapstones: Potato

Lattouce: Lettuce

Laurel: Bay

Lavose: Lovage

Leapord's Bane: Wolfsbane‡

Leaf of Patrick: Plantain

Leather Jackets: Potato

Lemon Balm: Balm, Lemon

Lemon Balsam: Balm, Lemon

Lent Lily: Daffodil

Leontopodium: Lady's Mantle

Levant Salep: Orchid

Libanotis: Rosemary

Licorice: Licorice

Lignam Aloes: Aloes, Wood

Lignam Sanctae Crucis: Mistletoe‡

Lily Constancy: Lily of the Valley‡

Lime: Linden

Lime Tree: Linden

Ling: Heather

Link: Broom

Linseed: Flax

Lion's Foot: Lady's Mantle

Lion's Herb: Columbine

Lion's Mouth: Foxglove‡

Lion's Tooth: Dandelion

Lippe: Cowslip

Little Queen: Meadowsweet

Little Stepmother: Pansy

Liverleaf: Liverwort

Liver Lily: Blue Flag‡

Liverweed: Liverwort

Lizzy-Run-up-the-Hedge: Ground Ivy

Llwyd Y Cwn: Horehound

Llygad Y Dydd: Daisy

Lorbeer: Bay

Lousewort: Betony, Wood

Love Fruit: Orange

Love Herbs: Lovage

Love Idol: Pansy

Love-in-Idleness: Pansy

Love-Lies-Bleeding: Amaranth, Pansy

Love Rod: Lovage

Love Root: Lovage

Love Vine: Dodder

Love-Will: Datura

Loving Herbs: Lovage

Loving Idol: Pansy

Loq John the Conqueroe: Galangal

Lubestico: Lovage

Lucerne: Alfalfa

Luib Na Muc: Pimpernel

Lunary: Honesty

Lurk-in-the-Ditch: Pennyroyal

Lusmore: Foxglove‡

Lus Na Mbau Side: Foxglove‡

Lycopod: Club Moss

Lycorys: Licorice

Lythrum: Loosestrife

M

Mackerel Mint: Spearmint

Mad Apple: Datura

Madder's Cousin: Bedstraw, Fragrant

Madherb: Datura

Mad Root: Briony

Madweed: Scullcap

Madwort: Alyssum

Magic Mushroom: Agaric

Maia: Banana

Maidenhair Fair: Maidenhair

Maid's Ruin: Southernwood

Maize: Corn

Male Lily: Lily of the Valley‡

Malicorio: Pomegranate

Mallaquetta Pepper: Grains of Paradise

Malum Punicum: Pomegranate

Madragen: Mandrake‡

Mandrake‡: Mayapple‡

Manicon: Datura

Mannikin: Mandrake‡

Manzanilla: Chamomile

Maracoc: Passion Flower

Marian Thistle: Thistle, Milk

Marigold of Peru: Sunflower

Marijuana: Hemp‡

Marrubium: Horehound

Marshmallow: Althea

Maruil: Horehound

Marybud: Marigold

Marygold: Marigold

Mary Gowles: Marigold

Master of the Woods: Woodruff

Masterwort: Angelica

Masticke: Mastic

Mate: Yerba Mate

Maudlinwort: Daisy

May: Hawthorn

Mayblossom: Hawthorn

May Buksh: Hawthorn

Mayglower: Hawthorn

May Lily: Lily of the Valley‡

Maypops: Passion Flower

Maythen: Chamomile

Meadow Anemone: Anemone

Meadow Cabbage: Skunk Cabbage

Meadowwort: Meadowsweet

Meadsweet: Meadowsweet

Mealberry: Uva Ursa

Melia: Plumeria

Mecca Balsam: Balm of Gilead

Medicine Plant: Aloe

Meet-Me-in-the-Entry: Pansy

Melampode: Hellebore‡, Black

Melequetta: Grains of Paradise

Melissa: Balm, Lemon

Michaelmas: Aster

Milfoil: Yarrow

Militaris: Yarrow

Military Herb: Yarrow

Millefolium: Yarrow

Minarta: Avens

Miracle Herb: Comfrey

Mirra Balsam Odendron: Myrrh

Mismin: Spearmint

Misseltoe: Mistletoe‡

Mizquitl: Mesquite

Money Plant: Honesty

Monkshood‡: Wolfsbane‡

Moonlight on the Grove: Jasmine

Moor Grass: Cinquefoil

Moose Elm: Slippery Elm

Mortification Root: Althea

Mother of the Herbs: Rue

Mother of the Wood: Sloe

Mountain Ash: Towan

Mountain Balm: Yerba Santa

Mountain Box: Uva Ursa

Mountain Cranberry: Uva Ursa

Mountain Mint: Marjoram

Mountain Tea: Wintergreen

Mousquito Plant: Pennyroyal

Muggons: Mugwort

Mum: Chrysanthemum

Murphies: Potato

Musquash Root: Calamus

Myrtle Grass: Calamus

Myrtle Sedge: Calamus

N

Narcissus: Daffodil

Nard: Lavender, Spikenard

Nardus: Lavender

Naughty Man: Mugwort

Naughty Man's Cherries: Belladonna‡

Neckweede: Hemp‡

Nelka: Carnation

Nepeta: Catnip

Nidor: Fumitory

Nine Hooks: Lady's Mantle

Nine Joints: Knotweed

Ninety Knot: Knotweed

Nion: Ash

Nip: Catnip

Nirvara: Rice

Noble Laurel: Bay

Noble Yarrow: Yarrow

No Eyes: Potato

Nosebleed: Yarrow

Nurse Heal: Elecampane

O

Oatmeal: Oats

Obeah Wood: Ebony

Ohe: Bamboo

Oingnum: Onion

Ofnokgi: Sumbul

Old Field Balsam: Life Everlasting

Old Gal: Elder

Old Lady: Elder

Old Mon: Mugwort, Southernwood

Old Man Fennel: Mullein

Old Man's Pepper: Yarrow

Old Man's Mustard: Yarrow

Old Uncle Henry: Mugwort

Old Woman: Wormwood‡

Olena: Turmeric

Olibans: Frankincense

Olibanum: Frankincense

Olibanus: Frankincense

Olivier: Olive

Onyoun: Onion

Orange Bergamot: Bergamot, Orange

Orange Mint: Bergamot, Orange

Orange Root: Golden Seal

Oregon Grape Root: Oregon Grape

Organ Broth: Pennyroyal

Organs: Pennyroyal

Organ Tea: Pennyroyal

Ortiga Ancha: Nettle

Osier: Willow

Ouchi: Sumbul

Our Herb: Basil

Our Lady's Glove: Foxglove‡

Our Lady's Keys: Cowslip

Our Lady's Mint: Spearmint

Our Lady's Tears: Lily of the Valley‡

Oval Buchu: Buchu

P

Paddock Pipes: Horsetail

Paeddy: Rice

Paeony: Peony

Paigle: Cowslip

Pain-de-Porceau: Cyclamen

Palma Christi: Castor

Palma Christi Root: Castor

Paraguay: Yerba Mate

Paralysio: Cowslip

Partyke: Loosestrife

Pad d'Ane: Coltsfoot

Pasque Flower: Anemone

Passe Flower: Anemone

Passions: Bistort

Passion Vein: Passion Flower

Password: Cowslip, Primrose

Patience Dock: Bistort

Patrick's Dock: Plantain

Patrick's Leaf: Plantain

Patterns and Clogs: Toadflax

Pimpinella: Pimpernel

Pinks: Potato

Pipe Tree: Elder

Pipul: Bodhi

Piss-a-Bed: Dandelion

Plumrocks: Cowslip

Pocan: Poke‡

Poison Flag‡: Blue Flag‡

Poison Hemlock‡: Hemlock‡

Poison Lily: Blue Flag‡

Poison Parsley: Hemlock‡

Poison Tobacco‡: Henbane‡

Polar Plant: Rosemary

Pole Cat Weed: Skunk Cabbage

Pokeberry Root‡: Poke‡

Poke Root‡: Poke‡

Polk Root: Poke‡

Poor Man's Meat: Beans

Por Man's Treacle: Garlic

Poorman's Weatherglass: Pimpernel

Porillon: Daffodil

Pot Marjoram: Marjoram

Pound Garnet: Pomegranate

Prickly Broom: Gorse

Priest's Crown: Dandelion

Princess Pine: Pipsissewa

Prince's Pine: Pipsissewa

Pucha-Pot: Patchouli

Pudding Grass: Pennyroyal

Puffball: Dandelion

Pukeweed: Lovelia

Purple Betony: Betony, Wood

Purple Medic: Alfalfa

Purple Willow Herb: Loosestrife

Pussy Willow: Willow

Q

Queen of the Meadow: Meadowsweet

Queen Elizabeth Root: Orris

Queen's Delight: Stillengia

Queen's Root: Stillengia

Quick: Hawthorn

Quickbane: Rowan

Quick Grass: Witch Grass

R

Rabbits: Toadflax

Raccoon Berry: Mandrake‡, Mayapple

Radix Viperina: Snakeroot

Ragweed: Ragwort

Rainbow Weed: Loosestrife

Ramsted: Toadflax

Ran Tree: Rowan

Rapuns: Radish

Rattle Root: Cohosh, Black

Red Bearberry: Uva Ursa

Red Campion: Bachelor's Buttons

Red-Cap Mushroom: Agaric

Red Cockscomb: Amaranth

Red Elm: Slippery Elm

Red Eyebright: Eyebright

Red Eyes: Potato

Red Pepper: Chili Pepper

Red Reapberry: Raspberry

Red Legs: Bistort

Red Robin: Notweed

Red Root: Bloodroot

Red Sage: Sage

Red Squill: Squill

Red Valerian: Valerian

Rewe: Rue

Rhizoma: Galangal

Ripple Grass: Plantain

Rob Elder: Elder

Robin-Run-in-the-Tongue: Ground Ivy

Rock Parsley: Parsley

Rocks: Potato

Rocky Mountain Grape: Oregon Grape

Roden-Quicken: Rowan

Roden-Quicken-Royan: Rowan

Roynetree: Chamomile

Roman Laurel: Bay

Rudbeckia: Echinacea

Ruddes: Marigold

Ruddles: Marigold

Rue, Meadow: Meadow Rue

Ruffett: Gorse

Run-by-the-Ground: Pennyroyal

Ruta: Rue

S

Sacred Bark: Cascara Sagrada

Sacred Herb: Yerba Santa

Sacred Mother: Corn

Sacred Mushroom: Agaric

Sacred Tree: Bodhi

Saffer: Saffron

Dagackhomi: Uva Ursa

Sage: Sagebrush

Sage Willow: Loosestrife

Sahlab: Orchid

Saille: Willow

Sailor's Tobacco‡: Mugwort

St. George's Herb: Valerian

St. James Wort: Ragwort

St. John's Plant: Mugwort

St. Joseph's Wort: Basil

St. Mary's Seal: Solomon's Seal

St. Patrick's Leaf: Plantain

Salap: Lucky Hand

Salep: Orchid

Salicaire: Loosestrife

Salicyn Willow: Willow

Saloop: Orchid

Samson: Groundsel

Sandberry: Uva Ursa

Sang: Ginseng

Sanguinary: Yarrow

Sanguis Draconis: Dragon's Blood

Sandal: Sandalwood

Santal: Sandalwood

Saracen Corn: Buckwheat

Satyrion: Orchid

Saugh Tree: Willow

Sawge: Sage

Scabwort: Elecampane

Scaffold Flower: Carnatkikon

Scaldweed: Dodder

Scheiteregi: Fumitory

Scoke: Poke‡

Scotch Broom: Broom

Scottish Heather: Heather

Sea Dew: Rosemary

Sea Holly‡: Eryngo

Sealroot: Solomon's Seal

Sealwort: Solomon's Seal

Sea Onion: Squill

Sea Parsley: Lovage

Sea Spirit: Bladderwrack

Seawrack: Bladderwrack

Seed of Horus: Horehound

Seed of Seeds: Corn

Seetang: Bladderwrack

Selago: Club Moss

Semihomo: Mandrake‡

Semgren: Houseleek

Sention: Groundsel

Septfoil: Tormentil

Serpentary Radix: Snakeroot

Serpent's Tongue: Adder's Tongue

Sete Wale: Valerian

Set Well: Valerian

Seven Barks: Hydrangea

Seven Year's Love: Yarrow

Shamrock: Clover

Shave-Grass: Horsetail

Sheep Lice: Houndstongue

Shepherd's Knot: Tormentil

Shepherd's Weatherglass: Pimpernel

Short Buchu: Cuchu

Siamese Banzoin: Benzoin

Silver Bough, the: Apple

Silver Cinuefoil: Cinquefoil

Silverweed: Cinquefoil

Silver Dollar: Honesty

Simple's Joy: Vervain

Skunk Weed: Skunk Cabbage

Slan-Lus: Plantain

Sleepwort: Lettuce

Slippery Root: Comfrey

Snagree: Snakeroot

Snagrel: Snakeroot

Snakebite: Plantain

Snake Grape: Briony

Snake Lily: Blue Flag‡

Snake's Friend: Indian Paint Brush

Snake's Grass: Yarrow

Snake's Matches: Indian Paint Brush

Snakeweed: Bistort, Plantain, Snakeroot

Snapping Hazelnut: Witch Hazel

Sola Indianus: Sunflower

Soldier's Tea: Horehound

Soldier's Woundwort: Yarrow

Solidago: Goldenrod

Solomon Seal: Solomon's Seal

Sol Terestis: St. John's Wort

Sops-in-Wine: Carnation

Sorb Apple: Rowan

Sorcerer's Berry: Belladonna‡

Sorcerer's Herb: Datura

Sorcerer's Violet: Periwinkle

Sourgrass: Sorrel, Wood

Sour Trefoil: Sorrel, Wood

Sow-Bread: Cyclamen

Spanish Arbor Vine: Wood Rose

Spanish Saffron: Saffron

Sparrow's Tongue: Knotweed

Spike: Lavender

Spider Lily: Spiderwort

Spindle Tree: Wahoo‡

Spire Mint: Spearmint

Sponnc: Coltsfoot

Spotted Alder: Witch Hazel

Spotted Corobane: Hemlock‡

Spotted Hemlock‡: Hemlock‡

Spousa Solis: Marigold

Spurge‡: Euphorbia

Squaw Mint: Pennyroyal

Squaw Root: Cohosh, Black

Staggerwort: Ragwort

Stammerwort: Ragwort

Stanch Griss: Yarrow

Stanch Weed: Yarrow

Stargrass: Ague Root

Star of the Earth: Avens

Starwort: Ague Root, Aster

Stellaria: Lady's Mantle

Steeplebush: Meadowsweet

Stepmother: Pansy

Sticklewort: Agrimony

Stillingia: Stillengia

Stinging Nettle: Nettle

Stinking Nanny: Ragwort

Stinking Willie: Ragwort

Stinkweed: Datura, Garlic

Strangle Tare: Dodder

Storm Hat: Wolfsbane‡

Stringy Bark Tree: Eucalyptus

Styrax: Liquidamber

Stubwort: Sorrel, Wood

Succory: Chicory

Summer's Bride: Marigold

Sunkfield: Cinquefoil

Suntull: Skunk Cabbage

Sureau: Elder

Surelle: Sorrel, Wood

Swallow Herb: Celandine‡

Swallow Wort: Celandine‡

Swamp Sassafras: Magnolia

Sweating Plant: Boneset

Sweet Balm: Lemon balm

Sweet Balsam: Lemon balm

Sweet Basil: Basil

Sweet Bay: Bay

Sweet Cane: Calamus

Sweet Cherry: Cherry

Sweet Dock: Bistort

Sweet Elder: Elder

Sweet Fennel: Fennel

Sweet Flag: Calamus

Sweet Gum: Liquidamber

Sweet Marjoram: Marjoram

Sweet Root: Calamus, Licorice

Sweet Rush: Calamus

Sweet Scented Goldenrod: Sweet-Scented Life Everlasting

Sweet Sedge: Calamus

Sweet Violet: Violet

Sweet Weed: Althea

Sweet Wood: Cinnamon

Sweet Woodruff: Woodruff

Swing Bread: Cyclamen

Swynel Grass: Knotweed

Symphonica: Henbane‡

Synkefoyle: Cinquefoil

T

Tabacca: Tobacco‡

Tamrindo: Tamaring

Tamus: Briony

Tansy: Yarrow

Taters: Potato

Tatties: Potato

Taubendripp: Fumitory

Teaberry: Wintergreen

Tear Grass: Job's Tears

Teasel: Boneset

Tekrouri: Hemp‡

Temple Tree: Plumjeria

Tetterberry: Briony

Tetterwort: Celandine‡

Thimbleberry: Blackberry

Thormantle: Tormentil

Thorn: Hawthorn

Thornapple: Datura

Thoroughwort: Boneset

Thor's Hat: Wolfsbane‡

Thor's Helper: Rowan

Thousand Seal: Yarrow

Three-Leaved Grass: Sorrel, Wood

Thrissles: Thistles

Thunderbesem: Mistletoe‡

Tickweed: Pennyroyal

Tipton Weed: St. John's Wort

Torches: Mullein

Tinne: Holly‡

Tittle-My-Fancy: Pansytoad, Toadflax

Toloache: Datura

Tojqua: Tonka

Tonquin Bean: Tonka

Trailing Grape: Oregon Grape

Tree of Chastity: Hawthorn

Tree of Death: Cypress

Tree of Doom: Elder

Tree of Enchantment: Willow

Tree of Evil: Walnut

Tree of Love: Apple

Trefoil: Clover

True Love: Troillium

True Unicorn Root: Ague Root

True Winter's Bark: Winter's Bark

Trumpet Flower: Be-Still

Trumpet Weed: Joe-Pye Weed, Meadow-sweet

Tumeric Root: Golden Seal

Tunhoff: Ground Ivy

Turnsole: Heliotrope

U

Unicorn Root: Ague root

Unshoe-Horse: Moonwort

Unyoun: Onion

V

Vada Tree: Banyan

Vandal Root: Valerian

Vanilla Leaf: Deerstongue

Van-Van: Vervain

Vapor: Fumitory

Vegetable Sulfur: Club Moss

Velvetback: Mullein

Velvet Dock: Elecampane

Velvet Flower: Amaranth

Velvet Plant: Mullein

Verbena: Vervain

Verge d'Or: Goldenrod

Vervan: Vervain

Vetivert: Vetivert

Virginia Dogwood: Dogwood

Virginian Pike: Poke‡

Virginian Snakeroot: Snakeroot

Virgin Mary's Nut: Molukka

Voodoo Witch Burr: Liquidamber

W

Wallwort: Walnut

Warnera: Golden Seal

War Poison: Yellow Evening Primrose

Water Flag: Blue Flag‡

Water Parsley: Hemlock‡

Way Bennet: Avens

Wax Dolls: Fumitory

Waybread: Plantain

Waybroad: Plantain

Weed: Hemp‡

Welcome-Home-Husband-Though-Never-So-Drunk: Houseleek

Welcome-Home-Husband-Though-Never-So-Late: Houseleek

Weybroed: Plantain

Whig Plant: Chamomile

Whin: Gorse

White Balsam: Life Everlasting

White Endive: Dandelion

White Squill: Squill

White Thorn: Hawthorn

White Willow: Willow

Whitty: Rowan

Wicken Tree: Rowan

White Horehound: Horehound

White Man's Foot: Plantain

White Sandalwood: Sandalwood

Wiggin: Rowan

Wiggy: Rowan

Wiky: Rowan

Wild Ash: Rowan

Wild Cherry: Chicory

Wild Curcurma: Golden Seal

Wild Endive: Dandelion

Wild Hops: Briony

Wild Lemon: Mandrake‡, Mayapple‡

Wild Oregon Grape: Oregon Grape

Wild Sage: Sagebrush

Wild Succory: Chicory

Wild Sunflower: Elecampane

Wild Vanilla: Deerstongue

Wild Vine: Briony

Wind Flower: Anemone

Wintera: Winter's Bark

Wintersweet: Marjoram

Wishing Thorn: Sloe

Witchbane: Rowan

Witchen: Rowan

Witches' Aspirin: Willow

Witches' Bells: Foxglove‡

Witches' Broom: Mistletoe‡

Witches' Grass: Witch Grass

Witches' Hair: Dodder

Witches' Herb: Basil

Witches' Thimble: Datura

Witch Burr: Liquidamber

Witch Herb: Mugwort

Witches' Berry: Belladonna‡

Witchwood: Rowan

Withe: Willow

Withy: Willow

Wolf Claw: Club Moss

Wolf's Hair: Wolfsbane‡

Wolf's Hat: Wolfsbane‡

Wolf's Milk: Euphorbia

Womandrake: Mandrake‡

Wonder of the World Root: Ginseng

Wood Aloes: Aloes, Wood

Wood Betony: Betony, Wood

Woodbine: Honeysuckle‡

Wood Boneset: Boneset

Wood of the Cross: Mistletoe‡

Wood-Rove: Woodruff

Wood Sorrel: Wood

Wood Vine: Briony

Woolmat: Houndstongue

Wound Weed: Goldenrod

Woundwort: Goldenrod

Wound Wort: Yarrow

Wuderove: Woodruff

Wymote: Althea

Y

Yakori Bengeskro: Elder

Yallus: Comfrey

Yarroway: Yarrow

Yaw Root: Stillengia

Yellow Avens: Avens

Yellow Dock: Dock

Yellow Gentian: Gentian

Yellow Oleander‡: Be-Still

Yellow Puccoon: Golden Seal

Yellow Root: Golden Seal

Yellow Sandalwood: Sandalwood

Yerba: Yerba Mate

Yerba Buena: Spearmint

Yerba del Diablo: Datura

Yerba Louisa: Lemon Verbena

Yerw: Yarrow

Yn-Leac: Onion

Ysopo: Hyssop

Yssop: Hyssop

Z

Zauberwurzel: Mandrake‡

Baneful Herbs

Some of these herbs possess highly potent medical properties, while some are poisonous in part or in whole. *CAUTION: Only an experienced herbalist should experiment with the herbs in the following list.*

Aconite	Elkweed
Arnica	Ergot
Asafoetida	Euphorbium
Baneberry	Fava Bean
Belladonna	Flag Lily
Bittersweet	Foxglove
Black Nightshade	Gelsemium
Blue Flag	Hashish
Burning Bush	Hellebore
Calabar Bean	Hemlock
Calico Bush	Hemp
Camphor	Henbane
Castor Oil Plant (seed)	Holly (seeds)
Celandine	Honeysuckle (vine and fruit)
Christmas Rose (root)	Horse Balm
Cowbane	Ilex
Daffodils	Impatiens Pallida
Deadly Nightshade	Indian Arrowroot
Dog's Mercury (seeds)	Indian Hemp

Indian Tobacco

Inkberry

Jack-in-the-Pulpit (root)

Jerusalem Cherry

Jimsonweed

Laurnum (seeds)

Lily of the Valley (seeds)

Lobelia

Mandrake

Mayapple (root, leaves, seeds)

Milkweed

Mistletoe (seeds)

Monkshood

Mountain Laurel

Nux Vomica

Oleander

Ordeal Bean

Opium Poppy

Pigeonberry

Poinsettia (leaves)

Poison Dogwood

Poison Flag

Poison Hemlock

Poison Ivy

Poison Oak

Poison Sumac

Poke

Pokeberry

Poke Root

Pokeweed

Rhubarb Leaves

Rosebay

Snow on the Mountain

Spingle Tree (seeds)

Spotted Hemlock

Spurge

Stramonium

Sulfur

Swallow Wort

Thorn Apple

Tobacco

Wahoo

Wake-Robin

Water Dropwort

Water Hemlock

White Bryony

White Hellebore

White Snakeroot

Winter Rose

Wolfsbane

Wood Anemone (seeds)

Wormwood

Yellow Jasmine

Yew (seeds and berries)

Bibliography

Ashley, Leonard R. N. *The Complete Book of Spells, Curses, and Magical Recipes*. New York, NY: Barricade Books, Inc., 1997.

Cabot, Laurie. *Celebrate the Earth*. New York, NY: Dell Publishing Group, Inc., 1994.

Cabot, Laurie and Tom Cowan. *Power of the Witch*. New York, NY: Dell Publishing Group, Inc., 1998

Conway, D. J. Animal Magick: *The Art of Recognizing and Working with Familiars*. St. Paul, MN: Llewellyn Publications, 1996.

———. *Dancing with Dragons*. St. Paul, MN: Llewellyn Publications, 1994.

———. *Moon Magick, Myth and Magick, Crafts and Recipes, Rituals and Spells*. St. Paul, MN: Llewellyn Publications, 1997.

Cunningham, Scott. *Encyclopedia of Magickal Herbs*. St. Paul, MN: Llewellyn Publications, 1994.

———. *Magical Herbalism*. St. Paul, MN: Llewellyn Publications, 1993.

———. *Wicca: A Guide for the Solitary Practitioner*. St. Paul, MN: Llewellyn Publications, 1993.

Cunningham, Scott and David Harrington. *Spell Crafts*. St. Paul, MN: Llewellyn Publications, 1994.

———. *The Magical Household Spell Crafts*. St. Paul, MN: Llewellyn Publications, 1993.

Dunwich, Gerina. *Candlelight Spells*. New York, NY: Carol Publishing Group, 1990.

————. *Wicca Craft, The Modern Witches' Book of Herbs, Magick, and Dreams*. New York, NY: Citadel Press, Carol Publishing Group, 1991.

Ellis, Peter Berresford. *The Druids*. Grand Rapids, MI: W.B. Berdmans Publishing Co., 1995.

Hahady D.A.C., Letha. *Asian Health Secrets: The Complete Guide to Asian Herbal Medicine*. New York, NY: Crown Publishers, Inc., 1995.

Jordan, Michael. *Encyclopedia of Gods, Over 2500 Deities of the World*. New York, NY: Facts on File, 1993.

Linn, Denise. *The Secret Language of Signs*. New York, NY: Ballantine Books, 1996.

Manning, Al G. *Helping Yourself with White Witchcraft*. West Nyack, NY: Parker Publishing Co. Inc., 1972.

Reed, Ellen C. *Invocations of the Gods, Ancient Egyptian Magick for Today*. St. Paul, MN: Llewellyn Publications, 1992.

Williams, Jude C. *Jude's Herbal Home Remedies*. St. Paul, MN: Llewellyn Publications, 1995.

Wippler, Migene Gonz'Alez. *Dreams and What They Mean to You*. St. Paul, MN: Llewellyn Publications, 1995.

————. *Spells, Ceremonies, and Magic*. St. Paul, MN: Llewellyn Publications, 1995.